HISTORIANS AT WORK

Whose Right to Bear Arms Did the Second Amendment Protect?

HISTORIANS AT WORK

Advisory Editor
Edward Countryman, Southern Methodist University

How Did American Slavery Begin?
Edward Countryman, Southern Methodist University

What Caused the Pueblo Revolt of 1680?
David J. Weber, Southern Methodist University

What Did the Declaration Declare?
Joseph J. Ellis, Mount Holyoke College

What Did the Constitution Mean to Early Americans?
Edward Countryman, Southern Methodist University

Whose Right to Bear Arms Did the Second Amendment Protect?
Saul Cornell, The Ohio State University

Does the Frontier Experience Make America Exceptional?
Richard W. Etulain, University of New Mexico

What Was Progressivism?
Glenda E. Gilmore, Yale University (forthcoming)

What Did the Internment of Japanese Americans Mean?
Alice Yang Murray, University of California, Santa Cruz

HISTORIANS AT WORK

Whose Right to Bear Arms Did the Second Amendment Protect?

Readings Selected and Introduced by

Saul Cornell

The Ohio State University

Selections by

Robert E. Shalhope

Lawrence Delbert Cress

Garry Wills

Don Higginbotham

Edmund S. Morgan

Michael A. Bellesîles

Bedford / St. Martin's   *Boston* ♦ *New York*

For Bedford/St. Martin's

Executive Editor for History and Political Science: Katherine E. Kurzman
Developmental Editor: Louise Townsend
Editorial Assistant: Chip Turner
Senior Production Supervisor: Dennis Conroy
Marketing Manager: Charles Cavaliere
Project Management: Books By Design, Inc.
Text Design: Claire Seng-Niemoeller
Cover Design: Donna Lee Dennison
Cover Art: Costumes de l'armée américaine en 1782, watercolor by Ludwig Van Closen,
   from the Milton S. Lathem journal, formerly in the Library of Congress
   Manuscript Division.
Composition: G & S Typesetters, Inc.
Printing and Binding: Haddon Craftsmen, an R. R. Donnelley & Sons Company

President: Charles H. Christensen
Editorial Director: Joan E. Feinberg
Director of Marketing: Karen R. Melton
Director of Editing, Design, and Production: Marcia Cohen
Manager, Publishing Services: Emily Berleth

Library of Congress Catalog Card Number: 99-63833

Manufactured in the United States of America.

5   4   3   2   1   0
f   e   d   c   b   a

For information, write: Bedford/St. Martin's, 75 Arlington Street, Boston, MA 02116
(617-399-4000)

ISBN: 0-312-24060-0 (paperback)
        0-312-22818-X (hardcover)

Acknowledgments

MICHAEL A. BELLESÎLES, "The Origins of Gun Culture in the United States,
   1760–1865," *Journal of American History,* Vol. 83, no. 2, pp. 425–55 (September
   1996). Copyright © 1996 by the *Journal of American History.* Reprinted by
   permission of the *Journal of American History.*
LAWRENCE DELBERT CRESS, "A Well-Regulated Militia: The Origins and Meaning of
   the Second Amendment," from *The Bill of Right of Rights: A Lively Heritage,* ed.
   Jon Kukla. Copyright © 1987 by The Library of Virginia. Reprinted by
   permission of The Library of Virginia.

Acknowledgments and copyrights are continued at the back of the book on page
188, which constitutes an extension of the copyright page.

Foreword

The short, inexpensive, and tightly focused books in the Historians at Work series set out to show students what historians do by turning closed specialist debate into an open discussion about important and interesting historical problems. These volumes invite students to confront the issues historians grapple with while providing enough support so that students can form their own opinions and join the debate. The books convey the intellectual excitement of "doing history" that should be at the core of any undergraduate study of the discipline. Each volume starts with a contemporary historical question that is posed in the book's title. The question focuses on either an important historical document (the Declaration of Independence, the Emancipation Proclamation) or a major problem or event (the beginnings of American slavery, the Pueblo Revolt of 1680) in American history. An introduction supplies the basic historical context students need and then traces the ongoing debate among historians, showing both how old questions have yielded new answers and how new questions have arisen. Following this two-part introduction are four to six interpretive selections by top scholars, reprinted in their entirety from journals and books, including endnotes. Each selection is either a very recent piece or a classic argument that is still in play and is headed by a question that relates it to the book's core problem. Volumes that focus on a document reprint it in the opening materials so that students can read arguments alongside the evidence and reasoning on which they rest.

One purpose of these books is to show students that they *can* engage with sophisticated writing and arguments. To help them do so, each selection includes apparatus that provides context for engaged reading and critical thinking. An informative headnote introduces the angle of inquiry that the reading explores and closes with Questions for a Closer Reading, which invite students to probe the selection's assumptions, evidence, and argument. At the end of the book, Making Connections questions offer students ways to read the essays against one another, showing how interesting problems emerge from the debate. Suggestions for Further Reading conclude each book, pointing interested students toward relevant materials for extended study.

Historical discourse is rarely a matter of simple opposition. These volumes show how ideas develop and how answers change, as minor themes turn into major considerations. The Historians at Work volumes bring together thoughtful statements in an ongoing conversation about topics that continue to engender debate, drawing students into the historical discussion with enough context and support to participate themselves. These books aim to show how serious scholars have made sense of the past and why what they do is both enjoyable and worthwhile.

EDWARD COUNTRYMAN

Preface

$\mathbf{M}$any aspects of the Bill of Rights have prompted controversy. Yet only the Second Amendment has led serious commentators to
consider repealing one of its original provisions. The meaning of the phrase
the "right to bear arms" has been examined in the pages of prestigious
scholarly journals such as the *Journal of American History* and the *William and
Mary Quarterly*. Dozens of law review articles have appeared in recent years
in such journals as the *Akron Law Review* and the *Yale Law Journal*. The editorial pages of newspapers and their letters to the editor have carried the
debate well beyond the walls of the academy. The Second Amendment has
also prompted some less serious commentaries. The debate over the meaning of this amendment has appeared on bumper stickers across America
and has even found its way onto late night talk shows.

As a teaching tool, the Second Amendment has several advantages over
more familiar topics such as freedom of the press. The subject of guns invariably produces strong reactions and the lines of ideological cleavage in
the classroom often defy one's expectations, a welcome and refreshing experience for any teacher. Supporters as well as opponents of the view that
the Second Amendment protects an individual right of gun ownership can
be found on both the left and the right.

While legal scholarship has focused almost entirely on the question of
whether the Second Amendment has protected an individual or collective
right to own guns, historians have used the subject to explore a wide range
of issues. Many of the topics dealt with both at the introductory level and
in upper-division courses in American history can be illuminated by the
Second Amendment. It is far easier to make abstract concepts such as republicanism and liberalism come alive for students when these concepts are
placed in the context of the original debates over the Amendment. The controversies over the Second Amendment also make clear why the issue of federalism was so important to both Federalists and Antifederalists. Finally, the
Second Amendment provides students with an opportunity to explore classic American Studies questions about the nature of American character and
culture. Recent historical scholarship offers a useful corrective to images

fashioned by Hollywood that have encouraged the view that the Second Amendment was a natural outgrowth of America's long and stormy love affair with guns. As is often the case with myths and unexamined assumptions, the historical reality is far more complex.

The purpose of this volume in the Historians at Work series is to expose students to the complexity of this issue through a range of unedited secondary sources written by leading scholars. These essays not only raise questions about whose right to bear arms the Second Amendment protected, but they also prompt further inquiry into what the Second Amendment tells us about the intellectual, social, and political world of the Founders of the American republic. All of the essays grapple with the problem of how historians interpret evidence and relate particular texts to their historical contexts. Equally important, the selections (and accompanying introduction, headnotes, and questions) showcase contemporary scholarly debate over the meaning of the Second Amendment and the controversies spawned by differing interpretations.

Studying the Second Amendment forces an examination of one of the most cherished assumptions about American political and legal culture. Should America continue to be held captive to a set of eighteenth-century ideas that some would argue have no relevance to life in the twenty-first century? American constitutional law accords a privileged position to the thought of the Founders. This deference to the authority of the past is evident in public discussions of gun control, which invariably lead back to questions about what the Founders intended by including the Second Amendment in the Bill of Rights. The essays collected here allow students to formulate their own questions about the meaning of the Second Amendment. However they choose to answer them, one thing remains certain. The continuing controversy over the Second Amendment is compelling proof that history does matter in all of our lives.

Acknowledgments

I have always been puzzled by efforts to draw a sharp line between scholarship and teaching. This particular volume is a good case in point. Before publishing a word on this topic, I had been teaching it for several years in both my introductory survey class and in upper-level courses. Once I began researching and writing about this subject, my approach to teaching it changed as I explored the sources and scholarship in greater detail. At Ohio State the introductory survey draws from an enormously varied student body. I have used the materials in this book with great success. This book owes much to the input provided by thousands of students I have taught and the dozens of teaching assistants I have had the good fortune to work with in the classroom.

I was especially pleased that this volume appeared in Edward Countryman's series on Historians at Work. Ed provided excellent guidance and encouragement. The Executive Editor for History and Political Science at Bedford/St. Martin's, Katherine E. Kurzman, was enthusiastic about this series and this particular project. My editor at Bedford/St. Martin's, Louise Townsend, made this a much better and more useful book through her keen insights. Her good cheer and patience made the editorial process a delight. Finally, I would like to thank Beth Morel for copyediting, and Chip Turner, Emily Berleth, and Nancy Benjamin for their careful and excellent work shepherding the manuscript through the production process. Robert Shalhope, Don Higginbotham, and Michael Bellesîles kindly shared their own experiences about teaching this topic. Lance Banning, Paul Finkleman, David Konig, Kenneth Stevens, and the other anonymous reviewers of this book made a host of thoughtful suggestions. Richard Groening's research assistance was invaluable.

My wife, Susan, and my daughters, Emma and Julia, lived with yet another book that had to compete with trips to the zoo and other important things. If this volume can help raise the level of public debate about this controversial topic above the trading of simple-minded slogans, it will certainly have been worth the effort.

SAUL CORNELL

A Note for Students

Every piece of written history starts when somebody becomes curious and asks questions. The very first problem is who, or what, to study. A historian might ask an old question yet again, after deciding that existing answers are not good enough. But brand-new questions can emerge about old, familiar topics, particularly in light of new findings or directions in research, such as the rise of women's history in the late 1970s.

In one sense history is all that happened in the past. In another it is the universe of potential evidence that the past has bequeathed. But written history does not exist until a historian collects and probes that evidence (*research*), makes sense of it (*interpretation*), and shows to others what he or she has seen so that they can see it too (*writing*). Good history begins with respecting people's complexity, not with any kind of preordained certainty. It might well mean using modern techniques that were unknown at the time, such as Freudian psychology or statistical assessment by computer. But good historians always approach the past on its own terms, taking careful stock of the period's cultural norms and people's assumptions or expectations, no matter how different from contemporary attitudes. Even a few decades can offer a surprisingly large gap to bridge, as each generation discovers when it evaluates the accomplishments of those who have come before.

To write history well requires three qualities. One is the courage to try to understand people whom we never can meet — unless our subject is very recent — and to explain events that no one can re-create. The second quality is the humility to realize that we can never entirely appreciate either the people or the events under study. However much evidence is compiled and however smart the questions posed, the past remains too large to contain. It will always continue to surprise.

The third quality historians need is the curiosity that turns sterile facts into clues about a world that once was just as alive, passionate, frightening, and exciting as our own, yet in different ways. Today we know how past events "turned out." But the people taking part had no such knowledge. Good history recaptures those people's fears, hopes, frustrations, failures, and achievements; it tells about people who faced the predicaments and choices that still confront us as we begin the twenty-first century.

All the essays collected in this volume bear on a single, shared problem that the authors agree is important, however differently they may choose to respond to it. On its own, each essay reveals a fine mind coming to grips with a worthwhile question. Taken together, the essays give a sense of just how complex the human situation can be. That point — that human situations are complex — applies just as much to life today as to the lives led in the past. History has no absolute "lessons" to teach; it follows no invariable "laws." But knowing about another time might be of some help as we struggle to live within our own.

EDWARD COUNTRYMAN

Contents

Foreword   *v*
Preface   *vii*
A Note for Students   *xi*

PART ONE   **The Document**   1

*Constitutional Amendments Proposed to
and Ratified by the States, Including the
Second Amendment*   *3*

PART TWO   **Introduction**   **7**

"To Keep and Bear Arms"   *9*

The Militia, the People, and the Problem of Rights
in Revolutionary America   9

Scholars and the Second Amendment   17

PART THREE   **Some Current Questions**   **25**

1. **Did the Second Amendment protect an individual's right
to own guns?**   27

Robert E. Shalhope

The Armed Citizen in the Early Republic

"While late eighteenth-century Americans distinguished
between the individual's right to *possess* arms and the need for a
militia in which to *bear* them, more often than not they
considered these rights inseparable."

2. Was the Second Amendment intended to protect the people's right to maintain a well-regulated militia?   51

Lawrence Delbert Cress

A Well-Regulated Militia: The Origins and Meaning of the Second Amendment, From *The Bill of Rights: A Lively Heritage*

"Unlike provisions of the Bill of Rights that guaranteed such individual rights as freedom of speech, due process, and religious choice, the Second Amendment to the United States Constitution was not written to assure private citizens the prerogative of carrying weapons."

3. Does the Standard Model of the Second Amendment favored by some legal scholars distort the original understanding of the right to bear arms?   63

Garry Wills

To Keep and Bear Arms, With *Letters in Rebuttal from Sanford Levinson, David C. Williams, and Glenn Harlan Reynolds*

"The Standard Model finds, squirreled away in the Second Amendment, not only a private right to own guns for any purpose but a public right to oppose with arms the government of the United States."

4. Was the Second Amendment primarily about the struggle between Federalists and Antifederalists over the nature of federalism?   97

Don Higginbotham

The Federalized Militia Debate: A Neglected Aspect of Second Amendment Scholarship

"In all the discussions and debates, from the Revolution to the eve of the Civil War, there is precious little evidence that advocates of local control of militia showed an equal or even a secondary concern for gun ownership as a personal right."

5. How did the reality of the militia differ from the ideal of the militia in Revolutionary America?   123

Edmund S. Morgan

The People in Arms: The Invincible Yeoman, From
*Inventing the People: The Rise of Popular Sovereignty in
England and America*

"In teaching the yeoman his place in the social order the
militia performed an undesignated but crucial function
as well as a social function and performed both more
successfully than its military function."

6. Was the Second Amendment an outgrowth of America's
gun culture?   145

Michael A. Bellesîles

*The Origins of Gun Culture in the United States,
1760–1865*

"Before we accept an individual right to gun ownership in the
Second Amendment, we must establish who were 'the people'
who were allowed to 'keep and bear arms.' Did they in fact own
guns? What was the popular attitude toward firearms? Did such
perceptions change over time?"

Making Connections   181
Suggestions for Further Reading   185

Whose Right to Bear Arms Did the Second Amendment Protect?

PART ONE

The Document

Constitutional Amendments Proposed to and Ratified by the States

Including the Second Amendment

Constitutional Amendments
Proposed to and Ratified by the States
Including the Second Amendment

Article I (rejected)

After the first enumeration required by the first Article of
the Constitution, there shall be one Representative for every thirty thousand, until the number shall amount to one hundred, after which, the proportion shall be so regulated by Congress, that there shall be not less than
one hundred Representatives, nor less than one representative for every
forty thousand persons, until the number of Representatives shall amount
to two hundred, after which the proportion shall be so regulated by Congress, that there shall not be less than two hundred representatives, nor
more than one Representative for every fifty thousand persons.

Article II (rejected)*

No law, varying the compensation for the services of the Senators and Representatives, shall take effect, until an election of Representatives shall have
intervened.

Article I (ratified)†

Congress shall make no law respecting an establishment of religion, or pro-
hibiting the free exercise thereof, or abridging the freedom of speech, or of
the press, or the right of the people peaceably to assemble, and to petition
the Government for a redress of grievances.

---

*Eventually ratified as the Twenty-seventh Amendment.
†Originally submitted as the Third Amendment.

Article II (ratified)*

A well regulated militia, being necessary to the security of a free State, the right of the people to keep and bear arms, shall not be infringed.

Article III (ratified)

No Soldier shall, in time of peace, be quartered in any House, without the consent of the owner, nor in time of war, but in a manner to be prescribed by law.

Article IV (ratified)

The right of the people to be secure in their persons, houses, papers, and effects, against unreasonable searches and seizures, shall not be violated, and no warrants shall issue, but upon probable cause, supported by oath or affirmation, and particularly describing the place to be searched and the persons or things to be seized.

Article V (ratified)

No person shall be held to answer for a capital, or otherwise infamous crime, unless on a presentment or indictment of [a] Grand Jury, except in cases arising in the land or naval forces, or in the militia, when in actual service in time of war or public danger; nor shall any person be subject for the same offence to be twice put in jeopardy of life or limb; nor shall be compelled in any criminal case to be a witness against himself, nor be deprived of life, liberty, or property, without due process of law; nor shall private property be taken for public use, without just compensation.

Article VI (ratified)

In all criminal prosecutions, the accused shall enjoy the right to a speedy and public trial, by an impartial jury of the State and district wherein the crime shall have been committed; which district shall have been previously ascertained by law, and to be informed of the nature and cause of the accusation; to be confronted with the witnesses against him; to have compulsory process for obtaining witnesses in his favor, and to have the assistance of counsel for his defence.

---

*Originally submitted as the Fourth Amendment.

Article VII (ratified)

In suits at common law, where the value in controversy shall exceed twenty dollars, the right of trial by jury shall be preserved, and no fact tried by a jury, shall be otherwise re-examined in any Court of the United States, than according to the rules of the common law.

Article VIII (ratified)

Excessive bail shall not be required, nor excessive fines imposed, nor cruel and unusual punishments inflicted.

Article IX (ratified)

The enumeration in the Constitution, of certain rights, shall not be construed to deny or disparage others retained by the people.

Article X (ratified)

The powers not delegated to the United States by the Constitution, nor prohibited by it to the States, are reserved to the States respectively, or to the people.

PART TWO

Introduction

"To Keep and Bear Arms"

"To Keep and Bear Arms"

The Militia, the People, and the Problem
of Rights in Revolutionary America

The history of the Second Amendment touches on all of the major constitutional questions that Americans faced in the years after the American Revolution. The debates over the connection between the right to bear arms and the militia forced Americans to consider the relationship between individual rights and the rights of communities to legislate on behalf of the public good. Arguments over the militia and the right to bear arms also focused attention on the problem of federalism: how would authority be divided between the states and the new federal government? Finally, the conflict over the militia and the right to bear arms posed questions about how Americans would deal with their own revolutionary heritage. Was the right of armed resistance that the colonists had asserted during the War of Independence something that later generations might claim? To understand the meaning of the Second Amendment one must reconstruct the political and legal ideas that shaped the Constitution and the Bill of Rights.

The ideal of the citizen militia was deeply rooted in American political culture. During the colonial period, Americans relied on militias composed of part-time citizen-soldiers who were responsible for local defense. American ideas about the militia also drew inspiration from English political theory. The seventeenth-century political philosopher James Harrington argued that a republic could maintain its freedom only when it was composed of virtuous yeomen — independent farmers — who would take up arms whenever their liberty was threatened. In contrast to the militia, who would provide a means of resisting tyranny, a standing army of professional soldiers was a potential threat to liberty, because that army might easily be used by corrupt politicians to oppress the people.

Over the course of the eighteenth century, the militia became less important as a means of defending the colonists against external enemies and grew increasingly devoted to the task of maintaining public order. In the South the militia protected slave owners from the threat of rebellion and formed the patrols that hunted fugitive slaves. Outside of the South the militia was used to put down civil disturbances. Among the most important functions of the militia was its role as a social and political institution that helped cement communities together. The rituals of the militia, particularly the muster days on which troops drilled, were festive occasions in which citizens came together for celebration.[1]

During the American Revolution the military record of the militia was mixed. Although individual militia units scored several impressive victories, in general the militia proved ill-suited to the demands of fighting a prolonged war against a well-trained professional army. Fortunately for the cause of the American Revolution, military leaders such as George Washington recognized the need for a regular army composed of professional soldiers and worked hard to persuade Congress to fund such an army.

Although the Revolution had done much to discredit the militia in the view of military leaders such as Washington, the ideal of the militia continued to have a powerful hold on the minds of most Americans. This influence is evident in the Virginia Declaration of Rights, drafted by George Mason in May 1776, a month before the Declaration of Independence. The Virginia Declaration of Rights affirmed

> That a well regulated militia, composed of the body of the people, trained to arms, is the proper, natural, and safe defence of a free state; that standing armies, in time of peace, should be avoided, as dangerous to liberty; and that in all cases, the military should be under strict subordination to, and governed by, the civil power.[2]

All of the former colonies followed Virginia's lead, and by the mid-1780s each had adopted a new state constitution. Seven of these documents included formal declarations of rights. All of the bills of rights prohibited peacetime standing armies and asserted the need to preserve civilian control of the military. Three of these bills of rights explicitly protected the right to bear arms.[3]

Although the press teemed with discussions about the various state constitutions, relatively little public scrutiny had been devoted to the Articles of Confederation, the first national constitution of the new United States of America. The relatively weak structure of government created by the Articles proved woefully inadequate to many of the problems confronting the new nation. A talented group of politicians intent on reforming the Articles, including Alexander Hamilton and James Madison, worked hard to persuade the states to revise the Articles and endow it with additional powers, especially the power to tax. Calls for reform of the Articles took on a new sense of urgency in 1786 when farmers in western Massachusetts took up arms to prevent their farms from being seized by creditors seeking to collect on outstanding debts. Led by a former Revolutionary War officer, Daniel Shays, the Shaysites closed courts and began organizing themselves into their own militia units. When the government of Massachusetts learned that the rebels had marched on the state arsenal in Springfield, the state militia was called out to put down the insurrection. Shays's Rebellion was routed, its leaders forced to flee the state.[4]

Prior to the outbreak of violence in Massachusetts, a call for delegates from all of the states to convene in Philadelphia to consider revisions to the Articles of Confederation had been made at a meeting in Annapolis, Maryland. When the delegates arrived in Philadelphia in the summer of 1787, their charge was reform of the Articles of Confederation. The participants in the Philadelphia Convention moved well beyond their instructions and created an entirely new frame of government. The Constitution they framed was sent to the states for approval. Special ratification conventions were convened in each of the states and charged with the task of either approving or rejecting the new frame of government. Discussion of the merits and defects of the Constitution were not restricted to these official bodies. As one contemporary commentator remarked, "The plan of a Government proposed to us by the Convention — affords matter for conversation to every rank of beings from the Governor to the door keeper."[5] Americans argued over the meaning of the Constitution in taverns and town squares. Hundreds of newspaper articles both for and against the new plan of government appeared.

In the process of debating the merits of the Constitution, Americans were forced to ponder a variety of questions about the nature of government, including the meaning of rights and the appropriate constitutional means to secure liberty. It was only natural that Americans would compare the new plan of government to those with which they were most familiar, the thirteen state constitutions. One of the most obvious differences that distinguished the new federal Constitution from the vast majority of state constitutions was the absence of a declaration of rights.

Opponents of the Constitution argued that the liberties of the people could not be secure without the inclusion of an explicit declaration of rights stating in clear terms the limits of government power. The absence of a bill of rights became the most powerful weapon in the Antifederalist arsenal. In the South Carolina state ratification convention, one Antifederalist leader remarked that his constituents were "opposed to this new Constitution, because, they say, they have omitted to insert a bill of rights." A declaration of rights was essential to preserve "the unalienable rights of men, without a full, free, and secure enjoyment of which there can be no liberty."[6]

Supporters of the Constitution, Federalists disputed this claim, arguing that a bill of rights was unnecessary. Unlike the individual state governments, the new federal government was one of delegated authority. All power not ceded to the new government was retained by the people of the states. The individual state bills of rights would therefore continue to protect citizens. "It would have been superfluous and absurd," James Wilson observed, to stipulate "that we should enjoy those privileges, of which we are not divested either by the intention or the act, that has brought that body into existence."[7] Some Federalists even went so far as to argue that a bill of rights was not only unnecessary, but might actually threaten liberty. James Iredell issued the following warning in the North Carolina state ratification convention: "No man, let his ingenuity be what it will, could enumerate all the individual rights not relinquished by this Constitution."[8] A bill of rights might undermine liberty by creating an impression that rights not explicitly listed in such a document were not protected.

In addition to their general complaints about the absence of a bill of rights, Antifederalists highlighted several specific rights that the Constitution failed to protect. Freedom of the press, freedom of religion, and the failure to provide assurances for the right of trial by jury were among the most frequently voiced complaints. Antifederalists also complained that the Constitution failed to guard against the dangers of a standing army and threatened the existence of the state militias. As Luther Martin, a Maryland Antifederalist noted, "when a government *wishes* to deprive their citizens of freedom, and reduce them to slavery, it *generally makes use of a standing army* for that purpose, and *leaves the militia in a situation as contemptible as possible."* Most Antifederalists viewed the new central government as the most serious threat to liberty. In keeping with this view, they argued that it was vital to maintain the strength of the state government, including their militias, to prevent the federal government from using its enormous powers to threaten the liberties of the people.[9]

While the need to maintain the effectiveness of the state-controlled militia prompted comment by many Antifederalist authors, far less attention was devoted to the threat that the new government posed to the right of individual citizens to own guns. One of the most important efforts to articulate such a right was framed by the Antifederalist Robert Whitehill in the Pennsylvania state ratification convention, and later reprinted in the press as part of the Dissent of the Minority of the Pennsylvania Convention. The Dissent of the Minority recommended the following amendments to the Constitution designed to protect the right to bear arms:

> That the people have a right to bear arms for the defense of themselves and their own state, or the United States, or for the purposes of killing game; and no law shall be passed for disarming the people or any of them, unless for

crimes committed, or real danger of public injury from individuals; and as standing armies in the time of peace are dangerous to liberty, they ought not to be kept up; and that the military shall be kept under strict subordination to and be governed by the civil powers.

   The inhabitants of the several states shall have the liberty to fowl and hunt in seasonable times, on the lands they hold, and on all other lands in the United States not enclosed, and in like manner to fish in all navigable waters, and others not private property, without being restrained therein by any laws to be passed by the legislature of the United States.[10]

It is worth noting that the second provision prevented the federal government, not the states, from passing legislation preventing citizens from hunting. The first provision also allowed individuals to be disarmed when they posed a threat to society. Although Pennsylvania Antifederalists were opposed to granting extensive powers to the new federal government, they showed little reluctance in allowing their own state government to take aggressive measures to restrict access to guns when the legislature deemed such actions necessary to promote the good of the community. The notion of rights and liberty that shaped this conception of law was rather different from modern ideas about individual rights. The Pennsylvania legislature enacted a sweeping law, the Test Act, that disarmed as much as 40 percent of the state's adult white male population who were deemed to be "disaffected to the liberty and independence of this state." For Pennsylvanians the concept of rights was understood in republican, not liberal, terms. Liberalism viewed rights as strong claims against government interference. The status of individual rights in republicanism was less secure, since personal liberty always had to be weighed against the good of the community. Legislatures enjoyed tremendous latitude to enact laws that might restrict the rights of citizens, if those laws were judged to be necessary for public welfare.[11]

   If Antifederalists were apt to trust their state government more than a distant federal government, the opposite was the case for Federalists who viewed the state governments as a much greater threat to liberty. It was the state governments, Federalists noted, not Congress, that had passed pro-debtor legislation that threatened the sanctity of contractual obligations. It was also the states that had enacted restrictions on political participation such as religious tests, which were designed to bar non-Protestants from holding public office. While Federalists differed from Antifederalists on the vital question of which level of government posed a greater threat to liberty, they were shrewd enough politicians to realize that the Constitution would never be ratified if assurances were not provided to calm popular concerns over the threat of standing armies and the need to retain a strong militia system.

Noah Webster, a leading Federalist, responded to Antifederalist complaints about the absence of a bill of rights. In response to their concerns over the militia, Webster reminded Americans that "Congress likewise are to have power to provide for organizing, arming and disciplining the militia, but have no other command of them, except when in actual service. Nor are they at liberty to call out the militia at pleasure — but only, to execute the laws of the union, suppress insurrections, and repel invasions."[12] The related charge that the new government did not prohibit a standing army drew a slightly different response from Webster, who turned the Antifederalist argument on its head: it was precisely because of the strength of state militias that there was no need to fear a standing army in America. The situation of Americans, Webster asserted, was different from that of any other country in the world.

> Before a standing army can rule, the people must be disarmed; as they are in almost every kingdom in Europe. The supreme power in America cannot enforce unjust laws by the sword; because the whole body of the people are armed, and constitute a force superior to any band of regular troops that can be, on any pretence, raised in the United States.[13]

Although Federalists won several impressive victories in the early state ratification contests, the issue of a bill of rights proved to be a significant political liability. For many who were otherwise supportive of the Constitution, the absence of a bill of rights remained a serious concern. A crucial turning point in the struggle over the Constitution occurred when the sixth state to vote for ratification, Massachusetts, recommended a list of amendments that would be taken up by the First Congress after the Constitution was adopted. The positive vote by the New Hampshire Convention, the ninth state to ratify, made the Constitution the new law of the land. Four days later Virginia ratified the Constitution. No state boasted a more articulate and well-organized Antifederalist opposition than Virginia. With the Massachusetts model in mind, Virginia also proposed a set of recommended amendments modeled primarily on its own Declaration of Rights. Regarding the right to bear arms and the militia, the Virginia State Ratification Convention proposed the following amendment:

> That the people have a right to keep and bear arms; that a well regulated Militia composed of the body of the people trained to arms is the proper, natural and safe defence of a free State. That standing armies in time of peace are dangerous to liberty, and therefore ought to be avoided, as far as the circumstances and protection of the Community will admit; and that in all cases the military should be under strict subordination to and governed by the Civil power.[14]

With ratification now an accomplished fact, Antifederalists were faced with a difficult decision. Should they continue to oppose the Constitution or work within the system for change? While the debate over the Constitution had been a long and in many instances a bitter struggle, the Antifederalists reconciled themselves to becoming a loyal opposition operating within the basic outlines of the new Constitution. Thus, rather than develop as an anti-Constitutional movement, Antifederalists sought to gain as many seats in the First Congress as possible. Once in Congress, they worked hard to obtain amendments that would provide greater protections for individual rights and return additional power back to the states.[15]

The subject of amendments was taken up by the First Congress. The task of guiding the amendments through the legislative process fell to one of the most important Federalist theorists, James Madison, who had been one of the most vocal opponents of Antifederalist calls for amendments. Madison's views of the desirability of amendments to the Constitution had shifted since ratification. One contributing factor to this change was the influence of Madison's good friend Thomas Jefferson, who was serving as America's minister to France, and had kept up an energetic correspondence with Madison on the progress of ratification. Jefferson had never considered himself an Antifederalist. Yet, he was convinced that the Antifederalists were correct to insist upon the inclusion of an explicit declaration of rights. Even more important than Jefferson's arguments was Madison's recognition of the political necessity of a bill of rights. Madison faced a difficult race in Virginia in his bid for a congressional seat in the House of Representatives. The issue that seemed most important to Virginians was a bill of rights. Madison realized that a properly worded bill of rights would do little harm and would assuage many moderate Antifederalists. With the fears of these moderates mollified, Madison hoped to isolate and effectively neutralize the efforts of those Antifederalists who sought to weaken the power of the new federal government.

The original proposal for amendments sent by the House of Representatives to the Senate contained seventeen provisions, the fifth of which dealt with the militia and the right to bear arms. It read

> A well regulated militia, composed of the body of the People, being the best security of a free State, the right of the People to keep and bear arms, shall not be infringed, but no one religiously scrupulous of bearing arms, shall be compelled to render military service in person.[16]

The Senate condensed and edited the House list, paring it down to twelve provisions. The original list of twelve amendments was sent to the states to ratify. The first two proposals dealing with legislative apportionment and congressional salaries were not adopted. When the states ratified the other ten amendments, what had been the fourth amendment sent by Congress to the states for ratification became the Second Amendment to the Constitution.

The Second Amendment did not end discussion about the role of the militia in American society. Although Americans continued to praise the ideal of the militia, the actual performance of the militia on the battlefield had been less of a cause for celebration. America's military leaders, most notably George Washington, were highly critical of the performance of the militia during the Revolution and worked hard to replace it with a more effective fighting force composed of professional soldiers and a select militia composed of highly trained volunteers. Indeed, shortly after the adoption of the Second Amendment, Federalist Henry Knox lobbied to create such a select militia, something akin to the modern National Guard. Congress rejected this idea and passed the Uniform Militia Act in 1792. This law directed the states to train all their free white citizens for militia service. The act did not, however, provide a mechanism to enforce the new law and most states failed to comply with its terms. From the point of view of military preparedness the act was a failure. Continued hostility between settlers and Indians along the western frontier finally prompted Congress to act in 1794 and create a corps of five thousand male professional soldiers. This new Legion of the United States played a decisive role in defeating Indians at the Battle of Fallen Timbers in 1794. The need for a professional army of trained soldiers to wage war had become an accepted part of American culture. While Federalists and Republicans could disagree over the size of the army and continued to disagree over the need to maintain an army during peacetime, no one believed that the militia alone could defend the new nation.[17]

Given the intensity of conflict over ratification, the absence of litigation based on the various provisions of the Bill of Rights in the ensuing decades is remarkable. Apart from the crisis caused by the Alien and Sedition Acts in 1798, which generated extensive discussion about the meaning of freedom of the press, the Bill of Rights was not at the center of American constitutional debate in the years following its adoption. Issues about federalism proved far more divisive than did questions of individual rights. The Second Amendment was no exception to this general pattern.

The individual states continued to enact laws regulating gun ownership. One such law produced the first serious test of the constitutional right to bear arms. In the 1840 case of *Aymette* v. *The State,* the Supreme Court of Tennessee upheld a state law against concealed weapons. The court argued that such a law did not violate the state's constitutional protection for the right to bear arms.[18]

Scholars and the Second Amendment

Although once neglected by historians and legal scholars, the Second Amendment has become one of the most controversial topics in American constitutional history. Interest in this aspect of the Bill of Rights among legal scholars has been fueled by contemporary debates about the merits and legality of gun control. While historians have not been blind to the policy implications of their research, historical scholarship on this topic has focused on the Amendment as a reflection of eighteenth-century American society. Reconstructing the context that gave rise to the Second Amendment necessarily leads to a consideration of the assumptions, ideals, and fears that shaped the world view of Americans during the struggle over the Constitution and the Bill of Rights.

The modern debate over the meaning of the Second Amendment among historians was inaugurated by Robert Shalhope. In the essay published in this volume, Shalhope makes a forceful case that Americans understood the right to bear arms as an individual right. His principal opponent among historians has been Lawrence Delbert Cress, who argues that the right to bear arms was part of a collective right of the people that was tied to participation in the militia. For Shalhope and Cress, the meaning of the Second Amendment provides a case study of the larger historical question about the relative influence and importance of republican and liberal ideas in early America. Cress supports the republican view that American thought was more community oriented than individualist in spirit. As a political and constitutional philosophy, republicanism placed a premium on the ideal of civic virtue. According to this view citizens were to be active participants in the political process and put the good of the community ahead of their private interest. One of the most important means for citizens to display civic virtue was through service in the militia. Although Shalhope does not deny that republican ideas were significant, he argues that liberal individualist ideas about rights were equally important to Americans during this period. The ideal of liberalism that Shalhope discusses in his essay, classical liberalism, is closer in spirit to libertarianism than it is to the common everyday meaning of the word *liberal* in modern American politics. Indeed, in contemporary usage liberals generally favor more active government involvement to achieve goals such as equality. Classical liberalism, the philosophy that Shalhope ascribes to early Americans, championed a vision of government in which citizens would pursue their own private interests with relatively little interference from the state. The goal of government was to protect liberty, not promote a virtuous citizenry.[19]

Contemporary legal interest in the subject of the Second Amendment was sparked by Sanford Levinson's provocative essay "The Embarrassing

Second Amendment." Levinson took constitutional scholarship to task for ignoring the subject of the Second Amendment. He also challenged the collective rights argument of Cress, asserting that the Second Amendment was intended to provide all citizens with the ultimate check on despotism. In essence, Levinson claims that the Second Amendment incorporated a right of revolution into the Constitution. A variety of legal scholars have built on the foundation laid by Levinson's essay. Indeed, in the view of legal scholar David Williams, "Virtually all modern Second Amendment theorists agree that one purpose of the provision was to make resistance to the federal government possible." The key difference for Williams is "who possesses the right, state militias or the mass of individuals."[20]

Additional support for the individual rights thesis was provided by Joyce Lee Malcolm, an English historian who saw the Second Amendment as an outgrowth of an English concept of liberty that recognized both an individual right and a collective right to gun ownership. Malcolm elaborated and refined Levinson's suggestion that the militia was understood to be the full body of citizens in arms. Her most significant contribution to the evolving debate on the meaning of the Second Amendment was her exploration of the difference between the idea of a select militia, the analogue of the modern National Guard, and a general militia composed of the body of the people.[21] During ratification, Antifederalists attacked the idea of a select militia and praised the ideal of a general militia. The Second Amendment was intended to protect the general militia from the federal government.

The work of Levinson and Malcolm formed the core of a new interpretation of the Second Amendment that legal scholar Glenn Harlan Reynolds has dubbed the "Standard Model." Borrowing a term that physicists use to describe the convergence among recent theories about the structure of the universe, Reynolds claimed that legal scholarship on the Second Amendment had arrived at scholarly consensus comparable to physicists' Standard Model. According to the Standard Model of the Second Amendment, the Bill of Rights protects both an individual right and a collective right to bear arms. The new theory also holds that this right was viewed by the Founders as the final check on tyranny. In his highly polemical critique of the Standard Model, historian Garry Wills assailed the supporters of this interpretation, going so far as to characterize their arguments as "wacky." Perhaps the most important aspect of this critique was the suggestion that supporters of the new interpretation tended to meld together the views of Antifederalists with those of Madison and the Federalists. For Wills, Antifederalist ideas about the right to bear arms were largely irrelevant. Antifederalists were defeated in their efforts to oppose the Constitution, and were a minority within the First Congress that drafted the Bill of Rights. For Wills, it is the intent of Madison and the Federalists, not the Antifederalists, that ought to guide interpretations of the Second Amendment. Supporters of the Standard Model, sometimes described as the individual rights school, including Levinson, Reynolds, and Williams, attacked Wills, reasserting the importance of understanding the voices of both Antifederalists and Federalists and denouncing him for violating the canons of polite scholarly debate.

Although the Standard Model has won converts among legal scholars, it generally has not been warmly received by early American historians. Indeed, Robert Shalhope, the historian most often cited by supporters of the Standard Model, has attacked this interpretation as anachronistic. The Standard Model asserts that there was a broad consensus on political and constitutional ideas in the years immediately following the adoption of the Constitution and Bill of Rights. Recent historical scholarship has demonstrated that the opposite was the case. American politics was exceedingly contentious in the Revolutionary era and these divisions only intensified after the adoption of the Constitution.[22]

Other aspects of recent legal scholarship on the Second Amendment have been challenged by historians. In particular, the claim that the Second Amendment incorporated a right of revolution into the Constitution has drawn the fire of historians. There is widespread agreement among historians that the state militias were far more likely to be employed to crush rebellion than to function as agents of revolution. The use of the militia in the South to police slaves and the actions of the militia in Shays's Rebellion are the most obvious examples of the counterrevolutionary function of the militia. Even more dramatic evidence is provided by the Whiskey Insurrection of 1794, the most serious popular rebellion to occur after the adoption of the Constitution and the Bill of Rights. Angered by federal taxes on distilled spirits, farmers in western Pennsylvania took up arms, claiming to be carrying forward the principles of the American Revolution. Legal scholars have either ignored the rebellion or relegated it to a minor footnote in their accounts. The failure to deal with the Whiskey Rebellion, perhaps the most important test case of the right of revolution in the new republic, reveals an important difference between the way historians and legal scholars approach primary source documents. Whereas legal scholars depend principally on published materials for their research, historians consult both published and unpublished materials, often traveling to historical archives and rare book libraries to find the sole surviving copies of important evidence. The unpublished sources on the Whiskey Rebellion provide striking evidence that contradicts the claims of the Standard Model that the Second Amendment protected a right of revolution. All the parties involved in drafting the Bill of Rights, former Federalists and Antifederalists, denounced the Whiskey Rebels' actions. There was also fairly widespread agreement that the example of the American Revolution did not support the rebels' actions but demonstrated that their behavior was unconstitutional. The American colonists did not enjoy the benefits of representative government, whereas farmers in western Pennsylvania were represented under the Constitution. In 1776 violent revolution was the only option available to people who did not enjoy representation and had no legal recourse available to redress their grievances.[23] In 1794 the Constitution provided citizens with several political and legal remedies to challenge unjust laws.

Although legal scholars have proclaimed the debate over the meaning of the Second Amendment closed, historians have not come to the same conclusion.[24] In an important article reproduced in this collection, Don Higginbotham has revisited the complex relationship between states' rights and individual rights. While most legal scholars have cast these two ideas as antagonistic, Higginbotham's focus on the problem of federalism seeks to reunite them. The struggle over the Constitution and the Bill of Rights pits two different conceptions of how rights would be protected in the new nation against each other. Antifederalists looked to the states as the appropriate guardian of rights and feared the new central government as the greatest threat to liberty. Federalists, by contrast, viewed the state governments as the primary threat to liberty and hoped that the new central government might serve as a check on the excesses of the states.

Historian Edmund Morgan's discussion of the meaning of the militia takes a different approach to reconstructing the context of the Second Amendment. For Morgan the stark contrast between the ideal of the militia and its actual performance suggests that the importance of the militia lay less in its role as a military institution and more in its ideological and social function. Invocations of the people, Morgan reminds us, are not always affirmations of a democratic ethos. In many instances, such rhetorical appeals were designed to mask an agenda that was anything but democratic. Extolling the myth of the virtuous citizen-soldier allowed members of the gentry elite to inculcate the principles of deference in the yeomanry, the broad rank of independent landholders who formed the numerical majority in Virginia.[25]

Some of the issues raised by Morgan about the connection between myth and reality have been taken up by historian Michael Bellesîles in an important study of gun ownership in American history. Contrary to the myth that America has always been a gun culture, an image that Hollywood has done much to perpetuate, Bellesîles finds that gun ownership was far less widespread in the era in which the Second Amendment was adopted. It was only after the Civil War and the creation of an industrial society that guns became widespread. One of the important developments in the evolution of a national gun culture was the creation of the National Rifle Association

(NRA), an organization that is now at the center of contemporary political debate over the meaning of the Second Amendment.

The answer to the question, Whose right to bear did the Second Amendment protect? turns out to be more complicated than scholars once thought. No historical consensus has emerged on the issue of how to interpret what the Second Amendment originally meant. Indeed, the most recent historical scholarship now accepts that there was a considerable range of opinions in America at the time the Bill of Rights was adopted. Although Americans shared a common political vocabulary in the eighteenth century, it appears there was far less agreement on what those shared terms meant in practice. The language of the Second Amendment, like virtually every aspect of American political thought, proved to be far more malleable than any of its authors might have ever intended.

Legal scholars intent on making a forceful case about the original meaning of the Second Amendment that will influence judges and lawmakers can ill afford to present the sort of nuance in their work on the Second Amendment that professional historians strive to create in their scholarship. As historian Gordon Wood has observed, "It may be a necessary fiction for lawyers and jurists to believe in a 'correct' or 'true' interpretation of the Constitution in order to carry on their business, but we historians have different obligations and aims."[26] While historians can help educate the public, it is unlikely that Congress, the media, or the many groups lobbying on either side of the gun debate will encourage the same level of sophistication that historians demand from scholarship on the Second Amendment. Still, the more the public can be made aware of the complexity of this topic, the more likely it is that contemporary policy debates will move beyond slogans to a substantive discussion of the issues. It is important to recall that original debate over the merits of the Bill of Rights included many thoughtful discussions and a fair amount of polemical excess. After more than two hundred years it appears that the meaning of the right to bear arms continues to provoke strong reactions. One thing seems clear, the current controversy over the Second Amendment shows no signs of disappearing anytime soon. Americans are likely to continue arguing over the meaning of this text for some time to come.

Notes

1. For more on this aspect of the militia, see the Edmund S. Morgan selection included in this volume.

2. "Committee Draft of Declaration of Rights, May 27, 1776" in Jack N. Rakove, ed., *Declaring Rights: A Brief History with Documents* (Boston, 1998), 84.

3. Donald S. Lutz, *A Preface to American Political Theory* (Lawrence, Ks., 1992), 64–67.

4. On Shays's Rebellion, see Robert A. Gross, ed., *In Debt to Shays: The Bicentennial of an Agrarian Rebellion* (Charlottesville, Va., 1993).

5. George Lee Turberville to Arthur Lee, Oct. 28, 1787, in Merrill Jensen et al., eds., *The Documentary History of the Ratification of the Constitution* (16 vols. to date, Madison, 1976–), 8:127.

6. Patrick Dollard, Speech in the South Carolina State Ratification Convention, in Cecelia Kenyon, ed., *The Anti-Federalists* (Indianapolis, 1966), 187.

7. James Wilson, "Statehouse Speech, Oct. 6, 1787," in Rakove, *Declaring Rights,* 122.

8. James Iredell, "Speech in the North Carolina Ratification Convention," in ibid., 146.

9. Luther Martin, "Genuine Information . . . ," in Herbert J. Storing, ed., *The Complete Anti-Federalist* (7 vols, Chicago, 1981), 2:59.

10. Although the Dissent was signed by the Antifederalist members of the state ratification convention, including Whitehill, it was drafted by Samuel Bryan, one of the most important Antifederalist essayists, [Samuel Bryan,] "The Address and Reasons of Dissent of the Minority . . ." in *Documentary History of the Ratification of the Constitution* 2:623–24. For further discussion, see the Garry Wills essay included in this volume.

11. Saul Cornell, "Commonplace or Anachronism: The Standard Model, the Second Amendment, and the Problem of History in Contemporary Constitutional Theory," *Constitutional Commentary* 16 (1999): 221–46.

12. [Noah Webster,] "A Citizen of America," *An Examination into the Leading Principles of the Federal Constitution,* in Colleen A. Sheehan and Gary L. McDowell, eds., *Friends of the Constitution: Writings of the "Other" Federalists, 1787–88* (Indianapolis, 1998), 394. Webster went on to edit the first dictionary of American English.

13. [Noah Webster,] "Leading Principles of the Constitution," ibid., 398.

14. Helen E. Veit et al., eds., *Creating the Bill of Rights* (Baltimore, 1991), 19.

15. For a discussion of this process, see Saul Cornell, *The Other Founders: Anti-Federalism and the Dissenting Tradition in America, 1788–1828* (Chapel Hill, N.C., 1999).

16. U.S. House of Representatives, "Constitutional Amendments Proposed to the Senate," in Rakove, *Declaring Rights,* 184.

17. For an excellent summary of recent work on the debates over the militia in the early republic, see E. Wayne Carp, "The Problem of National Defense in the Early Republic," in Jack P. Greene, ed., *The American Revolution: Its Character and Limits* (New York, 1987), 14–50.

18. *Aymette* v. *The State,* in Robert J. Cottrol, ed., *Gun Control and the Constitution: Sources and Explorations on the Second Amendment* (New York, 1994), 2–10.

19. In addition to the two essays reprinted in this volume, Shalhope and Cress have debated this issue in the pages of the *Journal of American History:* Robert E. Shalhope, "The Ideological Origins of the Second Amendment," *Journal of American History* 69 (1982), 599–614; Lawrence Delbert Cress, "An Armed Community: The Origins and Meaning of the Right to Bear Arms," ibid. 71 (1984), 22–42; and Shalhope and Cress, "The Second Amendment and the Right to Bear Arms: An Exchange," ibid. 71 (1984), 587–93. For an interesting effort to explore how republican and liberal ideas might be joined together, see James T. Kloppenberg, "The Virtues of

Liberalism: Christianity, Republicanism, and Ethics in Early American Political Discourse," ibid. 74 (1987): 9–33.

20. Sanford Levinson, "The Embarrassing Second Amendment," *Yale Law Journal* 99 (Dec. 1989), 637–59; David C. Williams, "Civic Republicanism and the Citizen Militia: The Terrifying Second Amendment," *Yale Law Journal* 101 (Dec. 1991), 551–615; and Williams, "The Militia Movement and the Second Amendment Revolution: Conjuring with the People," *Cornell Law Review* 81 (May 1996), 893. The importance of Levinson's and Williams's work to the emergence of a Standard Model is discussed by Glenn Harlan Reynolds, "A Critical Guide to the Second Amendment," *Tennessee Law Review* 62 (Spring 1995), 461–512. For a critique of Levinson's interpretation, see Dennis A. Henigan, "Arms, Anarchy and the Second Amendment," *Valparaiso University Law Review* 26 (1991), 107–29; and the Garry Wills essay included in this volume.

21. Joyce Lee Malcolm's *To Keep and Bear Arms: The Origins of an Anglo-American Right* (Cambridge, Mass., 1994) stresses the English origins of the Second Amendment. For a lively exchange on Malcolm's thesis, see Joyce Lee Malcolm and Michael A. Bellesîles, "Exchange: On the History of the Right to Bear Arms," *Law & History Review* 15 (Fall 1997), 339–45.

22. For a good sampling of this scholarship, see the essays collected in Edward Countryman, ed., *What Did the Constitution Mean to Early Americans?* (Boston, 1999).

23. Saul Cornell, "Commonplace or Anachronism" and Michael A. Bellesîles, "Suicide Pace: New Readings of the Second Amendment," ibid.; Robert Shalhope, "To Keep and Bear Arms in the Early Republic," ibid.; and Don Higginbotham, "The Second Amendment in Historical Context," ibid.

24. For evidence that legal scholars have pronounced the issue settled, see the article by Reynolds cited above and Randy E. Barnett and Don B. Kates, "Under Fire: The New Consensus on the Second Amendment," *Emory Law Journal* 45 (Fall 1996), 1139–259.

25. Although Morgan's study of Virginia demonstrates the conservative function of the militia, in other settings the militia could serve as an agent of political radicalization. The Pennsylvania militia provided a means for groups, marginal prior to the Revolution, to seize political power; on this point, see Steven Rosswurm, *Arms, Country and Class: The Philadelphia Militia and the "the Lower Sort," during the American Revolution, 1775–1783* (New Brunswick, N.J., 1987); and Gregory T. Knouff, "'An Arduous Service': The Pennsylvania Backcountry Soldiers Revolution," *Pennsylvania History* 61 (1994), 45–74. Recent work on Virginia also suggests that a comparable process of democratization began and was consciously thwarted by the gentry, who were eager to maintain their own dominance; see Michael A. McDonnell, "Popular Mobilization and Political Culture in Revolutionary Virginia: The Failure of the Minutemen and the Revolution from Below," *Journal of American History* 85 (1998), 946–81.

26. Gordon S. Wood, "Ideology and the Origins of Liberal America," *William and Mary Quarterly* 3rd Series 44 (1987), 632–33.

Some Current Questions

The selections that follow deal with some of the issues about the Second Amendment that now interest historians. Other questions and other selections could have been chosen, but these show the current state of the conversation. Each selection is preceded by a headnote that introduces both its specific subject and its author. After the headnote come Questions for a Closer Reading. The headnote and the questions offer signposts that will allow you to understand more readily what the author is saying. The selections are uncut and they include the original notes. The notes are also signposts for further exploration. If an issue that the author raises intrigues you, use the notes to follow it up. At the end of all the selections are more questions, under the heading Making Connections. Turn to these after you have read the selections, and use them to bring the whole discussion together. In order to answer them, you may find that you need to reread. But no historical source yields up all that is within it to a person content to read it just once.

1. Did the Second Amendment protect an individual's right to own guns?

Robert E. Shalhope

The Armed Citizen in the Early Republic

Robert E. Shalhope, George Lynn Cross Research Professor at the University of Oklahoma, has written widely on the topic of American political and constitutional thought. In this essay Shalhope focuses on the ways in which republicanism and liberalism were joined in what became the Second Amendment. Republican theory stressed the importance of virtuous citizens as a counterweight to the danger of government corruption. Virtue was most likely to be found in independent citizen farmers, precisely the sort of individuals who would form the core of a popular militia. Liberalism, by contrast, recognized that citizens would follow their individual interests and was more concerned with protecting personal liberty from the threat of government tyranny. For Shalhope, the Second Amendment reflects the complex melding of these two political traditions in American thought.

Questions for a Closer Reading

1. How would you define the philosophy of republicanism and liberalism in your own words?

2. What role did the right to bear arms play in republican thought?

3. What did the term *the right to bear arms* mean in liberal thought?

4. Shalhope surveys a wide range of sources including philosophical writings, the private correspondence of the Founders, the proceedings of state ratification conventions, and the debates within the First Congress over the Bill of Rights. What does each source tell us about the meaning of the Second Amendment? Whose point of view is represented in each of these bodies of evidence? How should historians weigh each of these sources? Are all of these sources equally important to understanding the Second Amendment?

5. Shalhope also discusses how later constitutional commentators such as Supreme Court Justice Joseph Story understand the original meaning of the Second Amendment. How should the views of later commentators such as Story be weighed against those of contemporary sources such as the debates of the state ratification conventions?

The Armed Citizen
in the Early Republic

Introduction

Over the past quarter century concerns about the private possession and use of firearms in the United States have greatly intensified. Indeed, citizens with alternative views of "what America is and ought to be" seem to be waging a great American gun war.[1] This "war," whose operations range from polite public forums to tragic confrontations between individual citizens and the police, finds both sides arrayed behind differing interpretations of the second amendment. Citizens anxious to protect the individual's right to possess firearms stress the "right to bear arms" portion of the amendment. Those concerned with collective rights and communal responsibilities, in contrast, emphasize the "well regulated Militia" phrase in their attempt to gain restrictive gun legislation. Each group rests its case upon an appeal to history. In fact, both sides frequently draw upon the same historical data to support opposing views.[2] Unfortunately, in their efforts to promote disparate views, these polemicists have obscured the historical context within which the second amendment originated.

To grasp the meaning of the amendment, as well as the beliefs of its authors, it is necessary to understand the intellectual environment of late eighteenth-century America. Attitudes toward an armed citizenry in that time had roots in classical philosophy, but drew most fully upon a tradition of "republicanism" received from Niccolò Machiavelli* through such intermediaries as James Harrington† and James Burgh.[3]‡ The belief system which emerged from the thought of these men joined the twin themes

---

**Niccolò Machiavelli:* sixteenth-century Italian Renaissance political theorist who helped revive and reshape republican thought.
†*James Harrington:* seventeenth-century English republican theorist.
‡*James Burgh:* eighteenth-century English political theorist.

Robert E. Shalhope, "The Armed Citizen in the Early Republic," *Law and Contemporary Problems,* Vol. 49, no. 1 (1986): 125–41.

of personal right and communal responsibility. In this belief system the collective right to arms was not antithetic to that of the individual, but rather inclusive of it, indeed, deduced from it. This integration of the individual and the community has escaped modern antagonists, but it is essential to understanding the second amendment and the role of the armed citizen in the early republic.

This article analyzes the influence of republican ideas in the political culture of early America. By focusing on arms, the individual, and society from an eighteenth-century perspective rather than a twentieth-century one, it attempts to recapture the relationship between the individual and the community characteristic of the early republic. Such an approach should provide useful insights into the beliefs of the founders, the intent of the second amendment, and the legacy of the nineteenth century to the modern gun controversy.

The Relationship between Arms and Society in Republican Theory

Within the last several decades scholars have recognized the centrality of republicanism, a distinctive universe of ideas and beliefs drawn primarily from the libertarian thought of the English commonwealthmen, in shaping the attitudes of late eighteenth-century Americans.[4] The fear of standing armies and the exaltation of a militia consisting of the ordinary citizenry are two important elements of republicanism which have received considerable attention. There is an equally important theme, however, which has largely been ignored except for the work of Pocock: the vital interrelationship linking arms, the individual, and society.[5] Therefore, to understand better the origins of the second amendment, this section analyzes the role of the armed citizen within libertarian thought as well as the manner in which Americans integrated this theme into their perception of republicanism.

To comprehend libertarian beliefs regarding the relationship between arms and society one should begin with the Florentine tradition upon which republican thought so strongly depended.[6] This tradition emanated from Niccolò Machiavelli's idealization of the citizen-warrior as the essential foundation of a republic. To Machiavelli the economic independence of the citizen and his ability and willingness to become a warrior were the most dependable protections against corruption. From these basic ideas he fashioned a sociology of liberty dependent upon the place of arms in society: Political conditions must allow every citizen to have arms; moral conditions must encourage all citizens to defend their republic with enthusiasm; and economic conditions must guarantee the citizen-soldier a livelihood upon leaving the army. The interrelation of arms and civic virtue was central to Machiavelli's thought and it fostered a belief in the inseparable nature of arms and a full array of civil rights. To prevent some citizens from possessing arms while allowing others this privilege constituted both a grievous breach of personal freedom and the erosion of a vital safeguard against tyranny.

The same themes surfaced (antithetically) in the philosophy of the French absolutist Jean Bodin. To him the widespread ownership of arms constituted an essential difference between the authoritarian monarchy he favored and popular government.[7] The latter depended upon, and there-fore encouraged, the armament of its individual citizens. Monarchs, on the other hand, only risked disaster by allowing commoners to arm: "[I]t is to be feared that they will attempt to change the state, to have a part in the gov-ernment."[8] In a monarchy, therefore, "the most usual way to prevent sedi-tions, is to take away the subjects' arms."[9] Although he saw individual arms possession as the source of political unrest, Bodin's reason for opposing popular possession of arms was thus identical to Machiavelli's for support-ing it: the power that the possession of arms might give the people relative to their governors.

Speaking from a value system much closer to Machiavelli's than Bodin's, Sir Walter Raleigh agreed with this point, suggesting that among the basic principles of the tyrant was "to unarm his people of weapons, money, and all means whereby they resist his power."[10] With reference to arms as a source of power, Raleigh amplified this point: "To unarm his people, and store up their weapons, under pretense of keeping them safe, and having them ready when service requireth, and then to arm them with such, and as many as he shall think meet, and to commit them to such as are sure men."[11]

These views, along with the Florentine tradition, were reiterated in light of changing conditions in the second half of the seventeenth century by English libertarian authors such as Marchamont Nedham. Believing that a republic thrived only if its citizens were familiar with the use of arms, Ned-ham felt that the popular possession of arms was no less indispensable than the regular election of magistrates and representatives.[12]

Most important to the development of this viewpoint, at least in the light of later American attitudes, was the contribution of James Harrington.[13] Like Machiavelli he believed that the preservation of popular and repub-lican institutions depended upon the continued existence of a "virtuous" citizenry. Moreover, he also defined the virtuous citizen in terms of his pos-session of arms and his self-reliant willingness to use them in defense of self, liberty, and property. Harrington's innovation, however, lay in joining land ownership with the possession of arms as the twin bases of virtuous citizenship. Because he was both armed and landed, Harrington's virtu-ous citizen had the necessary independence to maintain his life, liberty, and property against all who would deprive him of them. From Harring-ton, libertarians came to conceptualize civic virtue in terms of the armed freeholder: upstanding, courageous, self-reliant, individually able to repulse outlaws and oppressive officials, and collectively able to overthrow domestic tyrants and defeat foreign invaders.

Subsequent authors built upon Harrington's intellectual foundation by integrating the subject of arms to the basic themes of power and oppression which permeated libertarian thought. John Trenchard and Walter Moyle,* in an attack upon standing armies, elaborated upon the theme that citizens must jealously guard their liberties. Free nations, they warned, never maintained "any Soldiers in constant Pay within their Cities, or even suffered any of their Subjects to make War their Profession."[14] Those nations knew "that the Sword and Sovereignty always march hand in hand, and therefore they trained their own citizens and the Territories about them perpetually in Arms, and their whole Commonwealths by this means became so many several formed Militias."[15] Further,

> a general Exercise of the best of their People in the use of Arms, was the only bulwark of their Liberties; this was reckon'd the surest way to preserve them both at home and abroad, the People being secured thereby as well against the Domestick Affronts of any of their own Citizens, as against the Foreign Invasions of ambitious and unruly Neighbours.[16]

The idea that citizens must have the capability to protect themselves from their rulers played an important role in the essay of Trenchard and Moyle. Without this ability citizens might lose their liberties and live in tyranny. "It's the misfortune of all Countries, that they sometimes lie under a [*sic*] unhappy necessity to defend themselves by Arms against the Ambition of their Governours, and to fight for what's their own."[17] If those in government ignored reason, the people:

> must patiently submit to [their] Bondage, or stand upon [their] own Defence; which if [they] are enabled to do, [they] shall never be put upon it, but [their] Swords may grow rusty in [their] hands; for that Nation is surest to live in Peace, that is most capable of making War; and a Man that hath a Sword by his side, shall have least occasion to make use of it.[18]

Andrew Fletcher's† warning, "he that is armed, is always the master of the purse of him that is unarmed,"[19] lent subtle support to Trenchard and Moyle's suspicion of governmental authority, which became a central element in libertarian thought.

In *Cato's Letters* Trenchard and Thomas Gordon integrated the idea of an

---

John Trenchard and Walter Moyle: seventeenth-century English republican theorists who opposed the dangers of a standing army.

†*Andrew Fletcher:* Scottish republican theorist of the early eighteenth century who wrote about the militia.

armed citizenry with the eternal tension libertarians perceived between the realms of power and liberty. They said, "The Exercise of despotick Power is the unrelenting War of an armed Tyrant upon his unarmed Subjects: It is a War of one Side, and in it there is neither Peace nor Truce."[20] Rulers must be restrained by their subjects. An unarmed populace passively fosters their leaders' natural tendency toward oppression for "Men that are above all Fear, soon grow above all Shame."[21]

While those authors often discussed the people as a body set off against their rulers, others emphasized the individual citizen's right to defend himself against vicious fellow citizens as well as corrupt authorities — both banes of any republican society. This belief became manifest in observations by Cesare Beccaria* and Thomas Paine.† In his discussion of the "false ideas of utility,"[22] Beccaria expounded upon the wrongheaded nature of laws disarming the populace. He concluded that "such laws make things worse for the assaulted and better for the assailants; they serve rather to encourage than to prevent homicides, for an unarmed man may be attacked with greater confidence than an armed man."[23] A decade later Paine echoed these sentiments when he observed that "the peaceable part of mankind will be continually overrun by the vile and abandoned, while they neglect the means of self defence."[24] For Paine, "the supposed quietude of a good man allures the ruffian; while on the other hand, arms like laws discourage and keep the invader and the plunderer in awe, and preserve order in the world as well as property."[25] To protect themselves, responsible citizens must arm themselves. American colonists clearly articulated this belief in the months following the arrival of British troops in Boston on October 1, 1768. Demanding their rights as British citizens, "to whom the *privilege* of possessing arms is expressly recognized by the Bill of Rights,"[26] Bostonians claimed that it was

> a natural Right which the people have reserved to themselves, confirmed by the Bill of Rights, to keep arms for their own defence; and as Mr. Blackstone ‡ observes, it is to be made use of when the sanctions of Society and law are found insufficient to restrain the violence of oppression.[27]

Yet the philosophers of republicanism were not blind to the desirability of disarming certain elements within their society. The right to arms was to be limited to virtuous citizens only. Arms were "never lodg'd in the hand of any who had not an Interest in preserving the publick Peace. . . ."[28]

Cesare Beccaria: eighteenth-century Italian political philosopher who wrote an influential treatise on crime and punishment.

†*Thomas Paine:* American Revolutionary pamphleteer and Enlightenment philosopher.

‡*William Blackstone:* eighteenth-century English judge whose *Commentaries on the Laws of England* became the standard work on English law for Americans in the Revolutionary era.

James Burgh further refined the concepts of opposition to standing armies, dependence upon militias, and the need for the citizen to be armed in his own self defense in his *Political Disquisitions,*[29] which proved particularly useful to Americans as they articulated their vision of republicanism. Like his predecessors, Burgh stressed the relationship between arms and power in a society: "Those, who have the command of the arms in a country, says *Aristotle,* are masters of the state, and have it in their power to make what revolutions they please."[30] Thus, "there is no end to observations on the difference between the measures likely to be pursued by a minister backed by a standing *army,* and those of a court awed by the fear of an *armed people.*"[31] Burgh linked the very nature of society to whether or not individual citizens had arms and were vigorous in their use:

> No kingdom can be secured otherwise than by arming the people. The possession of arms is the distinction between a freeman and a slave. He, who has nothing, and who himself belongs to another, must be defended by him, whose property he is, and needs no arms. But he, who thinks he is his own master, and has what he can call his own, ought to have arms to defend himself, and what he possesses; else he lives precariously, and at discretion.[32]

Burgh's work epitomized the pessimism with which the English libertarians increasingly viewed their own people and, consequently, their society. Following Machiavelli and Harrington, the English libertarians perceived a dynamic relationship between the possession of arms and the spirit and character of the people. The hallmark of virtuous republican citizenship, Burgh reemphasized, was the individual's ability and willingness to arm himself in defense of his person, his property, and his state. Consequently, Burgh bewailed what he saw as the moral deterioration of English society. Interested only in luxury and commerce, Englishmen had surrendered their arms: "The common people of *England* . . . having been long used to pay an army for fighting for them, had at this time forgot all the military virtues of their ancestors."[33]

Thus Burgh joined the long line of English libertarians who, from Harrington's time, had grieved over what they perceived as the loss of virility and virtue within their society. An increasingly luxury-loving people had ceased to arm themselves and voluntarily abdicated their martial responsibilities to professionals. True virtue sprang from the agrarian world of self-sufficient farmers, which no longer existed in England. With its demise went all opportunity for a virtuous republic. Libertarians could, however, cling to one hopeful sign: America remained an agrarian society of armed, self-sufficient husbandmen. There, liberty's flame continued to burn brightly.

Americans quickly took up this flattering view of their society. Throughout the revolutionary period and beyond they continued to view the armed husbandman as both the quintessential element and indispensable safeguard in a healthy, virtuous republican state.[34] James Madison employed this theme in the *Federalist Papers*.[35] Noting "the advantage of being armed, which the Americans possess over the people of almost every other nation," he claimed that in Europe "the governments are afraid to trust the people with arms."[36] Several decades later Timothy Dwight* reiterated this view when he wrote that:

> [T]o trust arms in the hands of the people at large has, in Europe, been believed . . . to be an experiment fraught only with danger. Here by a long trial it has been proved to be perfectly harmless. . . . If the government be equitable; if it be reasonable in its exactions; if proper attention be paid to the education of children in knowledge and religion, few men will be disposed to use arms, unless for their amusement, and for the defence of themselves and their country.[37]

Joel Barlow† clearly articulated the vital relationship of armed citizens to American republican thought. For him, America's strength rested in "making every citizen a soldier, and every soldier a citizen; not only *permitting* every man to arm, but *obliging* him to arm."[38] In Europe this idea "would have gained little credit; or at least it would have been regarded as a mark of an uncivilized people, extremely dangerous to a well ordered society."[39] Quite the reverse characterized America where, "it is *because the people are civilized, that they are with safety armed*."[40] Such was the value of freedom and equality that Americans' "conscious dignity, as citizens enjoying equal rights," precludes any desire "to invade the rights of others."[41]

> [T]he danger where there is any from armed citizens, is only to the *government*, not to the *society* and as long as they have nothing to revenge in the government (which they cannot have while it is in their own hands) there are many advantages in their being accustomed to the use of arms, and no possible disadvantage.[42]

To the morally uplifting regime of free institutions Barlow contrasted despotisms characterized by professional soldiers

> who know no other God but their king; who lose all ideas of themselves, in contemplating their officers; and who forget the duties of a man, to practise

Timothy Dwight: New England Federalist political theorist and president of Yale College.
†*Joel Barlow:* New England Federalist poet.

those of a soldier,— this is but half the operation: an essential part of the military system is to disarm the people, to hold all the functions of war, as well the arm that executes, as the will declares it, equally above their reach.[43]

Then, by integrating Adam Smith's contention that individuals who lost their martial spirit suffered "that sort of mental mutilation, deformity, and wretchedness which cowardice necessarily involves in it"[44] with his own beliefs, Barlow articulated the vital nature of armed citizens in American republican thought: A government that disarmed its people "palsies the hand and brutalizes the mind: an habitual disuse of physical forces totally destroys the moral; and men lose at once the power of protecting themselves, and of discerning the cause of their oppression."[45] Only the individual capable of defending himself with arms if necessary possessed the moral character to be a good republican citizen. In democracies "the people will be universally armed: they will assume those weapons for security, which the art of war has invented for destruction."[46] A republican society might retain its vigor and virtue only so long as its individual citizens possessed arms and the capability of using them in the defense of themselves, their property, and their society.

This theme permeated the political observations of the eighteenth century. During the struggle over the ratification of the Constitution, Federalists and anti-Federalists alike had linked the preservation of liberty to an armed populace. Richard Henry Lee* considered it "essential that the whole body of the people always possess arms, and be taught alike, especially when young, how to use them."[47] In his defense of the Constitution, Noah Webster† echoed Madison's theme: "The supreme power in America cannot enforce unjust law by the sword; because the whole body of the people are armed, and constitute a force superior to any band of regular troops that can be, on any pretence, raised in the United States."[48] Thomas Jefferson, while not a participant in the ratification process, revealed a depth of feeling transcending politics with regard to the relationship among liberty, arms, and the character of the individual republican citizen. Writing to his nephew, Peter Carr, Jefferson advised that "health must not be sacrificed to learning."[49] A few hours each day should be set aside for physical exertion. "As to the species of exercise, I advise the gun. While this gives a moderate exercise to the body, it gives boldness, enterprize [sic], and independance [sic] to the mind."[50] In contrast, he believed that "[g]ames played with the ball and others of that nature, are too violent for the body and stamp no character on the mind. Let your gun therefore be the constant

---

Richard Henry Lee: Virginian Revolutionary leader and leading Antifederalist.
†*Noah Webster:* Federalist pamphleteer and author of America's first dictionary.

companion of your walks."[51] Here is perhaps the clearest indication that Americans perceived a vital link between the gun and the character of the individual citizen.

The Bill of Rights

When James Madison and his colleagues drafted the Bill of Rights, they did so at a time when Americans felt strongly about protecting individual rights from a potentially dangerous central government. Regarding the place of arms within their society, the drafters firmly believed in two distinct principles: (1) Individuals had the right to possess arms to defend themselves and their property; and (2) states retained the right to maintain militias composed of these individually armed citizens. Further, the drafters felt that professional armies should exist only in wartime and that, in any event, the military should always be subordinate to civilian control.

These principles had been clearly articulated in the several state bills of rights as well as in the amendments to the Constitution proposed by the various state ratifying conventions. The Pennsylvania Bill of Rights, for example, stated:

> That the people have a right to bear arms for the defense of themselves and the state; and as standing armies in the time of peace are dangerous to liberty, they ought not to be kept up; And that the military should be kept under strict subordination to, and governed by, the civil power.[52]

In their ratifying convention, New Hampshire men ignored the militia issue, but did claim that "no standing Army shall be Kept up in time of Peace unless with the consent of three fourths of the Members of each branch of Congress, nor shall Soldiers in Time of Peace be quartered upon private Houses without the consent of the Owners."[53] Then, they offered a separate admonition: "Congress shall never disarm any Citizen unless such as are or have been in Actual Rebellion."[54]

The Virginia convention exclaimed:

> That the people have a right to keep and bear arms; that a well regulated Militia composed of the body of the people trained to arms is the proper, natural, and safe defence of a free State. That standing armies in time of peace are dangerous to liberty, and therefore ought to be avoided, as far as the circumstances and protection of the Community will admit; and that in all cases the military should be under strict subordination to and governed by the Civil power.[55]

New Yorkers, who suggested over fifty amendments to the Federal Constitution, observed: "That the People have a right to keep and bear Arms;

that a well regulated Militia, including the body of the People *capable of bearing Arms,* is the proper, natural and safe defence of a free state."[56] Pennsylvania's minority report, a widely publicized anti-Federalist tract, was the most specific:

> That the people have a right to bear arms for the defence of themselves and their own State, or the United States, or for the purpose of killing game; and no law shall be passed for disarming the people or any of them, unless for crimes committed, or real danger of public injury from individuals; and as standing armies in the time of peace are dangerous to liberty, they ought not to be kept up; and that the military shall be kept under strict subordination to and be governed by the civil power.[57]

The Massachusetts Declaration of Rights claimed that the people had a "right of enjoying and defending their lives and liberties" (Article I)[58] and "to keep and to bear arms for the common defense" (Article XVII).[59] This wording caused a number of towns to demand more precise language in order to spell out the individual's right to possess arms in his own defense. The citizens of Northampton, for instance, resolved:

> We also judge that the people's right to keep and bear arms, declared in the seventeenth article of the same declaration is not expressed with that ample and manly openness and latitude which the importance of the right merits; and therefore propose that it should run in this or some such like manner, to wit, The people have a right to keep and bear arms as well for their own as the common defence. Which mode of expression we are of opinion would harmonize much better with the first article than the form of expression used in the said seventeenth article.[60]

For their part, inhabitants of Williamsburgh stated:

> Upon reading the 17th Article in the Bill of Rights. Voted that these words their Own be inserted which makes it read thus; that the people have a right to keep and to bear Arms for their Own and the Common defence.
>
> Voted Nemine Contradic. ———
>
> Our reasons gentlemen for making this Addition Are these. 1st that we esteem it an essential priviledge to keep Arms in Our houses for Our Own Defence and while we Continue honest and Lawful Subjects of Government we Ought Never to be deprived of them.[61]

Influential Americans clearly differentiated individual possession of arms from service in the militia. Samuel Adams offered an amendment at his state's convention that read: "And that the said Constitution be never construed to authorize Congress to infringe the just liberty of the press or the rights of conscience; or to prevent the people of the United States who are peaceable citizens from keeping their own arms."[62] Thomas Jefferson did not even mention the militia in his initial draft of a proposed constitution for the State of Virginia. He did, however, oppose standing armies except in time of actual war.[63] Then, in a separate phrase, he wrote: "No freeman shall ever be debarred the use of arms."[64] In succeeding drafts he amended this statement to read: "No freeman shall be debarred the use of arms within his own lands or tenements."[65] Clearly, Jefferson believed that the possession of arms could be entirely unrelated to service in the militia.

James Madison believed in balancing individual rights with communal responsibilities. Having buttressed the corporate nature of society with the Constitution, Madison and others set out to protect the individual from the potentially overweening power of the community. When he offered the amendments comprising the Bill of Rights, Madison suggested they be inserted directly into the body of the Constitution in article I, section 9, between clauses 3 and 4.[66] He did not separate the right to bear arms from other rights designed to protect the individual; nor did he suggest placing it in section 8, clauses 15 and 16, which dealt specifically with arming and organizing the militia.[67] When preparing notes for an address supporting the amendments, Madison reminded himself: "They relate 1st to private rights";[68] and when he consulted with Edmund Pendleton,* Madison emphasized that "amendments may be employed to quiet the fears of many by supplying those further guards for private rights."[69]

Others assumed the same stance. Madison's confidant, Joseph Jones, believed the proposed articles were "calculated to secure the personal rights of the people so far as declarations on paper can effect the purpose."[70] Tench Coxe,† writing as "Pennsylvanian," discussed individual guarantees and then, in reference to the second amendment, maintained that "the people are confirmed by the next article in their right to keep and bear their private arms."[71] "Philodemos"‡ exclaimed: "Every freeman has *a right to the use of the press,* so he has to *the use of his arms.*"[72] Clearly, Madison and his colleagues intended the right to bear arms, like that of free speech or the press, to be a guarantee for every individual citizen whether or not he served as part of the militia.

Edmund Pendleton: Virginia Federalist.
†*Tench Coxe:* Pennsylvania Federalist author.
‡*"Philodemus":* a classical pen name, literally, *friend of the people.* Eighteenth-century Americans often adopted classical identities when writing in the press to shield themselves from personal attacks and to focus attention on the content of their ideas.

When Madison and his select committee drafted the Bill of Rights, they did their best to combine briefly the essential elements of the various state bills of rights as well as the many suggestions made by state ratifying conventions. The effort resulted in a good deal of cutting, revising, and synthesizing.[73] This drafting approach was certainly used with the second amendment, as the committee incorporated two distinct, yet related, rights into a single amendment.[74]

The brief discussion of the amendment in Congress makes clear that the committee had no intention of subordinating one right to the other.[75] Elbridge Gerry* attacked the phrase dealing with conscientious objectors, those "scrupulous of bearing arms," that appeared in the original amendment. Revealing a libertarian distrust of government, Gerry maintained that the declaration of rights in the proposed amendment "is intended to secure the people against the mal-administration of the Government," and indicated that the federal government might employ the conscientious objector phrase "to destroy the constitution itself. They can declare who are those religiously scrupulous, and prevent them from bearing arms."[76] This would return America to a European-style society in which governments systematically disarmed their citizens. Thomas Scott of Pennsylvania also strenuously objected to this phrase for fear it might "lead to the violation of another article in the constitution, which secures to the people the right of keeping arms."[77]

While congressmen firmly believed in the right of individual citizens to possess arms, no consensus existed regarding whether or not these people should be required to bear arms in the militia. One representative declared: "As far as the whole body of the people are necessary to the general defence, they ought to be armed; but the law ought not to require more than is necessary; for that would be a just cause of complaint."[78] But another representative observed that "the people of America would never consent to be deprived of the privilege of carrying arms. Though it may prove burdensome to some individuals to be obliged to arm themselves, yet it would not be so considered when the advantages were justly estimated."[79] Other congressmen even went so far as to argue that the states should supply firearms to those Americans without them.[80] Regardless of their voicers' feelings about the militia, such statements clearly revealed an urge to get arms into the hands of all American males between the ages of eighteen and forty-five, and not to restrict such possession to those in militia service.[81]

While late eighteenth-century Americans distinguished between the individual's right to *possess* arms and the need for a militia in which to *bear* them, more often than not they considered these rights inseparable. Ob-

Elbridge Gerry: Massachusetts Antifederalist politician.

servations by Madison, George Washington, Dwight, and Joseph Story provide excellent insight into why it was so natural to combine these two rights into a single amendment.

Madison observed that in the case of oppressed Europeans "it is not certain that with this aid alone [possession of arms], they would not be able to shake off their yokes."[82] Something beyond individual possession of weapons was necessary:

> But were the people to possess the additional advantages of local governments chosen by themselves, who could collect the national will, and direct the national force; and of officers appointed out of the militia, it may be affirmed with the greatest assurance, that the throne of every tyranny in Europe would be speedily overturned, in spite of the legions which surround it.[83]

Similarly, Washington declared: "To be prepared for war, is one of the most effectual means of preserving peace. A free people ought not only to be armed, but disciplined; to which end, a uniform and well-digested plan is requisite."[84]

Several decades later, Dwight exalted the right of the individual to possess arms as the hallmark of a democratic society. But he observed: "The difficulty here has been to persuade the citizens to keep arms, not to prevent them from being employed for violent purposes."[85] A similar lament characterized the observations of Story, whose *Commentaries* captured the vital essence of the relationship between armed citizens and the militia. Regarding the second amendment, Story wrote:

> The right of the citizens to keep and bear arms has justly been considered, as the palladium of the liberties of a republic; since it offers a strong moral check against the usurpation and arbitrary power of rulers; and will generally, even if these are successful in the first instance, enable the people to resist and triumph over them. And yet, though this truth would seem so clear, and the importance of a well regulated militia would seem so undeniable, it cannot be disguised, that among the American people there is a growing indifference to any system of militia discipline, and a strong disposition, from a sense of its burdens, to be rid of all regulations. How it is practicable to keep the people duly armed without some organization, it is difficult to see. There is certainly no small danger, that indifference may lead to disgust, and disgust to contempt; and thus gradually undermine all the protection intended by this clause of our national bill of rights.[86]

Such observations divulge a fascinating relationship between the armed citizen and the militia. Clearly, these men believed that the perpetuation of a republican spirit and character within their society depended upon the freeman's possession of arms as well as his ability and willingness to defend both himself and his society. This constituted the bedrock, the "palladium," of republican liberty. The militia remained equally important to them, however, because militia laws insured that American citizens would remain armed and, consequently, retain their vigorous republican character. Beyond that, the militia provided the vehicle whereby the collective force of individually armed citizens might become most effectively manifest. By consolidating the power of individual Americans, the militia forced those in power to respect the liberties of the people and minimized the need for professional armies, the greatest danger a republican society could face. This belief lay behind Jefferson's oft-quoted statement: "[W]hat country can preserve it's [sic] liberties if their rulers are not warned from time to time that their people preserve the spirit of resistance. Let them take arms."[87] Thus, the armed citizen and the militia existed as distinct, yet dynamically interrelated elements within American thought; it was perfectly reasonable to provide for both within the same amendment to the Constitution.

Post-Revolution America and the Importance of the Individual

With the passage of time, the importance of the militia faded in American thought while the image of the privately armed citizen assumed increased importance. This shift in thought, resulting from changes in perceptions of republicanism during and after the Revolution, has exerted an enormous influence over time and plays a major role in the current discussion of the private ownership of guns.

Many Americans entered the Revolution with the millennial expectation of creating a new republican society comprised of virtuous citizens free of Old World corruption.[88] During the course of the war, however, American behavior manifested disturbing and disappointing signs of European vices. Public officials and contractors indulged in graft; farmers and merchants displayed greed; many Americans traded with the enemy; and the government had to rely on conscription of men and confiscation of property in order to prosecute the war.[89] Most important, the militia — the backbone of a republican society — proved ineffective; only the presence of a regular army saved the cause.[90] Despite these facts, following Yorktown, Americans chose to believe that their victory was a confirmation of their moral strengths.[91] In 1783 it was public virtue, not its failure, that was crucial. To preserve their millennial vision of the future, Americans could not recognize the reality of the many questionable expedients employed to win the war. Concerned about their failures and anxious about their bequest to posterity, the revolutionary generation redefined its experiences and made them as virtuous and as heroic as they ought to have been. Thus, victory — gained by the fallible, partial, and selfish efforts of most Americans — allowed an entire generation to ignore this unpleasant reality and to claim that it had remained true to the standard of 1775. They offered that standard and the image of a unified, virtuous republican citizenry to future generations.

The impulse to glorify the revolutionary effort led to exaggerated claims of success and helps to explain the significance accorded the militia by Americans in the 1780s. The popular interpretation of victory in the Revolution ignored the role played by the regular army and reinstated the people's militia as the vital pillar of American virtue and essential to the preservation of the nation's unique republican character. Thus, at the time the Founders drafted the Bill of Rights, reaffirmation of the militia principle seemed important along with the guarantee of arms to the individual. In the face of nineteenth-century developments, however, the symbolic importance of the militia would fade, while that of the armed individual gained increased stature.

Americans of the revolutionary generation had made a profession of virtue and committed their republic to the escape from corruption, but Enlightenment thought taught them that natural laws of social and economic development gripped all societies in an evolutionary process that carried them inevitably from brutal savagery to the decadent civilization of commerce and corruption.[92] In response, following Harrington's reasoning that commerce could not corrupt so long as it did not overwhelm agrarian interests, Americans believed that in order to accommodate both virtue and commerce a republic must be as energetic in its search for land as it was in its search for commerce. A vast supply of land, occupied by an armed and self-directing yeomanry, might establish an endless reservoir of virtue. This belief is what gave point to Jefferson's observations that "our governments will remain virtuous for many centuries; as long as they are chiefly agricultural; and this will be as long as there shall be vacant lands in any part of America."[93] If American virtue was threatened by the increase in commercial activity following the Constitution of 1787, it could revitalize itself on the frontier through the efforts of the armed husbandman. America might yet escape the evils of history by remaining forever in a "middle state" in which the people were constantly reinvigorated through their contact with nature. The "aggressive *virtu* of agrarian warriors" could thrive forever on the frontier.[94] Thus, Americans became caught up in a flight from history into nature.

A violently activist democratic ideology, based on nature's abundance and vitality, emerged in the nineteenth century.[95] Americans would not have to create their history in closed space, which could only foster decadence and decay. They could perpetually return to youthful vigor on the frontier.

There they could begin again and regenerate themselves and their society through heroic combat with the wilderness and its creatures.[96] The frontiersman gained self-realization through the prideful display of individual prowess and by a manly independence of social or other restraints. The myth of the frontiersman became one of self-renewal or self-creation through acts of violence. Believing in the possibility of regeneration, hunters, Indian fighters, and farmers gradually destroyed the natural conditions that supported their economic and social freedom as well as their democracy of social mobility. Yet the mythology and the value system it spawned survived long after the objective conditions that had justified it disappeared. By this process, the armed individual, free to act on his environment as he saw fit, free to control his own destiny, became an integral part of the nineteenth century's legacy to modern America. It is this inheritance that undergirds the emotional commitment of so many Americans today to the private ownership of guns. This is the legacy with which gun control advocates must contend.

Conclusion

When lawyers contest the "correct" interpretation of the past, history is often the loser. Angry polarization and distortion, rather than clarification and understanding, can be the result. This is certainly the case with the current argument between those emphasizing the right-to-bear-arms part of the second amendment and those stressing its well-regulated militia phrase. Such contentiousness obscures the Founders' efforts to create a nation that would foster communal responsibilities while at the same time guaranteeing the individual rights of its citizens. It may very well be true that *neither* the militia nor the armed citizen is appropriate for modern society. In any event today's needs, however urgently they are felt, must not be allowed to obscure our understanding of the origins of the second amendment and, in the process, our understanding of revolutionary America. The second amendment included *both* of its provisions because the Founders intended both of them to be taken seriously. They intended to balance as best they could individual rights with communal responsibilities.

Notes

1. Bruce-Biggs, "The Great American Gun War," *Public Interest* 45 (1976): 37, 61.

2. Inter alia, the following articles interpret the second amendment to guarantee an individual right to arms: Caplan, "Restoring the Balance: The Second Amendment Revisited," *Fordham Urban Law Review* 5 (1976): 31; Halbrook, "The Jurisprudence of the Second and Fourteenth Amendments," *George Mason University Law*

Review 4 (1981): 1; Hardy & Stompoly, "Of Arms and the Law," *Chicago-Kent Law Review* 51:62 (1974); Whisker, "Historical Development and Subsequent Erosion of the Right to Keep and Bear Arms," *West Virginia Law Review* 78:171 (1975). The following discussions reach the opposite position from what are essentially the same historical materials: G. Newton & F. Zimring, *Firearms and Violence in American Life* (1970); Levin, "The Right to Bear Arms: The Development of the American Experience," *Chicago-Kent Law Review* 48:148 (1971); Rohner, "The Right to Bear Arms: A Phenomenon of Constitutional History," *Catholic University Law Review* 16:53 (1966); Weatherup, "Standing Armies and Armed Citizens: An Analysis of the Second Amendment," *Hastings Constitutional Law Quarterly* 2:961 (1975).

In recent years the bulk of the literature has tended to support the individual right position. *See,* e.g., Staff of Subcomm. on the Constitution of Senate Comm. on the Judiciary, 97th Cong., 2nd Sess., The Right to Keep and Bear Arms (Comm. Print 1982); Caplan, "The Right of the Individual to Bear Arms," *Detroit College Law Review* 4:789 (1982); Dowlut, *The Right to Arms: Does the Constitution or the Predilection of Judges Reign?,* 36 *Oklahoma Law Review:* 65 (1983); Gardiner, "To Preserve Liberty — A Look at the Right to Keep and Bear Arms," *Northern Kentucky Law Review* 10:63 (1982); Halbrook, "To Keep and Bear Their Private Arms: The Adoption of the Second Amendment (1787–1791)," *Northern Kentucky Law Review* 10:13 (1982); Kates, "Handgun Prohibition and the Original Meaning of the Second Amendment," *Michigan Law Review* 82:204 (1983); Malcolm, "The Right of the People to Keep and Bear Arms: The Common Law Tradition," *Hastings Constitutional Law Quarterly* 10: 285 (1983).

3. For a discussion of these classical roots, see Halbrook, "The Second Amendment as a Phenomenon of Classical Political Philosophy," in *Firearms and Violence: Issues of Public Policy* (D. Kates ed., 1984), 363–83.

4. This literature is reviewed in Shalhope, "Toward a Republican Synthesis: The Emergence of an Understanding of Republicanism in American Historiography," *William and Mary Quarterly* 29:49–80 (1972), and Shalhope, "Republicanism and Early American Historiography," *William and Mary Quarterly* 39:334–56 (1982).

5. This theme appears throughout J. Pocock, *The Machiavellian Moment: Florentine Political Thought and the Atlantic Republican Tradition* (1975).

6. The discussion of Niccolò Machiavelli which follows in the text is drawn from J. Pocock, supra note 5, at 199–213, 290–92.

7. J. Bodin, *The Six Bookes of a Commonweale* (K. McRae ed., 1962), 542, 599–614, 605.

8. Id. at 605.

9. Id. at 542.

10. W. Raleigh, *The Works of Sir Walter Raleigh, Kt., Now First Collected: To Which Are Prefixed the Lives of the Author, by Oldys and Birch* (Oxford, 1829), 22.

11. Id. at 25.

12. *Mercurius Politicus* 103 (London, May 20–27, 1652): 1609–13.

13. The discussion of James Harrington which follows in the text draws upon J. Pocock, supra note 5, at 383–400; *see also* J. Harrington, *The Political Works of James Harrington* (J. Pocock ed., 1977).

14. J. Trenchard and W. Moyle, *An Argument Shewing, That a Standing Army Is Inconsistent with a Free Government, and Absolutely Destructive to the Constitution of the English Monarchy* (London, 1697), 7.

15. Id.

16. Id.

17. Id. at 12.

18. Id. at 7.

19. A. Fletcher, "A Discourse of Government with Relations to Militias," in *The Political Works of Andrew Fletcher, Esq.* (London, 1737).

20. J. Trenchard and T. Gordon, *Cato's Letters: Or, Essays on Liberty, Civil and Religious, and Other Important Subjects* (London, 1755), 189.

21. Id. at 255.

22. C. Beccaria, *An Essay on Crimes and Punishments* (1764).

23. Id. at 87–88.

24. T. Paine, *The Writings of Thomas Paine* (M. Conway ed., 1894–1896 and reprint 1967), 56.

25. Id. at 56.

26. "A Journal of the Times" for February 6, 1769, printed in the *Boston Evening-Post,* April 3, 1769.

27. "A Journal of the Times" for March 27, 1769, printed in the *Boston Evening-Post,* May 25, 1769.

28. J. Trenchard and W. Moyle, supra note 14, at 7. Nedham similarly declared that arms should not be "in the hands of any but such as have an Interest in the Publick." *Mercurius Politicus,* supra note 12, at 1610.

29. J. Burgh, *Political Disquisitions: Or, an Enquiry into Public Errors, Defects, and Abuses* (London, 1774), 2.

30. Id. at 345 (footnote omitted).

31. Id. at 476.

32. Id. at 390.

33. Id. at 415.

34. For an analysis of these attitudes, see Shalhope, "The Ideological Origins of the Second Amendment," *Journal of American History* 69 (1982): 599, 605–07.

35. *The Federalist* No. 46 [45], at 321–22 (J. Madison) (J. Cooke ed., 1961). (This essay, originally published as number 45, appears as number 46 in the Cooke edition. For an explanation of this discrepancy, see pp. xviii–xix in the Cooke edition.)

36. Id.

37. T. Dwight, *Travels in New-England and New-York* (London, 1823), xiv.

38. J. Barlow, *Advice to the Privileged Orders in the Several States of Europe: Resulting from the Necessity and Propriety of a General Revolution in the Principle of Government,* Parts I and II, at 16 (London 1792, 1795 and reprint 1956).

39. Id.

40. Id.

41. Id. at 17.

42. Id.

43. Id. at 45.

44. A. Smith, *An Inquiry into the Nature and Causes of the Wealth of Nations* (London, 1776), 373. For an excellent discussion of Adam Smith's attitudes toward the relationship between martial spirit and the public character, see D. Winch, *Adam Smith's Politics: An Essay in Historiographic Revision* (1978), 103–20.

45. J. Barlow, supra note 38, at 45.

46. Id. at 46.

47. R. Lee, *Letters from the Federal Farmer to the Republican* (W. H. Bennett ed., 1978) (1st ed. n.p. 1777–1778), 124. (*Author note:* Historians have now challenged Lee's authorship.)

48. Webster, "An Examination into the Leading Principles of the Federal Constitution," in *Pamphlets on the Constitution of the United States,* 56 (P. Ford ed., 1971).

49. T. Jefferson, "Thomas Jefferson to Peter Carr, August 19, 1785," in 8 *The Papers of Thomas Jefferson* (J. Boyd ed., 1950–1982), 405, 407 [hereinafter cited as *Jefferson Papers*].

50. Id.

51. Id.

52. *The Federal and State Constitutions, Colonial Charters, and Other Organic Laws of the States, Territories and Colonies Now or Heretofore Forming the United States of America* (F. Thorpe ed., 1909), 3083. [hereinafter cited as *F. Thorpe*]. All of the state bills of rights appear in this collection.

53. E. Dumbauld, *The Bill of Rights: And What It Means Today* (1957), 182.

54. Id. at 185.

55. Id.

56. Id. at 189. New York had the only state amendment that distinguished between keeping and bearing arms. It allowed all citizens to possess arms, but only those with the capability to bear them were asked to do so.

57. Id. at 174. For an excellent analysis of this report, see 2 *The Documentary History of the Ratification of the Constitution* (M. Jensen ed., 1976), 617–40.

58. *F. Thorpe,* supra note 52, at 1889.

59. Id. at 1892.

60. *The Popular Sources of Political Authority: Documents on the Massachusetts Constitution of 1780,* at 574 (O. Handlin and M. Handlin eds., 1966).

61. Id. at 624.

62. W. Wells, *The Life and Public Services of Samuel Adams, Being a Narrative of His Acts and Opinions, and of His Agency in Producing and Forwarding the American Revolution,* 267 (Boston, 1865).

63. *See Jefferson Papers,* supra note 49, at 344.

64. Id. at 353.

65. Id. at 363.

66. *The Papers of James Madison* (R. Rutland ed., 1977), 201.

67. *See* id. at 193, 201.

68. Id. at 193.

69. Id. at 306–07.

70. Id. at 258–59.

71. *Fed. Gazette and Philadelphia Evening Post,* June 18, 1789, at 2, col. 1.

72. *Pennsylvania Gazette* (Philadelphia), May 7, 1788, at 3, col. 2.

73. For an excellent analysis of this process, see B. Schwartz, *The Great Rights of Mankind: A History of the American Bill of Rights* (1977), 160–91.

74. There is nothing incongruous in the second amendment's combination in one article of such distinct, but related, ideas as that of the privately armed citizen and that of a militia composed of citizens bearing their own private arms. In this same manner the first amendment combines the distinct, yet closely related, principles of freedom of religion and separation of church and state with the more remotely related ones of freedom of speech and the press and the right of assembly and petitioning for grievances.

75. This is the manner in which contemporary as well as later nineteenth-century legal scholars interpreted the amendment. See Kates, supra note 2, at 240–43. Writing in 1829, William Rawle discussed the militia and then stated: "The corollary, from the first position, is, that *the right of the people to keep and bear arms shall not be*

infringed. The prohibition is general. No clause in the Constitution could by any rule of construction be conceived to give to congress a power to disarm the people." W. Rawle, *A View of the Constitution of the United States of America* (2nd ed., Philadelphia, 1829 and reprint 1970), 125 (emphasis in original). Fifty years later Thomas Cooley claimed that: "it might be supposed from the phraseology of this provision that the right to keep and bear arms was only guaranteed to the militia; but this would be an interpretation not warranted by the intent." Then, "the meaning of the provision undoubtedly is, that the people, from whom the militia must be taken, shall have the right to keep and bear arms; and they need no permission or regulation of law for the purpose." T. Cooley, *The General Principles of Constitutional Law in the United States of America* (1880), 271.

In their interpretations of the second amendment various authors have stressed the amendment's wording. See supra note 2. It is clear, however, that James Madison and the committee worked toward succinctness. Indeed, Madison's original suggestion read: "The right of the people to keep and bear arms shall not be infringed; a well armed and well regulated militia being the best security of a free country: but no person religiously scrupulous of bearing arms shall be compelled to render military service in person." E. Dumbauld, supra note 53, at 207.

76. *Annals of Cong.* (J. Gales ed., 1789), 779.

77. Id. at 749.

78. *See* id. at 1806.

79. Id.

80. *See* id. at 1807.

81. This was the opinion of St. George Tucker, one of the leading jurists of the day. When he edited Blackstone's *Commentaries,* Tucker noted the master's observation that the right of the people to bear arms constituted one of the essential rights necessary to protect life, liberty, and property. His footnote to this section read: "The right of the people to keep and bear arms shall not be infringed. Amendments to C. U. S. [Constitution of the United States] Art. 4, and this without any qualification as to their condition or degree, as is the case in the British government." 1 *William Blackstone, Commentaries,* 143 n.40 (Philadelphia, 1803 and reprint 1965). In another note Tucker observed that "whosoever examines the forest, and game laws in the British code, will readily perceive that the right of keeping arms is effectually taken away from the people of England." Id. at 144 n.41. Blackstone himself informed us that the "prevention of popular insurrections and resistance to government, by disarming the bulk of the people . . . is a reason oftener meant, than avowed, by the makers of the forest and game laws." 2 id. at 412 (footnote omitted).

82. *The Federalist* No. 46 [45], at 321–22 (J. Madison) (J. Cooke ed., 1961) (see supra note 35).

83. Id.

84. *Annals of Congress* (J. Gales ed., 1790), 933.

85. T. Dwight, supra note 37, at xiv.

86. J. Story, *Commentaries on the Constitution of the United States; With a Preliminary Review of the Constitutional History of the Colonies and States, Before the Adoption of the Constitution* (Boston, 1833), 746–47 (footnotes omitted).

87. *Jefferson Papers,* supra note 49, at 356.

88. G. Wood, *The Creation of the American Republic, 1776–1787,* at 91–124 (1969).

89. The discussion of the symbolic importance of the militia that follows in the text draws upon C. Royster, *A Revolutionary People at War: The Continental Army and American Character, 1775–1783,* at 331–68 (1979).

90. Id.

91. Id.

92. For an outstanding analysis of the republican perception of social progress and decay, see D. McCoy, *The Elusive Republic: Political Economy in Jeffersonian America* (1980), 13–47.

93. *Jefferson Papers,* supra note 49, at 442 (letter from Jefferson to James Madison).

94. These observations regarding the tension between commerce and virtue rest upon J. Pocock, supra note 5, at 506–52. The quotation appears id. at 537.

95. For excellent insight into the development of this ideology, see J. Ward, *Andrew Jackson, Symbol For an Age* (1953).

96. This analysis of the myth of regeneration draws upon M. Rogin, *Fathers and Children: Andrew Jackson and the Subjugation of the American Indian* (1975), and R. Slotkin, *Regeneration Through Violence: The Mythology of the American Frontier, 1600–1860* (1973).

2. Was the Second Amendment intended to protect the people's right to maintain a well-regulated militia?

Lawrence Delbert Cress

A Well-Regulated Militia: The Origins and Meaning of the Second Amendment

From *The Bill of Rights: A Lively Heritage*

Lawrence Delbert Cress is dean of the College of Liberal Arts and professor of history at Willamette University. In this essay, Professor Cress provides an alternative to Shalhope's interpretation of the Second Amendment as an expression of an individual and collective right to bear arms. For Cress, the meaning of the Second Amendment must be read as an affirmation of civic republican ideals. When the language of the Second Amendment is compared with the failed proposals for amendments suggested by Antifederalists, the true meaning of the amendment becomes clear. Although amendments explicitly affirming an individual right to bear arms were suggested during ratification, Madison and other members of the First Congress studiously avoided modeling the Second Amendment on these examples. The language of the Second Amendment, Cress concludes, followed the more typical language of the state constitutions that linked the right to bear arms to the necessity of maintaining a well-regulated militia.

Questions for a Closer Reading

1. What role did the militia play in American life during the Revolutionary era?

2. Why did Americans fear standing armies?

3. What does the militia's role in Shays's Rebellion reveal about the way Americans understood its purpose?

4. Who were the Antifederalists? What role did they play in the evolution of the Second Amendment? How should we weight Antifederalist ideas when seeking to understand the meaning of the Second Amendment?

5. Given that Cress and Shalhope cite many of the same sources, what accounts for the radically different interpretations each advances for understanding the meaning of the Second Amendment?

A Well-Regulated Militia: The Origins and Meaning of the Second Amendment

Unlike provisions of the Bill of Rights that guaranteed such individual rights as freedom of speech, due process, and religious choice, the Second Amendment to the United States Constitution was not written to assure private citizens the prerogative of carrying weapons. To the leaders of the American Revolution it meant something very different. The Second Amendment was intended to guarantee that the sovereign citizenry of the republic (armed, propertied, and able to vote) would always remain a vital force in America's constitutional order.[1] Despite the militia's poor showing during the revolutionary war, Americans remained convinced that republican government would fail without a "well-regulated militia."

Lawrence Delbert Cress, "A Well-Regulated Militia: The Origins and Meaning of the Second Amendment," in Jon Kukla, ed., *The Bill of Rights: A Lively Heritage* (Richmond, 1987), 55–65.

The lessons of history, they believed, were clear. Only a citizenry organized into local militia companies could deter ambitious tyrants or foreign invaders. Republics, whether ancient or modern, thrived only when their citizens were willing and able to leave the plow for the field of battle. When a professional army usurped the citizenry's role in national defense, especially as a consequence of political intrigue or moral decadence, republics withered and liberty fell victim to tyranny and oppression.

A well-regulated militia not only protected citizens against the intrigues of ambitious rulers, it also protected the body politic against civil disorder. Daniel Shays's Rebellion, an armed insurrection in western Massachusetts in 1786, had sent tremors through the nation. And, history suggested that republican governments were especially vulnerable to domestic turmoil. To the generation that wrote it, the Second Amendment was at once a declaration of a fundamental principle of good government and a means to protect the stability of republican institutions. It did not guarantee individuals, such as Daniel Shays and his followers, the right to stockpile armaments.

The Second Amendment had roots deep in Anglo-American political and constitutional theory. Since the mid-seventeenth century, English political theorists had linked the militia to the maintenance of a balanced, stable, and free constitution. James Harrington, whose *Commonwealth of Oceana* (London, 1656) was widely read by Americans of the revolutionary generation, recommended the militia both for national defense and to deter the misuse of political power. Political writers at the time of the Glorious Revolution of 1689 emphasized the militia's importance for constitutional stability. Algernon Sidney warned that tyranny arose whenever the militia was allowed to decay. John Trenchard, later popular in the colonies as the author with Thomas Gordon of *Cato's Letters,* began his career as a pamphleteer by chiding Parliament for providing William III with a standing army after the Treaty of Ryswick in 1697. Standing armies, he wrote, were the agents of political intrigue and corruption. Only a militia could be counted upon to protect both the territory and the liberties of free people.[2]

Between 1763 and 1776, Americans felt the truth of Trenchard's indictment. The occupation of Boston by British soldiers in 1768 and again in 1774, to say nothing of the Boston Massacre of 1770, confirmed the belief that hired soldiers were agents of political oppression. Although America did resort to professional soldiers in the revolutionary war, the country emerged from the Revolution no less persuaded by Trenchard's condemnation of standing armies. When they framed the Bill of Rights with an eye to preserving the republican gains of the Revolution, both the danger of standing armies and the militia's positive role as the armed manifestation of the sovereign people were important considerations.

The statutory antecedents of the Second Amendment reached far into the Anglo-American past. Magna Carta, a feudal compact accepted by King John at Runnymede in 1215 in exchange for renewed pledges of loyalty from his rebellious nobles, outlined the prerogatives of the nobility and the limits of royal authority. As an agreement between the king and the politically articulate community of the realm, Magna Carta served as an important touchstone for the development of Anglo-American law. Chapter 29 guaranteed every knight the right to serve in the castle-guard or to send someone of his own choosing to perform that duty and prohibited the king from forcing noblemen to pay taxes in lieu of personal service. The nobles in effect prevented King John from creating an army supported by their taxes but independent of their control. Magna Carta was the first step toward insuring the citizenry (then narrowly defined as the nobility) a role in the realm's defense.

Parliament grappled with similar matters during the Glorious Revolution. In the 1680s James II increased the number of Roman Catholic military officers and excluded Protestant officers in violation of the 1673 Test Act, and he imported Irish Catholics to fill the army's expanding ranks. Thus, as the English Bill of Rights phrased it, he "did endeavor to subvert and extirpate the Protestant religion, and the laws and liberties of this kingdom" by "raising and keeping a standing army . . . without consent of parliament" and by "causing several good subjects, being Protestants, to be disarmed, at the same time when papists were both armed and employed." To correct this, the Bill of Rights of 1689 prohibited the English monarchy from raising an army during peacetime without Parliament's consent and guaranteed that "subjects which are Protestants, may have arms for their defence suitable to their conditions, and as allowed by law." The English Bill of Rights did not create an unlimited right to bear arms, however, for Protestants were to "have arms for their defence" only as was "suitable to their conditions and as allowed by law." Arms were denied to men who did not own lands worth at least £100, unless they were the sons or heirs of an esquire, knight, or nobleman. Parliament also reserved the future option of restricting "by law" access to arms. These provisions were intended to ensure a stable government free from the threat of disruptions by Catholic Jacobites and the intrigues of future monarchs.[3]

A century later, the framers of the American states' declarations of rights also sought to lay the foundations for constitutional stability. When Thomas Jefferson indicted George III in the Declaration of Independence for keeping "among us in time of peace, standing armies without the consent of our legislatures," he underscored the American concern about the relationship between liberty and citizen soldiers, but the militia tradition had more than just rhetorical significance. Patriot leaders in the colonies during the winter and spring of 1774–1775 adopted resolutions declaring "that a well-regulated Militia, composed of the gentlemen, freeholders, and other freemen, is the natural strength and only stable security of free Government."[4] With independence at hand, the states' declarations of rights identified the militia as an institution necessary for the preservation of liberty.

Virginia's Declaration of Rights — adopted on 12 June 1776, nearly a month before the American colonies officially announced their independence — set the pattern. Article 13, drafted by George Mason and approved by a committee that included James Madison, declared "that a well regulated Militia, composed of the Body of the People, trained to Arms, is the proper, natural, and safe Defence of a free State." Two months later, Pennsylvania adopted in article 13 of its own declaration of rights the proposition that "the people have a right to bear arms for the defence of themselves and the state." The language was slightly different, but the meaning was the same. Only the trained, armed, and organized citizen militia could be depended upon to preserve republican liberties for "themselves" and to ensure the constitutional stability of the "state." Both Virginians and Pennsylvanians warned that standing armies were "dangerous to liberty" and stipulated that the military be kept "under strict subordination" to the civil government. Without a strong, popularly based militia, liberty would succumb to the dictates of tyrants.[5]

Delaware, Maryland, and North Carolina adopted similar declarations during the first year of independence, the first two states by borrowing language from Virginia's article 13, and North Carolina following Pennsylvania's lead by declaring that "the people have a right to bear arms, for the defence of the state." Vermont, though not formally a state until 1792, quoted Pennsylvania's article 13 in its 1777 declaration of rights. In the same year, New York incorporated an equally clear statement in the body of its constitution. Announcing it to be "the duty of every man who enjoys the protection of society to be prepared and willing to defend it," New Yorkers proclaimed that the "militia . . . at all times . . . shall be armed and disciplined."[6]

In Massachusetts, John Adams drafted the bill of rights that was ratified with the 1780 constitution. "The people," he wrote, "have a right to keep and bear arms for the common defence." New Hampshire's 1783 bill of rights made the same point, declaring "A well regulated militia is the proper, natural, and sure defence of a state." Both documents condemned standing armies and subordinated the military to civil authority, while affirming the citizen militia's collective role as the protector of personal liberty and constitutional stability against ambitious tyrants and uncontrolled mobs.[7]

Several states put limits on citizens' militia obligation. Pennsylvania, Delaware, and Vermont provided that no "man who is conscientiously scrupulous of bearing arms" could be "compeled" to serve in the militia, but they required that conscientious objectors meet their obligations with "equivalents," payments equal to the cost of their militia service. These clauses permitting conscientious objection to military service demonstrate yet again that for eighteenth-century Americans "to bear arms" meant militia service. State after state guaranteed a role in the common defense collectively to the "people" or the "militia." On the other hand, when describing individual rights such as freedom of conscience they used the terms "man" or "person." New Hampshire's bill of rights — the last written during the Confederation period and, as such, a compendium of previous thinking on the matter — is a case in point. It declared the importance of "a well regulated militia" to the defense of the state and exempted from service any "person . . . conscientiously scrupulous about the lawfulness of bearing arms." The individual right of conscience was asserted against the collective responsibility for the common defense. These same concerns surfaced in the debate about the Constitution.[8]

During the last days of the Philadelphia convention, Virginia delegate George Mason, having failed to secure a separate bill of rights, sought an explicit statement of the militia's place in republican government. He wanted a clause explaining that the congressional power to arm, organize, and discipline the militia was intended to secure "the Liberties of the People . . . against the Dangers of regular Troops or standing Armies in time of Peace." When the Convention failed to agree, Mason refused to sign the Constitution. As he explained in his widely read "Objections to the Constitution of Government formed by the Convention," the document contained "no Declaration of Rights" and specifically lacked a "declaration of any kind . . . against the danger of standing armies." To correct this omission, Mason backed an amendment, drafted on the eve of Virginia's ratification convention, declaring that the "People have a Right to keep & bear Arms" because "a well regulated Militia [is] the proper natural and safe Defence of a free State." Mason's proposal also rehearsed the dangers of standing armies and the need for the "strict Subordination" of military to civil authority. A separate amendment would have provided that a person "religiously scrupulous of bearing Arms" be allowed "to employ another to bear Arms in his Stead." Never did Mason challenge the Constitution's failure to guarantee individual access to weapons.[9]

During the debates over the Constitution, many critics worried that the proposed government threatened the militia's important role in the republic. Maryland Antifederalist Luther Martin challenged the proposed government's military prerogatives: "Instead of guarding against a standing army, . . . which has so often and so successfully been used for the subversion of freedom," Martin argued, the Constitution gave "it an express and constitutional sanction." Congress's authority over the state militias, he warned, could be used "even to disarm" them. Worse, the militia might be needlessly mobilized and sent marching to the far reaches of the Union so that the people would be glad to see a standing army raised in its stead. "When a government wishes to deprive its citizens of freedom," Martin noted, "it generally makes use of a standing army [while leaving] the militia in a situation as contemptible as possible, lest they might oppose its arbitrary designs."[10] Pennsylvania's Antifederalists demanded that the states be given a veto over any call for militia service outside a state's borders.

Concern arose too over the Constitution's failure to protect conscientious objectors. Antifederalist candidates for the New York convention charged that the Constitution left "men conscientiously scrupulous of bearing arms . . . liable to perform military duty."[11] Reflecting the sentiments of the state declarations of rights, the Antifederalists were determined to preserve the militia as a bulwark of republican government but also anxious to protect the individual's free exercise of conscience.

The notion that individual citizens should be guaranteed access to weapons surfaced several times during the debate over the Constitution. A minority report from the Pennsylvania ratifying convention borrowed language from the state's own declaration of rights to declare not only the people's right "to bear arms for the defence of themselves and their own State or the United States" but also the right to bear arms "for the purpose of killing game," while adding the proviso that "no law shall be passed for disarming the people or any of them." Samuel Adams, of Massachusetts, argued that the Constitution should never be construed "to authorize Congress to . . . prevent the people of the United States, who are peaceable citizens from keeping their own arms" but then renounced that position after reflecting on Shays's Rebellion in western Massachusetts. Finally, among a series of amendments recommended for consideration by the First Congress, New Hampshire proposed that "Congress shall never disarm any citizen unless such as are or have been in Actual Rebellion."[12]

The principles of these resolutions were close to the classical republican understanding of the armed citizenry. In each case, bearing arms was linked to the citizenry's collective responsibility for defense, familiar warnings about the danger of standing armies, and affirmations of the need to subordinate military to civil authority. Neither Pennsylvania's critics nor New Hampshire's cautious supporters of the Constitution had moved far, if at all, beyond the eighteenth-century notion that bearing arms meant militia service, and no other state followed their lead. Pennsylvania's Antifederalists provided for the disarming of criminals and conceded that further action would be appropriate if society faced "real danger of public injury from individuals." The order and safety of society always took precedence over the individual's claim to possess weapons, and constitutional stability remained the preeminent consideration. The only other hint that Americans may have viewed bearing arms as an individual right occurs in one of Thomas Jefferson's early draft proposals for Virginia's new state constitution. Jefferson's draft had a clause guaranteeing every freeman the use of arms "within his own lands or tenements," but this provision was not incorporated in the Constitution of 1776. Virginia's statesmen were satisfied that George Mason's thirteenth article of the Declaration of Rights protected the "Militia, composed of the body of the people, trained to arms" and accurately stated the armed citizenry's proper role in a republic.[13]

The amendments proposed in the state ratifying conventions reflected the concerns about national military power and the republican principles embodied in the states' declarations of rights. New York and North Carolina wanted to limit congressional power to raise a peacetime army by requiring "the consent of two thirds" of the House and Senate. Maryland suggested limiting a soldier's enlistment to four years to prevent Congress from creating a permanent military force. More than half of the states advocated strong state militias to counter the tyrannical potential of the Constitution. Fearing that the militia would be purposely neglected, some states proposed guarantees that the states could organize, arm, and discipline their citizens if Congress failed to fulfill its responsibilities. Against the more common fear that Congress's right to call out the militia would prove detrimental to republican liberties, New Yorkers recommended that a state's militia not be allowed to serve outside its borders longer than six weeks "without the consent of the legislature thereof." Others worried that the subjection of the militia to martial law might lead to abuses. The Maryland and North Carolina conventions asked Congress to amend the Constitution so that the militia could be placed under martial law only "in time of war, invasion, or rebellion." Finally, several state conventions stated firmly that no person "religiously scrupulous of bearing arms" should be compelled to serve in the military.[14]

Virginia's proposed amendments, which directly influenced Madison's draft of the Bill of Rights, bring into focus the concerns that ultimately produced the Second Amendment. Indeed, the changes proposed by the commonwealth's ratifying convention neatly defined the issues raised during later congressional debates. Declaring that "the people have a right to keep and bear arms," Virginians asked for constitutional recognition of the principle that "a well regulated Militia, composed of the Body of the People trained to Arms, is the proper, natural, and safe Defence of a free State." This proposition addressed the fear that the new government might disarm the citizenry while raising an oppressive standing army. To reinforce the point, the convention urged a constitutional declaration that standing armies "are dangerous to liberty, and therefore ought to be avoided, as far as the circumstances and protection of the community will admit." The Constitution was also found wanting for failing to pronounce the military "in all cases" subordinate to "civil power." The Virginia convention prepared a separate amendment "That any person religiously scrupulous of bearing arms ought to be exempted, upon payment of an equivalent to employ another to bear arms in his stead." No one expressed concern about an individual citizen's access to weapons.[15]

Madison had Virginia's recommendations in mind when, on 8 June 1789, he proposed to Congress that the Constitution be amended to provide that "The right of the people to keep and bear arms shall not be infringed; a well armed and well regulated militia being the best security of a free country: but no person religiously scrupulous of bearing arms shall be compelled to render military service in person." Six weeks later, a committee composed of Madison and ten representatives (one from each of the other states that had ratified the Constitution) began preparing a formal slate of amendments, using as a guide both Madison's recommendations and those proposed by the states. The committee revised Madison's original recommendation and stated more explicitly the armed citizenry's importance to the constitutional order.[16]

Such doubts as were raised remind us of the militia's importance in the political theory of the day. The failure to link freedom of conscience with the obligation to find a substitute or pay an "equivalent" troubled many members of the House. Requiring one part of the population to provide for the defense of the other was simply "unjust," argued James Jackson, of Georgia. Others believed that matters of "religious persuasion" had no place in an amendment designed to guarantee a fundamental principle of republican government. "It is extremely injudicious," warned one congressman, "to intermix matters of doubt with fundamentals." Such concerns brought the House of Representatives within two votes of striking the conscientious objection clause from the proposed amendment.[17]

Congressman Ædanus Burke, of South Carolina, proposed a clause declaring that a "standing army . . . in time of peace is dangerous to public liberty, and such shall not be raised . . . without the consent of two-thirds of the members present of both Houses" and an explicit statement of the subordination of military to civil authority. Burke's motion was defeated because some congressmen thought a simple majority vote was sufficient and other congressmen complained that the debate had already been closed. Nevertheless, Burke's amendment again demonstrates what Congress meant by the Second Amendment. The aim was to confirm a fundamental principle of republican government, that a well-regulated militia was "the best security of a free State."[18]

Little is known about the Senate debate on the Second Amendment; it seems to have been similar to that in the House. The Senate joined the House in rejecting the proposal to restrict Congress's power to raise armies during peacetime but denied approval to the controversial conscientious objection clause. The Senate's changes were accepted by a joint conference committee of both houses, and on 24 and 25 September 1789, the House and Senate respectively voted their approval.

We also know little about debate on the Second Amendment in the states. No state legislature rejected it. As a statement of republican principles already commonplace in state declarations of rights, it probably evoked little discussion. If any doubts were raised, they might have focused on the amendment's failure explicitly to describe the dangers of a standing army.

When Virginia ratified the Second Amendment on 15 December 1791 the statement that "A well regulated militia, being necessary to the security of a free State, the right of the people to keep and bear arms, shall not be infringed," became a part of the United States Constitution. The militia had played an important role in stemming the tide of oppression that necessitated independence from Great Britain, and it alone offered a republican remedy to domestic disorders such as Shays's Rebellion. The Second Amendment gave constitutional sanction to the idea that the militia was the institutional expression of the citizenry's collective obligation to bear arms against the internal and external enemies of the state — "a well regulated militia" to defend the liberties of the people against a demagogue's armed mob or a tyrant's standing army.

Notes

1. The Second Amendment has been the object of scholarly inquiry before. Most recently Robert E. Shalhope, "The Ideological Origins of the Second Amendment," *Journal of American History* 69 (1982–1983): 599–614, has argued that Americans of the revolutionary generation understood the Second Amendment to guarantee a personal right to bear arms. Robert A. Sprecher, "The Lost Amendment," *American Bar Association Journal* 51 (1965): 554–57, 665–69; and Stuart R. Hays, "The Right to Bear Arms, A Study in Judicial Misinterpretation," *William and Mary Law Review* 2 (1959–1960): 381–406, take a similar stand. Shalhope, consciously responding to the modern debate over gun control, has founded his argument in what he believes was the ideological context of late-eighteenth-century America. Sprecher and Hays focus more narrowly on the legal and legislative history of the amendment. Peter Buck Feller and Karl L. Gotting, "The Second Amendment: A Second Look," *Northwestern University Law Review* 61 (1966–1967): 46–70; Lucilius A.

Emery, "The Constitutional Right to Keep and Bear Arms," *Harvard Law Review* 28 (1914–1915): 473–77; George I. Haight, "The Right to Keep and Bear Arms," *Bill of Rights Review* 2 (1941): 31–42; and Ralph J. Rohner, "The Right to Bear Arms: A Phenomenon of Constitutional History," *Catholic University of America Law Review* 16 (1966–1967): 53–84, argue that the amendment supports the collective right of state militias to bear arms. Feller and Gotting, Emery, Haight, and Rohner also focus their analysis in legal and constitutional issues. What follows here places the legal and constitutional antecedents of the Second Amendment in America and England into an ideological context that differs fundamentally from that described by Shalhope.

2. For a detailed analysis of the debate over the militia and standing army in eighteenth-century thought, *see* Lawrence Delbert Cress, *Citizens in Arms: The Army and the Militia in American Society to the War of 1812* (Chapel Hill, 1982). J. G. A. Pocock, *The Machiavellian Moment: Florentine Political Thought and the Atlantic Republican Tradition* (Princeton, 1975), offers a penetrating analysis of classical republican theory from the sixteenth through the eighteenth century.

3. Bernard Schwartz, ed., *The Roots of the Bill of Rights: An Illustrated Source Book of American Freedom* (New York, 1971).

4. Thomas Jefferson, "A Summary View," [July 1774], *Jefferson Papers*, 1:133. The resolution cited here is from the Maryland convention, 8 Dec. 1774, in *American Archives*, ed. Peter Force, 4th ser. (Washington, 1837–1846), 1:1032.

5. Schwartz, *Roots*, 2:235, 266.

6. Ibid., 2:278, 282–87, 312, 324. For a summary of state constitutional provisions bearing on the militia and its relationship to civil authority, see Cress, *Citizens in Arms*, 60–62.

7. Schwartz, *Roots*, 2:342, 378.

8. Ibid., 2:265, 277, 312, 323, 377.

9. *Notes of Debates in the Federal Convention of 1787, Reported by James Madison* (Athens, Ohio, 1966), 630, 639–40; *Mason Papers*, 3:991–93.

10. Luther Martin, *Genuine Information* (delivered to the Maryland legislature, 29 Nov. 1787), in *Records of the Federal Convention of 1787*, ed. Max Farrand (New Haven, 1911–1937), 3:207–08; Luther Martin, "Letter on the Federal Convention of 1787," 27 Jan. 1788, Elliot, *Debates*, 1:371–72.

11. *Mason Papers*, 3:1070–71. Concern over the Constitution's failure to protect conscientious objectors was commonplace in Antifederalist tracts. "A Manifesto . . . from Albany County," in Kenyon, *Antifederalists*, 362, was typical in charging that "Men conscienciously scrupulous of bearing arms [were] made liable to perform military duty." *See also* note 10.

12. "Pennsylvania Minority Report," Kenyon, *Antifederalists*, 36; William V. Wells, *Life and Public Service of Samuel Adams* (Boston, 1865), 3:267; Elliot, *Debates*, 2:162; "New Hampshire Ratifying Convention to Congress," 21 June 1788, Elliot, *Debates*, 1:326.

13. "Pennsylvania Minority Report," Kenyon, *Antifederalists*, 36; *Jefferson Papers*, 1:344, 353, 363.

14. "Pennsylvania Minority Report," Kenyon, *Antifederalists*, 36–37; Elliot, *Debates*, for New York, 1:328, 330–31; for Rhode Island, 1:334–36; for Maryland, 2:550–52; for Virginia, 3:659–60; for North Carolina, 4:244–47. For the amendments proposed by New Hampshire, *see*, Schwartz, *Bill of Rights*, 2:760–61.

15. Elliot, *Debates*, 3:659–60.

16. *Annals of Congress,* 1:451 (8 June 1789); 1:685–691 (21 July 1789); 1:778 (17 Aug. 1789); "Committee of Eleven Report on Proposed Amendments," 28 July 1789, in Schwartz, *Roots,* 5: illustration following 1014.

17. *Annals of Congress,* 1:778–780 (17 Aug. 1789).

18. Ibid., 780.

Garry Wills

To Keep and Bear Arms

With letters in rebuttal by Sanford Levinson, David C. Williams, and Glenn Harlan Reynolds

Garry Wills is adjunct professor of history at Northwestern University. He has written extensively on the thought of the Founders and on a variety of other aspects of American political culture, including a Pulitzer Prize–winning study of Abraham Lincoln. Wills is also a frequent contributor to *The New York Review of Books,* an influential review of literature, art, politics, and current events. This essay reviews several works by scholars associated with the so-called Standard Model, an interpretation that supports the individual-rights view of the Second Amendment. In contrast to the dispassionate tone that characterizes much scholarly writing in professional journals, Wills's writing is more polemical. Wills takes issue with several features of the Standard Model. In particular, he faults legal scholars for blurring the differences separating Federalists from their Antifederalist opponents. Madison, the leading Federalist theorist and the primary architect of the Bill of Rights, viewed the Second Amendment as a means of thwarting the states'-rights agenda of his Antifederalist opponents. For Wills, the amendment was merely a restatement of widely accepted notions of the need to maintain a well-regulated militia in a republic. The Second Amendment, according to Wills, was never intended to protect an individual right of all citizens to own guns and was certainly not seen as incorporating a right of revolution into the Constitution. This selection also includes letters from Sanford Levinson, David C. Williams, and Glenn Harlan Reynolds, the legal scholars who are the primary objects of Wills's criticism in this review. In their responses, Levinson, Williams, and Reynolds restate the central beliefs of the Standard Model and take Wills to task for the scathing quality of his review, which they believe violates the standards of cordial academic exchanges.

Questions for a Closer Reading

1. What are the main beliefs associated with the Standard Model of the Second Amendment?

2. What role do Antifederalist ideas play in the Standard Model? Why does Wills believe these Antifederalist ideas should not control how the Second Amendment is interpreted?

3. What does Wills say in response to the suggestion that the Second Amendment incorporates a right of armed resistance into the Constitution?

4. Wills was originally trained as a Latin scholar. One of the most fascinating aspects of his argument is his discussion of how concepts such as bearing arms were derived from Latin terms. How important is this linguistic analysis to understanding the meaning of the Second Amendment? What role did Latin play in the world of the Founding Fathers?

5. This essay adopts a polemical tone, chiding supporters of the Standard Model for their "wacky" ideas. Do you find this a persuasive strategy? Is there any danger that such a strategy can backfire?

6. Which, if any, of the points made in the letters responding to Wills's essay do you find convincing? How do you think Wills might respond?

7. Exactly who would have been part of the militia in the period in which the Second Amendment was ratified? What groups would have been excluded from militia service?

To Keep and Bear Arms *

Over the last decade, an industrious band of lawyers, historians, and criminologists has created a vast outpouring of articles justifying individual gun ownership on the basis of the Second Amendment: "A well-regulated militia being necessary to the security of a free State, the right of the people to keep and bear arms shall not be infringed."

This body of commentary, much of it published in refereed† law journals, has changed attitudes toward the Second Amendment. The National Rifle Association's lobbyists distribute it to legislators. Journalists like Michael Kinsley and George Will disseminate this school's views. Members of it now claim, on the basis of their work's quantity and what they believe is its quality, that scholarship on this subject is now all theirs — so that even to hold an opposing view is enough to "discredit its supporters," according to the historian Joyce Lee Malcolm.[1]

The *Tennessee Law Review* devotes most of its Spring issue to a collection of articles by members of this school, including one that says its authors have created "the Standard Model" for interpreting the Second Amendment. To this mood of self-congratulation can be added the fact that a majority of Americans tell pollsters that they believe the Second Amendment protects private ownership of guns. So the defenders of that position feel they hold both the scholarly high ground and the popular consensus. The five who constitute a kind of inner circle of Standard Modelers — Robert J. Cottrol, Stephen P. Halbrook, Don B. Kates, Joyce Lee Malcolm, and Robert E. Shalhope — recycle each other's arguments energetically. Three of the five write in the *Tennessee Law Review* issue, one of them (Malcolm)

---

*Notes for this selection begin on p. 84.

†Legal journals are edited by law students, while professional history journals use a process of blind peer review in which articles are sent out to experts anonymously for comment, and decisions are made by professional editors in consultation with editorial boards composed of historians.

Garry Wills, "To Keep and Bear Arms," *New York Review of Books*, Vol. 42, no. 18 (1995): 62–73; and letters by Sanford Levinson, David C. Williams, Glenn Harlan Reynolds, ibid. 42 (1995): 61–62.

devoting her essay to the fourth (Cottrol), while the fifth (Shalhope) is frequently cited.

Then why is there such an air of grievance, of positive victimhood, in the writings of the "Standard Model" school? They talk of the little honor they are given, of the "mendacious" attitude of the legal establishment, of a rigidity that refuses to recognize their triumph. Don Kates (with co-authors) sputters in mixed metaphors of an opposition that "exists in a vacuum of lock-step orthodoxy almost hermetically sealed from the existence of contrary data and scholarship."[2] Randy E. Barnett, introducing the *Tennessee Law Review* symposium, predicts dire things if people do not "accord some respect to those citizens (and academics) whose views it [the Standard Model Scholarship] supports."[3] Glenn Harlan Reynolds, in the article stating the Standard Model thesis, argues that militia extremism may be fueled by the Model's opponents, who are "treating the Constitution, too, as a preserve of the elite."[4]

Their own reciprocating nods and citations of approval are apparently not enough for these authors. Nor is popular support enough. They still talk like Rodney Dangerfield, getting no respect. They should ask themselves more penetratingly why this should be. Perhaps it is the quality of their arguments that makes them hard to take seriously.

Take the case of Stephen P. Halbrook, one of the central figures in this new literature. His imaginative manipulation of evidence runs to arguments like this, from his 1989 book, *A Right to Bear Arms:* the Second Amendment cannot be referring only to military weapons, since a Federal-period dictionary (Noah Webster's), under "bear," lists "to bear arms in a coat" as one usage, and only a handgun could be carried in a coat pocket.[5] Mr. Halbrook does not recognize the term "coat of arms," a decidedly military form of heraldry presided over by the College of Arms (by Mr. Halbrook's interpretative standards, a medical institution specializing in the brachium).

The quality of the school's arguments can be seen in the very article that proposes the "Standard Model" as the norm of scholarship in this area. Glenn Harlan Reynolds "proves" that the Second Amendment looked to private ownership of guns by quoting Patrick Henry, in these words (and these words only): "The great object is that every man be armed. . . . Everyone who is able may have a gun."[6]

That quotation comes from the debate over adopting the Constitution. It cannot, therefore, be concerned with the Second Amendment, which was not proposed until after the Constitution was in effect. Henry is not discussing the Amendment's text, which the Standard Model says looks to other weapons than those used by the militias (citizens' armies) of the states. Henry is talking precisely about the militia clause in the Constitution, which refers *only* to military weapons ("Congress shall have the power to provide for organizing, arming, and disciplining the militia," Article I, Section 8, Clause 16). Henry argues that federal arming of militias will either supplant or duplicate the states' arming of their own forces (the arrangement under the Articles of Confederation and in colonial times). He says that, in the case of duplication,

> Our militia shall have two sets of arms, double sets of regimentals, &c.; and thus, at a very great cost, we shall be doubly armed. The great object is that every man [of the militia] be armed. But can the people afford to pay for double sets of arms, &c? Every one who is able may have a gun. But we have learned, by experience, that, necessary as it is to have arms, and though our Assembly has, by a succession of laws for many years, endeavored to have the militia completely armed, it is still far from being the case.[7]

The debate throughout is on ways to arm the militia. The "arms" referred to are cognate with "regimentals, etc." as military equipment. The attempts to get guns in every hand are the result of state laws for equipping the militia. Henry is saying that if the states could not do this heretofore, how is the federal government to do it?

Time after time, in dreary expectable ways, the quotes bandied about by Standard Model scholars turn out to be truncated, removed from context, twisted, or applied to a debate different from that over the Second Amendment. Those who would argue with them soon tire of the chase from one misquotation to another, and dismiss the whole exercise — causing the angry reaction from Standard Modelers that they are not taken seriously. The problem is that taking them seriously is precisely what undermines their claims.

Yet both the general public, which has a disposition to believe that the Second Amendment protects gun ownership, and the NRA lobby are bolstered in that view by the sheer mass of the articles now being ground out and published in journals. It is difficult to sort out all the extraneous, irrelevant, and partial material daily thrown into the debate. Even to make a beginning is difficult. One must separate what the Second Amendment says from a whole list of other matters not immediately at issue. Some argue, for instance, that there is a natural right to own guns (Blackstone* is often quoted here) antecedent to the right protected by the amendment, or that such a right may be protected in other places (common law, state constitutions, statute, custom, etc.). All that could be true without affecting the original scope of the Second Amendment. One could argue for instance, that owners of property

---

*William Blackstone: eighteenth-century English judge whose *Commentaries on the Laws of England* became the standard work on English law for Americans in the Revolutionary era.

have a right to charge rental on it — but that is not the point at issue in the Third Amendment (against quartering federal troops on private property).

In order to make any progress at all, we must restrict ourselves to what, precisely, is covered by the Second Amendment. That is not hard to determine, once the irrelevant debris adrift around its every term has been cleared away. Each term exists in a discernible historic context, as does the sentence structure of the amendment.

That amendment, as Madison first moved it, read:

> The right of the people to keep and bear arms shall not be infringed; a well armed and well regulated militia being the best security of a free country; but no person religiously scrupulous of bearing arms shall be compelled to render military service in person.[8]

The whole sentence looks to military matters, the second clause giving the reason for the right's existence, and the third giving an exception to that right. The connection of the parts can be made obvious by using the same structure to describe other rights. One could say, for instance: "The right of free speech shall not be infringed; an open exchange of views giving the best security to intellectual liberty; but no person shall be free to commit libel." Every part is explained in relation to every other part. The third clause makes certain what Madison means *in this place* by "bear arms." He is not saying that Quakers, who oppose war, will not be allowed to use guns for hunting or sport.

Did the changes made to Madison's proposed amendment remove it from its original (solely military) context? Only two substitutions were made in the wording — "country" became "state" and "the best security of" became "necessary to." This latter change might demote the right to bear arms by comparison with other rights (perhaps, say, free speech is the very *best* security of freedom), but it does not alter the thing being discussed.[9] Beyond that, nothing was *added* to the text, so it could not be altered by addition. Was it altered by deletion? "Well armed and" was dropped, in drafting sessions that generally compressed the language, but "well regulated" includes "well armed" (see below, Number 3). Then the whole third clause was omitted — but for a reason that still dealt with the military consequences of the sentence.

Elbridge Gerry* objected to the third clause on the grounds that rulers might *declare* some people "scrupulous" and then exclude them from service — as some tended to declare Quakers ineligible for office since they take no oaths; or as Catholics were once declared incapable, without

---

* *Elbridge Gerry:* Massachusetts Antifederalist politician.

scruple, of defending a Protestant government.[10] Gerry was clearly talking of public service, not whether Quakers should go hunting or target shooting. His objection resembles the one Samuel Johnson made to limiting militia service by the imposition of a religious oath.[11]

One transposition was made in Madison's sentence, but it *strengthened* the military context, as even the Standard Modeler, Joyce Lee Malcolm, admits.[12] The basis for the asserted right was put first, as is normal in legal documents. The preamble, the "whereas," the context-establishing clause — these set the frame for what follows: "A well regulated militia being necessary to the security of a free State, the right of the people to keep and bear arms shall not be infringed." To use again the parallel sentence on free speech, transposition would produce: "An open exchange of views being necessary to the security of intellectual liberty, the right of free speech shall not be infringed." Such preceding declaration of intent is found, for example, in the Constitution's copyright clause (Article I, Section 8, Clause 8), where the simple listing of granted powers "to coin money . . . to declare war," etc., is varied by a prior statement of purpose: "to promote the progress of science and useful arts by securing for limited times to authors and inventors. . . ." The prefixed words give the reason for, and scope of, what follows.

So nothing was added or changed that affected Madison's original subject matter. The things removed did not change the sentence's frame of reference. The transposition fixed the sentence even more precisely in a military context. How, then, did the ratification alter Madison's terms? The Standard Modelers draw on an argument made by Stephen Halbrook, an argument often cited by the NRA:

> The Senate specifically rejected a proposal to add "for the common defense" after "to keep and bear arms," thereby precluding any construction that the right was restricted to militia purposes and to common defense against foreign aggression or domestic tyranny.[13]

His proof of deliberate preclusion is this passage in the Senate records: "It was moved, to insert the words, 'for the common defence,' but the motion was not successful." We are not told why the motion failed. We know the Senate was mainly compressing and combining the amendments, not adding to the language. There are several possible reasons for the action, all more plausible than Halbrook's suggestion that "for the common defense" could have *imported* a military sense that is lacking without it. The military sense is the obvious sense. It does not cease to become the obvious sense if something that *might* have been added *was* not added.

The obvious reason for excluding the term "common defense" is that it could make the amendment seem to support only joint action of the state militias acting in common (shared) defense under federal control. The Articles of Confederation had used "common defense" to mean just that, and the defenders of state militias would not want to restrict themselves to that alone.[14] The likelihood that this is the proper reason is strengthened when it is considered in relation to another change the drafters made in Madison's text, from "free country" to "free state." We are not expressly given the reason for that change, either; but most people (including Standard Modeler Malcolm) agree that the reason was to emphasize the state's separate militias, not the common defense of the country.[15] If that is the obvious reason there, it is also the obvious reason for omitting "common defense."

There are other possible (though less plausible) reasons for the omissions — e.g., to prevent tautology. What is neither warranted nor plausible is Halbrook's certitude that these words were omitted *deliberately* to *preclude* militia-language. The whole context of the amendment was always military. Halbrook cannot effect an alchemical change of substance by bringing two words, "common defense," near to, but not into, the amendment.

1. *Bear arms.* To bear arms is, in itself, a military term. One does not bear arms against a rabbit. The phrase simply translates the Latin *arma ferre.* The infinitive *ferre,* to bear, comes from the verb *fero.* The plural noun *arma* explains the plural usage in English ("arms"). One does not "bear arm." Latin *arma* is, etymologically, war "equipment," and it has no singular forms.[16] By legal and other channels, *arma ferre* entered deeply into the European language of war. To bear arms is such a synonym for waging war that Shakespeare can call a just war "just-borne arms" and a civil war "self-borne arms."[17] Even outside the phrase "bear arms," much of the noun's use alone echoes Latin phrases: to be under arms (*sub armis*), the call to arms (*ad arma*), to follow arms (*arma sequi*), to take arms (*arma capere*), to lay down arms (*arma ponere*). "Arms" is a profession that one brother chooses as another chooses law or the church. An issue undergoes the arbitrament of arms. In the singular, English "arm" often means a component of military force (the artillery arm, the cavalry arm).

Thus "arms" in English, as in Latin, is not restricted to the meaning "guns." The Romans had no guns; and they did not limit *arma* to projectile weapons (spears, arrows). It meant weaponry in general, everything from swords to siege instruments — but especially shields. That is why the heraldic use of "arms" in English (the very case Stephen Halbrook invokes) refers to *shields* "coated" (covered) with blazonry.

Of course, even the Latin *arma ferre* can be used figuratively, metaphorically, poetically (bear arms in Cupid's wars, animals bear arms in their fighting talons or tusks). But these are extensions of the basic meaning, and the

Second Amendment is not a poetic text. It is a legal document, the kind in which *arma ferre* was most at home in its original sense; a text, moreover, with a preamble establishing a well-regulated militia as the context.

Standard Modelers try to get around this difficulty by seeking out every odd, loose, or idiosyncratic use of "bear arms" they can come up with — as if the legal tradition in which the Second Amendment stands must yield to marginal exceptions, in defiance of the solid body of central reference. Or they bring in any phrase that comes near "bear arms" without being that phrase. Stephen Halbrook cites a law concerning deer hunting that refers to "bearing of a gun" in the hunt.[18] Not only is the context different from the amendment's, but "bearing of a gun" is not the canonical formulation with a plural noun. In Latin a hunter could be seen to carry a bow (*arcum ferre*) without that altering the military sense of *arma ferre*.

It is impossible to follow the gun people into every thicket of their linguistic wild-hare chase, but one passage must be considered since it comes up again and again in the new writings. Even the sensible essay in the *Tennessee Law Review* by Colonel Charles J. Dunlap, Jr., says that "the minority of the Pennsylvania state convention that voted to adopt the Constitution" put "killing game" among the objects of a "right to bear arms."[19] That is now the customary way for the Standard Modelers to refer to the passage at issue: it is the position of "the minority" in the Pennsylvania ratifying convention. That makes it sound like the view of a considerable body of men (though not the majority). Dunlap took his information from an article written in a law journal by Robert Dowlut, the General Counsel of the National Rifle Association — an affiliation that helps explain the wide dissemination of this argument.[20]

It is true that an omnium gatherum of arguments against the Constitution was hastily assembled and published five days after Pennsylvania's ratification of the Constitution. The author was probably the propagandist Samuel Bryan, not himself a delegate in the convention, but one who took what the minority delegates gave him, including a hastily scribbled last-minute set of objections raised by Robert Whitehill.[21]

Whitehill is well described in his *Dictionary of American Biography* entry:

He was one of the small group which in this period fanned jealousies and suspicions of the Pennsylvania back country into an opposition which was probably the most vehement experienced by any state and nearly resulted in armed conflict . . . At no period of his official career did Whitehill reflect better his back-country views than as a member of the Pennsylvania convention to ratify the federal Constitution (1787). In the Assembly he sought a delay in the election of delegates . . . In the convention he resorted to every device to delay and defeat ratification. He insisted that there were inadequate safe-guards against a tyranny and on the day of ratification attempted, without avail, to have fifteen articles incorporated as a bill of rights.

Whitehill brought his fifteen proposals into the convention, on the day scheduled for a final vote, in order to abort the process. He made them the basis of a motion to adjourn without voting. The record of the Convention describes the turmoil over this last-minute effort at obstruction:

> Some confusion arose on these articles being presented to the chair, objec-tions were made by the majority to their being officially read, and, at last, Mr. [James] Wilson desired that the intended motion might be reduced to writing in order to ascertain its nature and extent. Accordingly, Mr. White-hill drew it up, and it was read from the chair . . .[22]

Whitehill's motion to adjourn was denied, the majority voted for the Con-stitution, and Whitehill's fifteen destructive proposals were never even de-bated by the convention. Some of Whitehill's fifteen points resembled other calls for a bill of rights, calls later answered in the first ten amendments; but others were merely frivolous, or were aimed at entirely gutting the draft Constitution. In the latter category was proposal fifteen, which began, "That the sovereignty, freedom, and independence of the several states shall be retained . . ." (exactly the state's position under the existing Articles).

Whitehill's objection to the militia clause of the Constitution was put in these words:

> 11. That the power of organizing, arming, and disciplining the militia (the manner of disciplining the militia to be prescribed by Congress) remains with the individual states, and that Congress shall not have authority to call or march any of the militia out of their own state, without the consent of such state and for such length of time only as such state shall agree.[23]

This would not only have canceled the militia clause in the draft Constitu-tion but would have repealed Articles VII and VIII of the Articles of Confed-eration. Not even Whitehill had any real hope of doing that. It is a measure of his desire to throw up any, even the wildest, objection to the Constitution that he could have drafted this proposal, one surely not backed by others in the minority.[24]

Following his throw-in-the-kitchen-sink approach, Whitehill introduced some language going back to English gaming laws and "enclosures,"[25] as if hunting were in peril from the Constitution.

8. The inhabitants of the several states shall have liberty to fowl and hunt in seasonable times, on the lands they hold, and on all other lands in the United States not enclosed . . .

It is in the context of these scattershot objections, hastily assembled to be purely destructive, that we should read the part of Whitehill's list that gun advocates like to quote as the "minority position":

7. That the people have a right to bear arms for the defense of themselves and their own state, or the United States, or for the purpose of killing game . . .

This sentence turns out to be redundant when he goes on, in Proposal 8, to protect a separate right to hunt. He begins a complex sentence with "right to bear arms" and then throws in everything he can think of—illogically, since he is about to take up hunting in a different proposal. He has confused, in his haste, different things—war and killing game—under one head ("bear arms"). He is a desperate man by now, unable to make his own motion coherently enough for the convention to understand it, until he is forced to put it in writing.

It is a sign of the desperation of the Standard Modelers that they take these ill-conceived phrases of Whitehill as the deliberated position of a whole "minority," and want to make *them* the text that controls our interpretation of "bear arms" in the Second Amendment—a text which was still to be drafted, debated, and clarified in the entirely military context Madison would give it. Did even Whitehill mean what he was saying? Or, as in his attack on the Articles along with the Constitution, was he just babbling to head off the impending vote? This was not a serious proposal, and it was not treated seriously by the convention. That Bryan included it in his response to the act of ratification just shows that he needed to add quick bulk to a publication that is not itself well organized or particularly coherent, but repetitive, random, full of discordant elements.[26]

I must apologize for pursuing this one instance of the gun advocates' mode of argument. It shows how difficult it is to track down their many misrepresentations. They take an isolated odd usage by an idiosyncratic man in a moment of little reflection, misrepresent it as the considered position of a group, and pit it against the vast body of normal usage, as that is qualified by legal usage and military context. Yet this is the argument that many gun advocates consider their "clincher." Robert Whitehill did them a favor they repay by hiding his name and confusing the responsibility for his frantic "proposals."

An indirect argument is made by Joyce Lee Malcolm—that the Second Amendment refers to the private use of arms, since that is what is intended by the 1689 British Bill of Rights, Article 6: "That the subjects which are Protestants may have arms for their defence suitable to their conditions and as allowed by law." But to have arms is not to "bear arms," and the British document lacks Madison's context-establishing language of a "well-regulated militia." Even if Malcolm's argument were true of seventeenth-century England (I argue elsewhere that it is not), it is irrelevant to an amendment phrased like Madison's.[27]

2. *To keep.* Gun advocates read "to keep and bear" disjunctively, and think the verbs refer to entirely separate activities. "Keep," for them, means "possess personally at home"— a lot to load into one word.[28] To support this entirely fanciful construction, they have to neglect the vast literature on militias. It is precisely in that literature that to-keep-and-bear is a description of one connected process. To understand what "keep" means in a military context, we must recognize how the description of a local *militia*'s function was always read in contrast to the role of a *standing army*. Armies, in the ideology of the time, should not be allowed to keep their equipment in readiness.

The constitutional ideology formulated in seventeenth-century England recognized that the realm's wealthy landowners and merchants were invited to share in the national government only or mainly when the king called parliaments into session, and he did that largely when he needed funds. One of the greatest urgencies for funds arose from war. If the king needed to raise and equip a new army for each war, he was dependent on the fresh revenues only a parliament could bring him in sufficient quantities. Thus it was to parliament's interest not to give any king the means to *continue* an army at his disposal. The more discontinuous his military efforts, the more was it necessary to call new parliaments, which could bargain for new powers of their own.

An army must be prevented from standing — from existing on a permanent basis. A pamphleteer against absolute monarchy wrote in 1675 that the king must not be allowed to "*keep up* a standing army."[29] In 1697, the great ideologue of the militia movement, John Trenchard, warned against any situation where "a standing army must be *kept up* to prey upon our entrails."[30] That applied not only to troops, standing in readiness but to "stands" (stores) of arms.

To preclude, so far as possible, the maintenance of extraordinary forces by the king, local rulers (the squirearchy) kept in readiness a force — a militia — to handle all normal peacekeeping activity. Royal forces, except for those abroad in the navy or guarding Channel forts, were to be disbanded after each specific campaign, their arsenals broken up. Those who could not be reabsorbed into the normal economy should go to the militias, according to Trenchard.[31] These latter *were* to maintain arsenals and all the equipment needed for "trained bands" (the normal term for individual militia bodies). In fact, at a time when more men were likely to have crossbows than "firelocks," Trenchard advised that "a competent number of them [firelocks] be *kept* in every parish for the young men to exercise with on holidays."[32] These would be used on a rotating basis, since Trenchard proposed that only a third of the militia should be exercised at one time.[33]

The idea of militia "stands" in common depots or arsenals was not confined to England. In America, the Articles of Confederation required that "every state shall always *keep up* a well regulated and disciplined militia, sufficiently *armed* and accoutred, and shall *provide and constantly have ready for use, in public stores,* a due number of field pieces and tents, and a proper quantity of arms, ammunition and equipage" (equipage being the etymological sense of *arma*).[34] Thus it is as erroneous to suppose that "keep" means, of itself, "keep at home" as to think that "arms" means only guns. As Patrick Henry tells us, the militia's arms include "regimentals, etc."— the flags, ensigns, engineering tools, siege apparatus, and other "accoutrements" of war.

Some arms could be kept at home, of course. Some officers kept their most valuable piece of war equipment, a good cross-country horse, at home, where its upkeep was a daily matter of feeding and physical regimen. But *military* guns were not ideally kept at home. When militias were armed, it was, so far as possible, with guns of standard issue, interchangeable in parts, uniform in their shot, upkeep, and performance — the kind of "firelocks" Trenchard wanted kept "in every parish" (not every home). The contrast with armies was not to be in performance (Trenchard and others boasted of the *high* degree of efficient organization in militias).[35] The contrast was in continuity. The militia was always at the ready, its arms "kept." Armies came and went — their "continuation" was what Trenchard attacked.[36]

Trenchard talked of militia arms being lodged in the proper hands — neither in an army's, on the one side, nor in the lower orders, on the other (Trenchard's was a militia of property owners).[37] In America, "deposition" of arms from the proper hands occurred, most famously, when the King's troops seized the militia's arsenals at Concord in the north and at Williamsburg in the south. That is where arms were kept, lodged, maintained.

To keep-and-bear arms was the distinguishing note of the militia's permanent readiness, as opposed to the army's duty of taking up and laying down ("deponing" is Trenchard's word) their arms in specific wars. The militia was maintained on a continuing basis, its arsenal kept up, its readiness expressed in the complex process specified by "keep-and-bear." To separate one term from this context and treat it as specifying a different right (of home possession) is to impart into the language something foreign to each term in itself, to the conjunction of terms, and to the entire context of Madison's sentence.

3. *Well-regulated.* One of the modern militia leaders who testified before Congress said, in answer to a question by Representative Patricia Schroeder about his insignia, that the militia movement is informal, spontaneous, and without fixed leadership. No eighteenth-century defender of the militias would have spoken that way. Sensitive to the charge that militias could be mobs, they always stressed that they were talking of a *proper* militia, a *good* militia, a *correct* militia, one well-trained, well-disciplined, well-regulated.

The use of the last term is especially significant, since the king's soldiers and sailors were called "regulars" in the eighteenth century. The militias, too, were "regular," existing under rules (*regulae*). They did not boast a lesser *discipline,* just a right to continual *upkeep* of themselves and their equipment. Adam Smith took regulated to mean, principally, "regimented"—divided into bodies of troops.[38]

General discussion of regulation concentrated on three matters: composition of the bands, arming (which included financing) them, and disciplining them. These three concerns are reflected in the Constitution's militia clause, which speaks of a congressional power "to provide for organizing, arming, and disciplining the militia" (Article I, Section 8, Clause 16).

To organize a militia, the most basic question is: Who should belong to it? The answer, prompted by reliance of the militia ideology on classical republicanism, was "the people." Greece and Rome were military states in which each *civis* was a *miles.* But "the people" in seventeenth-century England had a meaning as narrow in military affairs as in all others. Few could vote in that era. Few held land. Few had patents or grants for commerce. Since one of the roles of the militia was to serve as a local police power (in conjunction with the constabulary of the parish), not just any transient, or guild member, or wage laborer automatically belonged to the militia. They were the ones *being* policed. A landholder could use his own "retainers" (equipping them out of his store) to serve under him, at war as in peace. Or he could buy the services of another if he wished to evade service. But in general the social structure of a very deferential society was reflected in the makeup of the militias, whose officer class was the ruling class.[39] Suspect elements in society—Catholics, Jews, some members of dissenting sects—were kept at various times from access to military equipment. Traces of this attitude survived in the American colonies, where John Adams described the militia as led by "*gentlemen* whose *estates,* abilities and benevolence" made them obeyed.[40] As we shall see, the meaning of "the people" is different at differing periods, but at no time preceding the passage of the Second Amendment could any man be considered a militia member just by picking up his gun and proclaiming himself one.

The arming of the militia was a delicate matter, since that meant financing it — its wages, supplies, equipment, training facilities. Royal money could not be accepted, since permanent militia costs would give the king a claim upon permanent revenues. The gentry could provide much of the cost, or parish authorities. The local residence of the bands made barracks unnecessary. Use of public facilities was not considered "quartering" when local authorities and residents were the users. The ideological furor against quartering troops had the same source as the support of militia. Since the king was denied the standing barracks of a standing army, he might maintain an army on the cheap, without having to call on parliament, if he used public buildings, landed estates, taverns and inns, and even some private homes to lodge his military men, horses, and arsenals.[41] To this concern we owe the Third Amendment, which is as solely (and anachronistically) military in focus as is the Second Amendment. A fear of "taking the King's pence" lay behind the objections of Patrick Henry and others to federal financing of the militias. Yet that became the law of the land under the Constitution. All authorized militias under our government have been financed by the central government, which also establishes their code of discipline.

Discipline was the third item of concern for eighteenth-century defenders of militias. No one was a member of the militia who had not joined an authorized "trained band" *and been trained.* So important is proper training that we often find "well-regulated" followed by an epexegetic phrase, spelling out the meaning of the term: "a well regulated militia, trained to arms" was the form Elbridge Gerry preferred for the Second Amendment.[42] More expansively the Virginia ratifying convention suggested "a well-regulated militia, composed of the body of the people trained to arms."[43]

In England, the need for a *common* discipline for militias was recognized, in order that the establishment of ranks, order, drill, maneuver, military obedience and punishment would be the same in neighboring counties, and even between the temporary army and the continuing militia (since some of the same men would go in or out of service in both). As early as Henry IV's time, an overall "commission of army," meant "to muster and array (or set in military order) the inhabitants of every district," was accepted.[44]

In America, the Constitution gives the federal government the power and duty to "discipline" the state militias — i.e., set their order of military rank, procedure, drill, and punishment. The so-called militias that wear the private insignia of Representative Schroeder's interlocutor are not "well-regulated" in the constitutional sense. The only militia recognized by the Second Amendment is one "regulated" by the militia clauses of the Constitution — one organized, armed, and disciplined by the federal government. Though the state militias (the National Guard financed by Congress) are under the ordinary jurisdiction of the states' governors, the common discipline insures that the guard will be efficient if it is federalized (by a procedure also in the Constitution).

Only fantasts can think the self-styled militias of our day are acting under the mandate of, or even in accord with, the Second Amendment. Only madmen, one would think, can suppose that militias have a *constitutional* right to levy war against the United States, which is treason by constitutional definition (Article III, Section 3, Clause 1). Yet the body of writers who proclaim themselves at the scholarly center of the Second Amendment's interpretation say that a well-regulated body authorized by the government is intended to train itself for action *against* the government. The proclaimer of the Standard Model himself says that the National Guard cannot be the militia intended by the Second Amendment since that militia was meant to oppose the government, and the National Guard is required to swear an oath of *loyalty* to the government that funds and organizes it.[45]

The Standard Model finds, squirreled away in the Second Amendment, not only a private right to own guns for any purpose but a public right to oppose with arms the government of the United States. It grounds this claim in the right of insurrection, which clearly does exist whenever tyranny exists. Yet the right to *overthrow* government is not given by government. It arises when government no longer has authority. One cannot say one rebels by right of that nonexistent authority. Modern militias say the government itself instructs them to overthrow government — and wacky scholars endorse this view. They think the Constitution is so deranged a document that it brands as the greatest crime a war upon itself (in Article III: "Treason against the United States shall consist only in levying war against them . . .") and then instructs its citizens to take this up (in the Second Amendment). According to this doctrine, a well-regulated group is meant to overthrow its own regulator, and a soldier swearing to obey orders is disqualified for true militia virtue.

Gun advocates claim that a militia is meant to oppose (not assist) the standing army. But even in England the militia's role was not to fight the king's army. The point of the militias was to make it unnecessary to establish a standing army. That no longer applied when the Second Amendment was adopted, since the Constitution had already provided Congress the powers to "raise and support armies" (Article I, Section 8, Clause 12), to "provide and maintain a navy" (Clause 13), and "to make rules for the government and regulation of the land and naval forces" (Clause 14). The battle against a standing army was lost when the Constitution was ratified, and nothing in the Second Amendment as it was proposed and passed altered that.[46] Nor did it change the Constitution's provision for using militias "to suppress insurrections" (Clause 15), not to foment them.

Yet gun advocates continue to quote from the ratification debates as if those arguments applied to the interpretation of the Second Amendment. They were aimed at the military clauses in the proposed Constitution. Patrick Henry and others did not want the Constitution to pass precisely because it would set up a standing army — and it did.

One of the Standard Modelers' favorite quotations, meant to prove that the militia was designed to fight against, not for, the federal government, is James Madison's argument, in *Federalist* No. 46, that any foreseeable national army could not conquer a militia of "half a million citizens with arms in their hands." But Madison says this while making what he calls a "visionary supposition"— that the federal government has become a tyranny, overthrowing freedom.

> That the people and the States should for a sufficient period of time elect an uninterrupted succession of men ready to betray both; that the traitors should throughout this period, uniformly and systematically preserve some fixed plan for the extension of the military establishment; that the governments and the people of the States should silently and patiently behold the gathering storm, and continue to supply the materials, until it should be prepared to burst on their own heads, must appear to every one more like the incoherent dreams of a delirious jealousy, or the misjudged exaggeration of a counterfeit zeal, than like the sober apprehensions of genuine patriotism.[47]

Madison says he will grant, *per impossible,* such a hypothesis in order to consider the result:

> A correspondence would be opened. Plans of resistance would be concerted. One spirit would animate and conduct the whole. The same combination in short would result from an apprehension of the federal, as was produced by the dread of the foreign yoke . . .

Madison is describing the Revolution, when Committees of Correspondence, Minutemen, and other bodies of resistance to tyranny sprang into being. It is not the "well-regulated militia" under the Constitution that is being described, but the revolutionary effort of a people overthrowing any despotism that replaces the Constitution and makes it void. Tyrannicides do not take their warrant from the tyrant's writ. In Madison's dire hypothesis, all bets are off and the pre-government right of resistance replaces governmental regulations *including the Second Amendment.* He is not describing the militia as envisioned in the Second Amendment. To use his words as if they explained the amendment's proper functioning is absurd.

It is from such material that the Standard Model makes its case that militias are supposed to oppose the government that organizes, funds, and regulates them. They have been helped along by two frivolous but influential articles supposedly written "from the left," published in *The Yale Law Journal.* In 1989, Sanford Levinson found the idea of a right to revolution in the Second Amendment so "interesting" that it, along with other things in the text, could be "embarrassing" to liberals like himself.[48] One sign of this article's influence is that it dazzled the eminent constitutionalist George Will, whose praise for the article has been disseminated ever since by the National Rifle Association.[49]

In 1991, David C. Williams upped Sanford Levinson's bid, calling the Second Amendment not only "embarrassing" but "terrifying" because it imports republican resistance into a merely liberal document.[50] If no modern militia meets the standards of republican virtue, then the courts should try to enforce the Second Amendment by other "republican" steps — like universal service, broader distribution of property, and other things Professor Williams agrees with. Any document would be terrifying if it mandates whatever a professor has on his wish list.

Both Levinson and Williams quote indiscriminately from republican literature and the ratification debates as if the question of a standing army were still "up" when the amendment was framed and ratified. With scholars like these, the NRA hardly needs to hire its own propagandists. They all agree, for their own circuitous reasons, that Second Amendment militias are organized, funded, and regulated by the federal government so that they may take arms against the federal government. It sometimes seems as if our law journals were being composed by Lewis Carroll* using various other pseudonyms.

4. *The people.* Gun advocates claim that the "right of the people" to keep and bear arms is distributive, the right of every individual taken singly. It has that sense in, for instance, the Fourth Amendment ("the right of the people to be secure in their persons"). But the militia as "the people" was always the *populus armatus,* in the corporate sense (one cannot be a one-person militia; one must be formed into groups). Thus Trenchard calls the militia "the people" even though as we have seen, the groups he thought of were far

---

**Lewis Carroll:* Author of *Alice in Wonderland.*

from universal.[51] The militia literature often refers to "the great body of the people" as forming the militia, and body (*corpus*) is a necessarily corporate term. The great body means "the larger portion or sector of " (OED, "great," 8:c). This usage came from concepts like "sovereignty is in the people." This does not mean that every individual is his or her own sovereign. When the American people revolted against England, there were loyalists, hold-outs, pacifists who did not join the revolution. Yet Americans claimed that the "whole people" rose, as Madison wrote in the *Federalist*, since the connection with body makes "whole" retain its original, its etymological sense — wholesome, hale, sound (*sanus*). The whole people is the *corpus sanum*, what Madison calls "the people at large."[52] Thus "the people" form militias though not every individual is included in them. The people as a popular body (*corpus*) was often contrasted with the rulers (*senatus populusque*), which is not a distributive sense (that would exclude senators from individual rights).

Gun advocates like to quote republican literature, based on classical history, to say that every citizen should be a soldier. That was true of Greece and Rome, where slaves gave citizens far greater freedom to be devoted to political and military life. But we should remember two things. Ancient citizens were not trained to be *militiamen,* a force supplementary to regular troops. Athenians were trained to *be* the regular troops (hoplites), as Romans were trained to be legionaries. And, second, initiation into citizenship was part of the same process that inducted one into religious duties to the state.[53] No modern republic has contemplated such militarization and regimentation of political life, which is the very farthest thing from the individualism of those who would read the Second Amendment distributively. Political life was *corporate* life in antiquity.

A false universalism makes the Standard Modelers say that the militia mentioned in the Second Amendment is made up of the entire citizenry. Enrollment of a segment of the populace in the National Guard does not count, since that is what the British described negatively as a "select" militia.[54] The attempt to raise a volunteer force for royal use across local lines was seen, in the seventeenth century, as a step toward assembling the elements of a standing army. But that does not mean that the ordinary local militia was ever universal. No locale could empty out its fields and shops to train all males of the appropriate age. The militia was in fact "select" in that it represented the local squirearchy and its dependents. The very operation of the militia depended on some people continuing their ordinary work — civil officials, food suppliers, sowers and harvesters, ostlers, blacksmiths, and the like. The very term "trained bands" means that the militia was not universal: only those with the time, opportunity, acceptance, and will to be exercised in training were actual "bandsmen," on whose discipline depended the effectiveness of the trained bands in precluding the need for a standing army. Any breakdown of order at the local level would destroy the argument that militias were a sufficient defense of the kingdom under ordinary circumstances.

It is true that Congress passed a militia law in 1792 providing that every able-bodied man should equip himself with a musket to serve in the militia — but it was a dead letter, since no organized training was provided for.[55] This was like defining the jury pool as the citizenry at large without providing for voir dires, so that no jury panels could be formed. Not until Congress passed the Dick Act in 1903 was the overall organization of a trained militia (the Guard) put on a regular basis. The gun advocates' talk of a time when the militia of the United States was universal is not nostalgia for a past reality, but a present dream about a past dream. The militia actions of the nineteenth century were sporadic, "select," and largely ineffectual.[56]

Adam Smith predicted in the eighteenth century, and Max Weber confirmed in this century, that modern principles of the division of labor, specialization of scientific warfare, and bureaucratization of responsibility would shift the functions of the eighteenth-century militia to professional armies and to local police forces, giving the state a "monopoly on force" as a matter of efficiency. George Washington, who had bitterly criticized the militias during the Revolution, tried to adhere to the Second Amendment by proposing what was known as the Knox Plan, for a small but well-trained militia. Congress, instead, gave him the Militia Act of 1792, which made of the militia a velleity.

Why, in fact, did Madison propose the Second Amendment? Not to prevent a standing army. That was already established by Article I, and the amendment did not overthrow it. Not to organize the militia. That, too, was mandated by Article I. Even a Standard Modeler like Joyce Lee Malcolm treats the amendment as, constitutionally, a gesture: "A strong statement of preference for a militia must have seemed more tactful than an expression of distrust of the army."[57] Constitutional law normally enacts more than "a strong statement of preference."

Why, then, did Madison propose the Second Amendment? For the same reason that he proposed the Third, against quartering troops on the civilian population. That was a remnant of old royal attempts to create a standing army by requisition of civilian facilities. It had no real meaning in a government that is *authorized* to build barracks, forts, and camps. But it was part of the anti-royal rhetoric of freedom that had shown up, like the militia language, in state requests for amendments to the Constitution.

Madison knew that the best way to win acceptance of the new government was to accommodate its critics on the matter of a bill of rights. He had opposed that during the ratification debates, recognizing that people like Robert Whitehill and Patrick Henry were using the demand to kill the document, not to improve it. His assessment was confirmed when Antifederalists like Henry and Whitehill changed their stance and *opposed* the amendments when Madison offered them. Henry

> thought that the amendments would "tend to injure rather than serve the cause of liberty" by lulling the suspicions of those who had demanded amendments in the first place . . . The Antifederalist strategy, it seems, was to reject the most popular of the amendments, thus making it necessary for Congress to take up the whole matter again.[58]

Henry feared that Madison was doing in the Antifederalists with sweet talk, and he was right. Madison confided to a friend: "It will kill the opposition everywhere."[59] Sweet-talking the militia was a small price to pay for such a coup — and it had as much impact on real life as the anti-quartering provisions that arose from the same motive. Thus he crafted an amendment that did not prevent the standing army (and was not meant to) but drew on popular terms that were used for that purpose in the past. His sentence structure set as totally military a context for this amendment as for the Third. Every term in the Second Amendment, taken singly, has as its first and most obvious meaning a military meaning. Taken together, each strengthens the significance of all the others as part of a military rhetoric.

Against this body of evidence we have the linguistic tricks of the Standard Model which wrench terms from context and impose fanciful meanings on them. The Standard Model takes apart the joint phrasing of keep-and-bear arms to make "keep" mean only keep-in-the-home-for-private-use and "bear arms" mean carry-a-gun-in-the-hand. The ratification-debate attacks on the militia clause of the Constitution are illegitimately applied to the support of the later amendment. Madison is made to talk as if obliterating the government could be a way to obey the government. We are told that the Second Amendment is deliberately insurrectionary and proclaimed (in an absent-minded way) the right of armed rebellion as a method of regulating the military. We are told that arms, all the equipage of war, can be borne in a coat pocket. Heraldry is mixed with haberdashery, humbug with history, and scholarly looking footnotes with simple-minded literalism. By the methods used in the Standard Model, we could argue that a good eighteenth-century meaning for "quarter" shows that the Third Amendment was intended to prevent soldiers from having their limbs lopped off in private homes.

As I said at the beginning, my argument does not deny any private right to own and use firearms. Perhaps that can be defended on other grounds — natural law, common law, tradition, statute. It is certainly true that most people assumed such a right in the 1780s — so naturally, in fact, that the question was not "up" and calling for specific guarantees. All I maintain is that Madison did not address that question when drafting his amendment. When he excepted those with religious scruple, he made clear that "bear arms" meant wage war — no Quaker was to be deprived of his hunting gun.

The recent effort to find a new meaning for the Second Amendment comes from the failure of appeals to other sources as a warrant for the omnipresence of guns of all types in private hands. Easy access to all these guns is hard to justify in pragmatic terms, as a matter of social policy. Mere common law or statute may yield to common sense and specific cultural needs. That is why the gun advocates appeal, above pragmatism and common sense, to a supposed sacred right enshrined in a document Americans revere. Those advocates love to quote Sanford Levinson, who compares the admitted "social costs" of adhering to gun rights with the social costs of observing the First Amendment.[60] We have to put up with all kinds of bad talk in the name of free talk. So we must put up with our world-record rates of homicide, suicide, and accidental shootings because, whether we like it or not, the Constitution tells us to. Well it doesn't.

Notes for Wills

1. Joyce Lee Malcolm, "Gun Control and the Constitution: Sources and Explorations on the Second Amendment," *Tennessee Law Review* (Spring 1995), 815.

2. Don B. Kates, Henry E. Schaffer, John K. Lattimer, George B. Murray, and Edwin H. Cassem, "Guns and Public Health: Epidemic of Violence or Pandemic of Propaganda?" *Tennessee Law Review* (Spring 1995), 519.

3. Randy E. Barnett, "Guns, Militias, and Oklahoma City," *Tennessee Law Review* (Spring 1995), 452.

4. Glenn Harlan Reynolds, "A Critical Guide to the Second Amendment," *Tennessee Law Review* (Spring 1995), 512.

5. Stephen P. Halbrook, *A Right to Bear Arms* (Greenwood Press, 1989), 101. The author had published this argument five years earlier in his book *That Every Man Be Armed: The Evolution of a Constitutional Right* (University of New Mexico Press, 1984), 219, and no scholar of the movement had the heart (or perhaps the head) to correct him in the interval.

6. Reynolds, "A Critical Guide to the Second Amendment," 469.

7. Jonathan Elliot, *The Debates in the Several State Conventions on the Adoption of the Federal Constitution* (Washington, 1836), 3:386.

8. Bernard Schwartz, *The Bill of Rights: A Documentary History* (Chelsea House, 1971), 2:1026.

9. It was a commonplace that a proper militia was "the best security" to a state — meaning best physical guarantor of "national security." Adam Smith uses just those words in his *Lectures on Jurisprudence* (Oxford University Press, 1978), 543. But Madison broadened the issue by distinguishing a free country's protection.

10. Bernard Schwartz, *The Bill of Rights*, 2:1107; "They can declare who are religiously scrupulous, and prevent them from bearing arms."

11. *See* Johnson's texts analyzed by J. C. D. Clark, in *Samuel Johnson: Literature, Religion and English Cultural Politics From the Restoration to Romanticism* (Cambridge University Press, 1994), 120–126.

12. Joyce Lee Malcolm, *To Keep and Bear Arms: The Origins of an Anglo-American Right* (Harvard University Press, 1994), 160–61: "The language had also been tightened by reversing the reference to the military and the right of the people to bear arms, perhaps intentionally putting more emphasis on the militia."

13. Stephen P. Halbrook, *That Every Man Be Armed*. For the motion that failed, see Schwartz, *The Bill of Rights*, 2:1143–54.

14. *See* Articles of Confederation, draft Articles X, XI, and XII, all of which used "common defence" for confederated action, and Articles VII and VIII as passed. *See The Documentary History of the Ratification of the Constitution*, edited by Merrill Jensen (State Historical Society of Wisconsin, 1976), 1:81, 89. Article VIII stated: All charges of war, and all other expenses that shall be incurred *for the common defence or general welfare*, are allowed by the united states in congress assembled, shall be defrayed out of a common treasury . . . according to such mode as the united states in congress assembled shall from time to time direct and appoint. [italics added] Alexander Hamilton used "common defence" in the same way in *Federalist* No. 25 (Jacob E. Cooke, ed., Wesleyan University Press, 1961, 158).

15. Malcolm, *To Keep and Bear Arms*, 160: "In keeping with state proposals, the word 'state' had been substituted for Madison's 'country.' 'State' was a more precise term and, since a state was a polity, it could refer either to one state or to the United States."

16. Though the Greek equivalent of *arma* has a singular (*hoplon*), meaning shield, the plural (*hopla*) refers to all kinds of military (including naval) equipment.

17. Shakespeare, *King John* 2.1.345, *Richard II* 2.3.80. In the last line the emphasis on *native* ("And fright our native peace with self-borne arms") shows that Berkeley is describing citizens who bear arms against themselves.

18. Halbrook, *A Right to Bear Arms*, 56.

19. Colonel Charles J. Dunlap, Jr., "Revolt of the Masses: Armed Civilians and the Insurrectionary Theory of the Second Amendment," *Tennessee Law Review* (Spring 1995): 650, fn. 35.

20. Robert Dowlut, "Federal and State Constitutional Guarantees to Arms," *University of Dayton Law Review* (Fall 1989): 62–63.

21. *See* "The Dissent of the Minority of the Convention" (September 18, 1787), in Jensen, ed., *The Documentary History of the Ratification of the Constitution*, 2:617–49.

22. "Debates of the Convention" (September 12, 1787), in Jensen, ed., *The Documentary History of the Ratification of the Constitution*, 2:599.

23. "Debates" in Jensen, ed., *The Documentary History of the Ratification of the Constitution*, 2:598.

24. That other members of the minority did not agree with Whitehill's desire to rescind the Articles is seen in the completely different treatment of the militia also contained in Bryan's hodgepodge "dissent." The treatment, on pp. 637–39 of the

"Dissent," says nothing of service beyond state borders, or other powers granted in the Articles.

25. "Debates," in Jensen, ed., *The Documentary History of the Ratification of the Constitution,* 598.

26. The signers of the dissent were agreeing with the things they had contributed to the whole, not with the parts in discord with their own contributions. (See footnote 24.)

27. Malcolm, *To Keep and Bear Arms,* Chapters 7 and 8. It should be observed that the British "complaint" is a gun-control measure, setting three restrictions on having arms — Protestantism, social condition, and the allowance of unspecified gun laws. Furthermore it is a *grant* ("may have") not a statement of antecedent *right.*

28. For the assumption that "keep" means "keep in the house" *see* Dowlut, "Federal and State Constitutional Guarantees to Arms," 69: "The bearing of arms in a public place is different from the keeping of arms in the home on account of the home's special zone of privacy." *Private* gun ownership is guaranteed, he claims, by the keeping of guns in the privacy zone. For keep as *individual possession, see* Robert E. Shalhope on "two distinct, yet related rights — the individual possession of arms and the need for a militia made up of ordinary citizens." "The Ideological Origins of the Second Amendment," *Journal of American History* (December 1982): 599–614. Glenn R. Reynolds, one proponent of the Standard Model, quotes with approval the disjunction formulated by Donald B. Kates that "the term 'keep' refers to owning arms that are kept in one's household; the term 'bear' refers to the bearing of arms while actually taking part in militia duties" ("A Critical Guide to the Second Amendment," 482).

29. Anonymous pamphlet cited in Richard Ashcraft, *Revolutionary Politics and Locke's 'Two Treatises of Government'* (Princeton University Press, 1986), 118. Italics added.

30. John Trenchard, *An Argument, Shewing that a Standing Army Is Inconsistent with a Free Government and absolutely destructive to the Constitution of the English Monarchy* (London, 1697), 6. Italics added. A good brief description of the militia ideology is in Adam Smith, *Lectures on Jurisprudence,* 268–69, 420–21. *See also* J. G. A. Pocock, *The Machiavellian Moment* (Princeton University Press, 1975), Chapter 12, 401–22, and Lois G. Schwoerer, *'No Standing Armies!': The Antiarmy Ideology in Seventeenth-Century England* (Johns Hopkins University Press, 1974), 174–87 (on Trenchard as "the great tutor" on militias). Hamilton says the objection to standing armies was to "*keeping them up* in a season of tranquility" (*Federalist* No. 25, 160). Italics in original.

31. Trenchard, *An Argument,* 21.

32. Trenchard, *An Argument,* 21. Italics added.

33. Trenchard, *An Argument,* 21.

34. "Articles of Confederation," in Jensen, editor, *The Documentary History of the Ratification of the Constitution,* Article VI, 88. Italics added. As an English noun, "keep" meant the permanently holdable part of a castle (the equivalent of the Italian military term *tenazza*).

35. Trenchard defends the "well-trained militia" against the arming of "an undisciplined mob" (*An Argument,* 20).

36. A "continuation" of the army would make it an "establishment" (*An Argument,* 15).

37. Trenchard, *An Argument,* 7, 10.

38. Adam Smith, *An Inquiry Into the Nature and Causes of the Wealth of Nations*, ed. W. B. Todd (Oxford University Press/Clarendon Press, 1976), Vol. 2, 698.

39. *See* Trenchard, *An Argument*, 22: "There can be no danger from an army where the nobility and the gentry of England are the commanders, and the body of it made up of the freeholders, their sons and servants . . ." Because the militia was an extension of the landed class's authority, it was a Tory enthusiasm, denounced as such by the Whig author, Sir John Hawkins, when he condemned his friend Samuel Johnson for "his invectives against a standing army." Bertram H. Davis, ed., *The Life of Samuel Johnson, LL.D., by Sir John Hawkins, Knt.* (Macmillan, 1961), 45. Adam Smith said a laborer should not join the military since his "constant labour hurt the shape and rendered him less fit for military exercises . . . (We can know a tailor by his gait.)" *See Lectures on Jurisprudence*, 231.

40. Robert J. Taylor et al., eds., *Papers of John Adams* (Harvard University Press/Belknap Press), Vol. 2 (1977): 253 ("Novanglus" No. 2, February 6, 1775).

41. *See* Schwoerer, *'No Standing Armies!'*, 20–22.

42. Schwartz, *The Bill of Rights*, 2:1109.

43. Elliot, *Debates in the Several State Conventions*, 3:659.

44. William Blackstone, *Commentaries on the Laws of England*, facsimile of the first edition of 1765–1769, ed. Stanley N. Katz (University of Chicago Press, 1979), 1:398.

45. Reynolds, "A Critical Guide to the Second Amendment," 476–77: "The National Guard was never designed to resist a tyrannical government. . . . And they are required to swear an oath of loyalty to the United States government, as well as to their states."

46. Of course, the original point of British resistance to standing armies was lost in America. The militias were parliament's tool to keep the king from having a regular revenue for standing forces. In America, the parliament (Congress) had established itself as the organizer and founder of the military forces, a point made both by Hamilton in *The Federalist* (Nos. 24, 26, 28) and Madison (Elliot, *Debates in the Several State Conventions*, 3:383).

47. James Madison, *The Federalist* No. 46, 320–21.

48. Sanford Levinson, "The Embarrassing Second Amendment," *Yale Law Journal* (December 1989): 637–59.

49. *See* Wayne LaPierre, *Guns, Crime, and Freedom* (Regnery Publishing, 1994), 12, 175. For the constitutionalism of George Will, see Garry Wills, "Undemocratic Vistas," *New York Review of Books*, November 19, 1992, 28–34.

50. David C. Williams, "Civic Republicanism and the Second Amendment: The Terrifying Second Amendment," *Yale Law Journal* (December 1991), 551–615.

51. Trenchard, *An Argument*, 15.

52. Madison, *The Federalist* No. 46, 316.

53. *See*, for instance, S. D. Lambert, *The Phratries of Attica* (University of Michigan Press, 1993), 25–58, 205–36.

54. Ironically, the private militias of our day like to compare themselves with the Minutemen of the Revolutionary era — yet those were volunteer forces joined only by the ideologically compatible, something far closer to the "select militia" of the eighteenth century than is the contemporary National Guard. For the lack of universal service in colonial militias, *see* John Shy, *A People Numerous and Armed* (Oxford University Press, 1976), 21–33.

55. The best summary of this matter is by Frederick Bernays Wiener, "The Militia Clause of the Constitution," *Harvard Law Review* (December 1940), 181–219.

56. Wiener, "The Militia Clause," 188–93.

57. Malcolm, *To Keep and Bear Arms,* 164.

58. Richard R. Beeman, *Patrick Henry* (McGraw-Hill, 1974), 170–72. There is a good contemporary description of Henry's attempt to kill the Bill of Rights he had earlier demanded in *The Papers of James Madison* (University Press of Virginia, 1979), 12:463–65.

59. Madison, *Papers,* 12:347. Madison called the Bill of Rights "the nauseous project of amendments," which he considered unnecessary in a republic, but "not improper in itself," and useful for preempting a position it would be inconvenient to surrender to the Antifederalists (346–47). This is hardly the stubborn call to a last bastion of freedom that gun advocates find in the Second Amendment.

60. Levinson, "The Embarrassing Second Amendment," 657–59.

To Keep and Bear Arms:
Letters in Rebuttal to Garry Wills

Sanford Levinson,
David C. Williams,
and Glenn Harlan Reynolds

To THE EDITORS:

Garry Wills interprets the Second Amendment as a cynical maneuver by James Madison ["To Keep and Bear Arms," *NYR*, September 21]. Anti-nationalists (misleadingly labeled "anti-federalists") had threatened rejection of the 1787 Constitution unless its proponents agreed to add certain guarantees to protect the American people against a potentially corrupt and tyrannical national government. For Wills, Madison's acquiescence to this demand was disingenuous, for he managed to place in the Constitution new text that only appeared to assuage anti-Federalist fears. Wills reads the opening clause of the 1791 amendment, "A well regulated Militia, being necessary to the security of a free State" as entirely subordinated to the 1787 language of Article I, Section 8 giving Congress the power "[t]o provide for organizing, arming, and disciplining, the Militia. . . ." Thus, the final clause of the Amendment, referring to "the right of the people to keep and bear Arms" and commanding that this right "shall not be infringed" for Wills *really* means that Congress faces no constitutional barriers at all if, for example, it determines that the Militia should consist only of a relatively few number of people, all vetted by federal authority, and that no one else shall have *any* protected constitutional right "to keep and bear arms."

This may be a logically possible meaning of the Second Amendment, even though, by Wills's own admission, it changes (or even clarifies) nothing in the 1787 Constitution. Far more plausible, though, is Justice Joseph Story's analysis in his 1833 *Commentaries on the Constitution:*

> The importance of this article will scarcely be doubted by any persons, who have duly reflected upon the subject. The militia is the natural defense of a free country against sudden foreign invasions, domestic insurrections, *and domestic usurpations of power by rulers.* . . . [L]arge military establishments and standing armies in time of peace . . . *afford to ambitious and unprincipled rulers* [means] *to subvert the government, or trample upon the rights of the people. The right of the citizens to keep and bear arms . . . offers a strong moral check against the usurpation and arbitrary power of rulers; and will generally, even if these are successful in the first instance, enable the people to resist and triumph over them.* . . .[1]

American political thought, including its constitutional dimension, must be read against the background of our origin, both actual and mythic, in the armed popular overthrow of a well-established government that was, nonetheless, deemed corrupt and illegitimate. And the 1787 Constitution was, as Madison emphasized, only an "experiment," one that could conceivably emulate the British constitution by allowing the descent into intolerable corruption.

American thought is significantly anti-statist, and "We the People" retain what might be deemed an "inalienable right" to judge our agents who fill governmental positions. The first alternative open to us if we fear that our agents are becoming corrupt is to write angry letters to the editor, march in demonstrations, and, of course, throw the rascals out in free elections. But what if all of these fail? Unless one believes that such failure is literally unthinkable, there must remain the possibility of a Lockean "appeal to heaven," including armed revolt against the government.

The Second Amendment is most plausibly read as acknowledging the right of otherwise peaceable and law-abiding American citizens "to keep and bear arms" against the dreaded possibility that they will find it necessary to join with other citizens in making the Lockean appeal against an overweening national government. I believe that most ordinary Americans in 1791 were likely to agree with George Mason, a Virginia delegate to Philadelphia who refused to sign the Constitution because it lacked sufficient protection of popular rights: "Who are the Militia? They consist now of the whole people." To be sure, as Wills suggests, the 1787 notion of "the whole people" was egregiously less inclusive than our own. That, however, is true in regard to far more than the right to bear arms, and one wonders if Wills generally embraces a constitutional hermeneutic of "original intent" that would limit constitutional meaning to the most crabbed interpretation possible. One is curious, for example, about Wills's readings of the Commerce Clause or of the First and Fourteenth Amendments.

The clause "A well regulated Militia being necessary to the security of a free State" was, I think, likely to be translated by most (though perhaps not all) state legislators of the time — and the views of ratifying state legislators trump any private views held by Madison — as (something like) "an armed citizenry being necessary to maintaining a state of freedom," with it then following that the general mass of citizens retains a right protected against congressional interference to keep and bear arms. This interpretation is faithful to anti-nationalist impulses behind the Bill of Rights, and it avoids the "maximalist" interpretation of the Amendment that would prohibit even much state regulation. (The maximalist interpretation depends on one's understanding of the limitations on state power imposed by the Ninth or Fourteenth Amendments, though one notes that Story even in 1833 referred to generalized "rulers.") What limits the attraction of this interpretation, at least to those who support further regulation of guns, is that the constitutions of some forty states offer some degree of protection to private gun ownership.

There are good reasons to believe that historical fidelity is not particularly important when interpreting the Constitution. But that is not Wills's argument; he offers an historical account claiming that the Second Amendment as originally understood leaves the national government unfettered in regulating firearms in any ways it sees fit. It is that claim that I dispute.

SANFORD LEVINSON
University of Texas Law School
Austin, Texas

Note for Levinson

1. Quoted in Ralph Lerner and Philip Kurland, eds., *The Framer's Constitution* (University of Chicago Press, 1987), 5:214 (emphasis added). Story's comment is consistent with other material presented from case law and commentary by St. George Tucker, the editor of the first American edition of *Blackstone's* Commentaries, and William Rawle's *A View of the Constitution of the United States* (2nd ed., 1829). None offers an interpretation similar to Wills's.

To the Editors:

Something in the Second Amendment seems to cause otherwise careful scholars to engage in oversimplification, distortion, and caricature. I regret that Garry Wills, whose past work I have admired, has so succumbed in his recent article "To Keep and Bear Arms" [*NYR*, September 21]. His thesis is that the framers of the Second Amendment did not intend to create a right to own arms so as to resist federal tyranny. To reach that conclusion, he selectively uses evidence and misrepresents the present state of Second Amendment scholarship.

The historical events leading up to the Second Amendment are not a matter of controversy. In 1776, the American colonies made a revolution against the British imperial government. Shortly thereafter, the colonies created a weak federal government under the Articles of Confederation. Dissatisfied with its impotence, the framers of the Constitution created a stronger federal government in 1787. Among the national government's new powers was the authority to organize, arm, and discipline the state militias. Concerned about the possibility for tyranny in these new powers, the state legislatures urged Congress to adopt a Bill of Rights so as to curb federal overreaching. Among the new limits on government was the Second Amendment.

While the importance of these events is not in question, their constitutional significance is the subject of great disagreement. Wills argues that James Madison — the sponsor of the Bill of Rights — was an ardent nationalist and did not really want a Bill of Rights. To placate the state legislatures, he introduced the Second Amendment, but he had cleverly worded that amendment so that it would legally be meaningless. Before the amendment, the federal government had broad power over the state militias; after the amendment, it had the same power. The provision, in Madison's mind, was only a rhetorical gesture to the worrywarts in the state legislatures. Frankly, I cannot believe that Wills really means that we should interpret the Constitution in this way. According to his view, we should ignore the intent of those many state legislators who wanted an amendment and instead heed only the intent of one opportunistic politician who did not want it. But that tactic would allow representatives — with a nod and a wink to their colleagues — to fob off the public with meaningless, cannily worded amendments.

Once we look beyond Madison's own discomfort with the Bill of Rights, we find that its proponents meant for someone — the exact identity of that someone is harder to determine — to have a right to arms so as to resist federal tyranny. In proposing the Second Amendment, the state legislatures' worry was that the federal government might disarm or fail to arm the state militias, so as to destroy their ability to resist federal tyranny. Wills argues that the state debates over the ratification of the Constitution are irrelevant to the Bill of Rights, which was adopted later. In fact, however, the states proposed the Bill of Rights *at the same time* that they ratified the Constitution, precisely because of their lingering disquiet over the wisdom of a strong central government. The origin of the Bill of Rights thus lies in the ratification struggle.

At a minimum, then, the amendment extends some sort of protection for the state militias so that they can protect the people from federal tyranny. The amendment *might* mean more than that; some have argued that it is a protection for the individual ownership of arms. With Wills, I believe that these arguments are on shaky ground. But the amendment plainly means *something,* and Wills reaches the contrary conclusion only by selective use of the evidence. His other recourse is to leave the historical evidence altogether and argue, on abstract principles, that a legal order cannot protect a legal right to overthrow that very legal order. But that way of putting the matter confuses the legal order with a particular set of office-holders. If government authorities have abandoned the Constitution, then the people armed may become the true defenders of the legal order. Only if we assume that the government will always hew to the Constitution may we assume that a revolt against government is a revolt against the Constitution. The framers were plainly not prepared to make that assumption.

To be sure, the right of revolution might not hold under present circumstances. Indeed, I have argued that it does not,[1] although Wills lumps my work in with those who endorse a private right to arms. This distortion is part of Wills's general misrepresentation of the state of debate on the Second Amendment. In Wills's account, every scholar in the field argues that the amendment guarantees a private right to arms. In fact, a group of writers believes that the amendment protects only the right of the states to raise and arm militias — now manifest in the National Guard system. The proponents of this view include advocates for Handgun Control, Inc., and yet they give the amendment more meaning than Wills does. In fact, Wills is alone in reducing the provision to a nullity.

In other words, the field of debate is rich in controversy and disagreement. Wills, however, flattens the picture: previous writers have offered one and only one view. Dominated by an "inner circle" of five, they have attempted to deceive the American people, but Garry Wills has arrived in time to expose this nefarious conspiracy and save the citizenry from its plots. In this rendition, it is perfectly understandable that Wills is alone in his view that the amendment means nothing, because the other writers have conspired to suppress the truth. This kind of caricature is more than tiresome; it makes intelligent, subtle, and responsible debate in this field almost impossible, yet Wills is only mimicking a viciousness evident in the field before he arrived. Before Wills's article, I had hoped that a major intellect from outside the field might help to curb these vices; Wills certainly had the stature and the ability to initiate such a transformation. Instead, the field's vices seem to have infected him. His later work on the other subjects might return to his usual high standards, but our understanding of the Second Amendment will be no greater as a result of his review — and neither will our manners.

DAVID C. WILLIAMS
Indiana University School of Law
Bloomington, Indiana

Note for Williams

1. David C. Williams, "Civic Republicanism and the Citizen Militia: The Terrifying Second Amendment," *Yale Law Journal* (December 1991), 551.

TO THE EDITORS:

As someone interested in a civil and sensible debate on the Second Amendment, I am deeply disappointed in Garry Wills's "To Keep and Bear Arms" [*NYR*, September 21]. Much like Robert Bork's writings on the Ninth Amendment, Wills's effort shows how strong feelings can provoke the very sins the author deplores. Wills's article is a pastiche of *ad hominem* attacks, out-of-context quotes, *non sequiturs,* deliberate misreadings, and simple sneers. Because of length, a few examples must suffice.

Wills's greatest *non sequitur* is his identification of Don Kates, Joyce Malcolm, Robert Shalhope, Robert Cottrol, and Stephen Halbrook as the core group among Second Amendment scholars, after which he immediately turns to an article of mine in an effort to discredit that group.[1] Wills suggests my quotation of Patrick Henry is misleadingly out of context, but in fact his reprinting of a lengthier excerpt changes nothing. Patrick Henry was talking about the necessity of having a universally armed citizenry, from which a militia of the whole could be drawn. Nothing in the extended quote changes that, and that purpose is emphasized by the Second Amendment scholarship.[2] Wills also complains that it comes from the debate over the Constitution, predating the Second Amendment itself. Well, yes. It is hard to see why this matters, as it simply demonstrates that such issues were important before the Bill of Rights debate. (Anyway, Wills is not one to talk, as he similarly quotes Trenchard's 1697 *Argument.*) Wills also seems to think

Second Amendment scholars claim the right to arms applies only to non-military weapons; here he has things pretty much backward, as my article makes clear.[3]

However, if it's quotes that Wills wants, how about this one, from Tench Coxe at the time of the Second Amendment debate:

> As civil rulers, not having their duty to the people duly before them, may attempt to tyrannize, and as the military forces which must be occasionally raised to defend our country, might pervert their power to the injury of their fellow citizens, the people are confirmed by the next article [i.e., the Second Amendment] in their right to keep and bear their private arms.

This statement (which, a footnote points out, James Madison endorsed) appears in my article just prior to the Patrick Henry quote and seems rather inconsistent with Mr. Wills's view of the Second Amendment, yet he fails to discuss it. Nor are Wills's quotes irreproachable: to demonstrate the defensiveness of Second Amendment scholars he quotes a passage from Don Kates that actually discusses the public health debate over gun safety and has nothing to do with the Second Amendment.

Wills's quote quibbles are particularly inappropriate because my article does not purport to be original historical research. As it states plainly, it is a survey of the literature, whose main thesis is that the scholarship in the field demonstrates considerable consensus, making it appropriate to talk about a "Standard Model" (a term borrowed from physicists) of Second Amendment interpretation that I then proceed to summarize and critique. Like the physicists', this model does not preclude disagreement (my article has already been criticized by some Standard Model scholars for suggesting that gun registration does not violate the Second Amendment) but it does mean that the general framework for debate is regarded as settled.

Wills obviously does not disagree with my characterization, as he repeatedly uses the term "Standard Model" in his article in just the fashion I do. But in his haste to demolish straw men he completely fails to mention any of my significant criticisms of some aspects of Standard Model thinking, or my criticisms (shared by virtually all the Standard Model scholars) of the modern "militia movement." Indeed, Wills's hostility causes him to overlook the considerable agreement between him and the scholarly community on this subject: the similarities between his August 10 article on the militia movement in this *Review* (which I enjoyed) and the discussion of that subject in Randy Barnett's contribution to the *Tennessee Law Review* are positively eerie.

Finally, Wills was obviously unpersuaded by the part of my article that called for better manners in this debate, given his shrill condescension and his characterization of Standard Model scholars as "wacky." The "wacky" scholars to whom he refers include not only those named earlier, but also Akhil Amar of Yale Law School, Randy Barnett of Boston University, Raymond T. Diamond of Tulane, Sanford Levinson of Texas, William Van Alstyne of Duke, and David Williams of Indiana — all leading figures in constitutional law. They are judged "wacky" only by Wills, whose apparent criterion is that they disagree with him. Wills's characterization of these scholars is the proverbial thirteenth chime of the clock: not only wrong in itself but discrediting all that has come before.

Like Robert Bork's writings on the Ninth Amendment, Wills's essay may comfort those who already agree with him, but, also like Bork, he has not seriously engaged his opponents' arguments. That's too bad. A clearly reasoned and civil response to the Standard Model scholarship would be a real contribution to the literature. Despite Wills's efforts, however, no such response has yet been made.

GLENN HARLAN REYNOLDS
University of Tennessee
Knoxville, Tennessee

Notes for Reynolds

1. Glenn Harlan Reynolds, "A Critical Guide to the Second Amendment," *Tennessee Law Review* (Spring, 1995), 461.

2. Reynolds, 473; William Van Alstyne, "The Second Amendment and the Personal Right to Arms," *Duke Law Journal* (Spring, 1994), 1244 (armed populace is predicate for "well regulated militia").

3. Reynolds, 479–80.

4. Was the Second Amendment primarily about the struggle between Federalists and Antifederalists over the nature of federalism?

Don Higginbotham

The Federalized Militia Debate: A Neglected Aspect of Second Amendment Scholarship

Don Higginbotham, Dowd Professor of History at the University of North Carolina, is an expert in early American military history. In this essay, he focuses on the way in which the problem of federalism, the distribution of power between the states and the federal government, colored debate over the Second Amendment. The issue for Antifederalists in Higginbotham's view was federal control of the militia, not an individual right of gun ownership. Antifederalists feared that the new government would use its authority over the state militia to impose its will on the states. The struggle over the militia was part of a larger battle to define how power would be allocated under the Constitution. Although Federalists paid lip service to the ideal of the militia, the poor showing of the militia in the Revolution convinced leading Federalists of the need for reform. George Washington and his Federalist allies labored to transform the militia and even advocated the creation of an elite select militia. Efforts at reforming the militia failed; neither Congress nor the individual states showed any willingness to make the necessary changes to bolster the military effectiveness of the militia.

Higginbotham also supports Cress's and Wills's contention that a militia was more likely to be used to suppress radical challenges than to serve as an instrument of revolution.

Questions for a Closer Reading

1. What is federalism? How did Antifederalist and Federalist views of federalism differ? How does the debate over the militia relate to the problem of federalism?

2. Why did leading Federalists seek to create a select militia and a professional army?

3. Did the Bill of Rights mean the same thing to Federalists and Antifederalists? Did the Bill of Rights answer the main Antifederalist objections to the Constitution?

4. Higginbotham's description of the subsequent history of the militia demonstrates that Americans were not all in agreement about the role of the militia in the new nation. What can the subsequent history of the militia tell us about the Founders' vision of the Second Amendment?

5. Several scholars have observed that in the long run many Antifederalist predictions came true. Does the case of the militia support this contention?

The Federalized Militia Debate: A Neglected Aspect of Second Amendment Scholarship

The past fifteen years or so have brought heated debate on one aspect of the Second Amendment. Does its gun ownership language provide both a personal right to keep firearms — for protection and other private purposes such as hunting and recreation — and a collective right to defend society as a member of the militia? Historians such as Robert E. Shalhope, Lawrence Delbert Cress, and Joyce Lee Malcolm have addressed these issues.[1] They have been joined in increasing numbers by members of the legal academy. The lawyers have concentrated on the individual rights question, which the great majority of them answer affirmatively.[2]

Virtually absent from these gun ownership and gun rights arguments, in both the legal and the historical literature, is what Americans had to say about control of the state militias before, during, and after the writing of the Constitution. The subject is important because it shows how radical was the shift from the states' total control of their militias to the sharing of that authority under the Constitution, how disturbing this development was to the Antifederalists, how James Madison dealt with Antifederalist concerns in the Second Amendment, and, finally, how the issue was gradually resolved in the first half of the nineteenth century. In all the discussions and debates, from the Revolution to the eve of the Civil War, there is precious little evidence that advocates of local control of the militia showed an equal or even a secondary concern for gun ownership as a personal right.

The language of the Constitution provides the base for the militia-control controversy in the late 1780s. Article I, Section 8 declares that "The Congress shall have power . . . To provide for calling forth the militia to execute the laws of the Union, suppress insurrections and repel invasions."

Don Higginbotham, "The Federalized Militia Debate: A Neglected Aspect of Second Amendment Scholarship," *William and Mary Quarterly,* Vol. 55, no. 1 (1998): 39–58.

Although the states retain the authority to train the militia and to appoint its officers, Congress has the power "to provide for organizing, arming, and disciplining the militia, and for governing such part of them as may be employed in the service of the United States." The Antifederalists gave initial definition and drive to the controversy over the meaning and application of these terms, but none of their proposals for limitations or prohibitions on the federalized militia appears in the Second Amendment, which, writes Leonard W. Levy, is "as vague as it is ambiguous."[3] It therefore became the responsibility of Congress, with some assistance from the Supreme Court, to implement the Constitution's militia clauses.

After showing that colonial and Revolutionary Americans were virtually of one mind in espousing a well-regulated militia under local authority, this article reviews the breakdown of that consensus brought about by the militia's performance in the War of Independence and during Shays's Rebellion. After looking into the militia provisions of the Constitution, it examines the Antifederalists' negative reactions to those provisions and their failure to accomplish their agenda in the Second Amendment. It then shows how Congress and the Supreme Court resolved the constitutional questions concerning the federalization of the militia for domestic purposes. That resolution, together with the limited extent to which the national government actually called out the militia in peacetime — the subject of the final part of this article — explains why, for all practical purposes, a long and hotly disputed ideological issue disappeared. That the states were rarely called on to send their militias into national service, however, proved no guarantee that the institution itself was, in the classic phrase, the great palladium of liberty that Antifederalists and other states' rights advocates claimed it to be.

In their newspaper and pamphlet responses to Britain's new imperial policy after the Seven Years' War, the colonists decried, among other ominous developments, the decline of the metropolitan militia and the increasing use of redcoats to preserve law and order in both the parent kingdom and its transatlantic dominions.[4] Americans asserted that if their civil officials encountered domestic commotions, they should appeal only to their local militias for support, a contention that reflected both their reading of the dangers of standing armies in English history and their own colonial experience. It became a tenet of faith that colonial authorities should retain jurisdiction over their provinces' militias and other forces. That view brought displeasure to royal governors during the imperial wars, for the provincial assemblies claimed and exercised such power over the militia to set salaries, to authorize the stores and equipment to be raised, to determine the number of men called for service, to prescribe organization and training, and to forbid or limit duty outside their provinces. Consequently, American law-makers hamstrung royal administrators and British officers who sought to establish control over colonial fighting men.[5] The colonists predictably reacted vigorously when royal governors in 1775 attempted to seize militia arsenals at Williamsburg and Concord, the latter episode igniting the War of Independence.

The pattern of home control of local military organizations continued in the Revolution. Both conviction and precedent explain why the language of the thirteenth article of the Virginia Declaration of Rights in 1776 resounded through similar state charters. The Virginia document declared "that a well-regulated militia, composed of the body of the people trained to arms, is the proper, natural and safe defence of a free state . . . and that in all cases, the military should be under strict subordination to, and governed by, the civil power." The new state constitutions gave the legislatures the power to mobilize the militia, and mustering them for campaigns usually required the approval of the state executive council, which the legislatures themselves elected in most states. For Congress or the army to attempt to take over the militias or to send them against their will outside their own states would constitute "a Subvertion of all Liberty," asserted Abraham Clark of New Jersey, who lectured the speaker of his state's assembly on the need to "Oppose Tyranny in all its Strides."[6] Noting that few if any structures symbolized state sovereignty more than the militia, Cress calls the institution "central to the political stability and constitutional balance that sustained a republican constitution."[7]

George Washington, critical of a system that at best provided poorly trained men for limited service in his Continental army, addressed the sensitive issue of militia control near the war's end in 1783. His "Sentiments on a Peace Establishment," a document that anticipates crucial elements of military policy debate for the next two centuries, proposed that America retain its Revolutionary practice of regular and state forces but with fundamental alterations in the militia system. Congress should create two classes of militia within each state, each more effectively organized than the present militias. The first and larger class would, as in the past, include all men from ages sixteen to fifty. It would represent an improvement over the old system in that its establishment, exercise, and weapons would be uniform in all the states. Even so, the class could hardly be trusted to meet the nation's most critical needs. For "amongst such a Multitude of People . . . there must be a great number, who from domestic Circumstances, bodily defects, natural awkwardness, or disinclination, can never acquire the habits of Soldiers." The second class, drawn from the first, would be composed solely of young, able-bodied volunteers or draftees. While on active duty, this class would be under direct federal jurisdiction. Its primary task would be to resist "any sudden impression which might be attempted by a foreign Enemy," affording time for Congress to begin full-scale mobilization.[8]

Militia reform, like other schemes for empowering Congress under the Articles of Confederation, found a chilly reception. Washington's "Sentiments," though approved in revised form by a Congressional committee, elicited scant support in the full legislative body. In 1786, Henry Knox, secretary at war for the Confederation, advanced a militia plan that resembled Washington's blueprint in some respects and also responded to parochialists' fears that a nationalized militia might be corrupted and cease to embody republican virtue. Knox proposed that militiamen in federal training would hear lectures on the glories of republican institutions and would engage only in recreation and amusements that were morally and physically uplifting. Moreover, militia units called outside their states to deal with threats and emergencies would be returned in no more than a year, a provision Knox believed would dampen apprehensions of misusing the militia or turning the state troops into a standing army. Even so, Knox's recommendations suffered the fate of Washington's "Sentiments."[9]

The Articles referred to every state's maintaining "a well regulated and disciplined militia," yet they contained no authorization for the central government under any circumstance to assemble for training or any other reason even some small part of the state militias. Only the broadest interpretation of Congressional authority could read into the Articles a power to dictate militia regulations or responsibilities to the states. Short of amendments — and they required unanimous approval from the thirteen states — Congress could not reform the militias, even had it a mind to do so.[10]

Although the Confederation's main line of defense in the post-1783 years consisted of a single regiment under the control of Congress, the states proved unwilling to upgrade the militias on their own initiative. David Ramsay, a former South Carolina congressman, complained that "our governments are too relaxed to bear any [militia] system . . . attended with . . . time & expense."[11] Part of the problem stemmed from opposition of local elites. In Virginia, for example, the legislature, responding to Washington's recommendation that the states replace their militia officers with former officers of the Continental army "so far as can be done without creating uneasiness and jealousy," authorized Governor Patrick Henry to make wholesale replacements.[12] Henry made a number of appointments but ran into strong resistance, for loss of office also meant diminution of the senior officers' local standing and influence. As one appointee who declined to accept his commission explained, he did not hail from one of the foremost Augusta County families and did not wish to be "an object of . . . utmost resentment." The following year, the legislature, beating a retreat, returned the displaced militia officers to their commands.[13]

The nationalists, persistent advocates of a more consolidated political union, saw the uneven performance of the Massachusetts militia in Shays's Rebellion as a further indication of the need for improving militia by the central government. In 1786, several thousand men took up arms, closed the courts in western counties, and threatened the Confederation's arsenal at Springfield. Some militia units in the insurgent counties supported the rebels. A battle between state troops and dissidents at Springfield produced defections to the rebel ranks. In time, the government forces prevailed, but not before the Confederation was gravely shaken.[14] Other states likewise suffered from postwar economic dislocation; would they be spared similar tumults? A less publicized confrontation had occurred almost simultaneously in New Hampshire. There, angry debtors led by militia officers surrounded the building in Exeter where the legislature was in session and announced that none could leave until the besiegers obtained an acceptable response to their petitions for relief. The following day, militia from the state's eastern towns dispersed the insurgents.[15] Everywhere, newspaper essays and letters echoed Washington's exclamation that "combustibles in every State" menaced the tranquility of the states and the stability of the union itself.[16]

The authors of the federal Constitution saw a critical need to impose controls over the internal affairs of the states in general and over the state militias specifically, to counter domestic turmoils. They added a new component to the idea of a federalized militia as detailed by Washington, Knox, and several other generals of the Continental army. It now appeared insufficient to provide better training and a measure of Congressional oversight. Consequently, the Philadelphia Constitutional Convention gave Congress authority to employ the militia against the states or any of their citizens in certain cases involving internal disturbances and breaches of federal law.

Owing to a preoccupation with such major concerns as the structure of the central government and representation issues, the subject of militia control was not formally addressed by the full convention until August 6, when the committee of detail reported the first draft of a constitution. Surprisingly, in light of earlier negative views on militia reform and the presence in the convention of men who held such views, the delegates agreed with little debate to accept the committee's all-embracing language empowering the national legislature "to call forth the aid of the militia" not only to "repel invasions" but also "to execute the laws of the Union" and to "suppress insurrections." Some of the more state-minded delegates, however, favored a limit on the portion of any state's militia that might be subject to federally imposed rules for training and that might be called up for national service at one time. But these were mainly differences of degree; the idea of some measure of federal oversight and control in these two areas was questioned on the floor by only two delegates: Elbridge Gerry of Massachusetts and Luther Martin of Maryland. The task of dealing with the delegates' differences over this part of the militia wording fell on August 18 to a committee of eleven. Three days later, the committee reported militia language almost identical to that in the final document: Congress was "to make laws for organizing, arming, and disciplining the militia, and for governing such part of them as may be employed in the service of the United States, reserving to the States respectively, the appointment of the Officers, and the authority of training the militia according to the discipline prescribed by the United States." The convention then agreed to accept the committee report in two votes: 9–2 and 7–4, the four negatives in the second vote coming from states that wished to reduce the federal role in training the militia.[17]

The militia provisions of the Constitution flew in the face of so much American thinking and experience and so became subject to Antifederalist attack. On December 12, 1787, at the Pennsylvania ratifying convention, the first to be held, Robert Whitehill introduced one of the most detailed Antifederalist resolutions on the militia to appear during the ratification contest. It stated "that the power of organizing, arming, and disciplining the militia (the manner of disciplining the militia to be prescribed by Congress) remain with the individual states, and that Congress shall not have authority to call or march any of the militia out of their own state, without the consent of such state and for such length of time only as such state shall agree."[18] Whitehill's resolutions set the stage for the militia debate that would be repeated in subsequent conventions and the press.

The absence of stated limits to Congressional control, asserted the Antifederalists, would generate repeated military interventions in the domains of the states and the lives of the people, especially because, as Patrick Henry warned, the Constitution did not define the meaning of executing the laws or suppressing insurrections.[19] Critics of the Constitution feared that only military coercion could hold together a consolidated republic in a sprawling country like the United States, with its diverse regions and heterogeneous population, but such use of force, declared the "Federal Farmer," would "very soon destroy all elective governments in the country, produce anarchy, or establish despotism."[20] Antifederalists warned that the people's resistance to unjust and discriminatory taxation would prompt the federal government to resort to arms. "Is it not well known," asked Virginia's George Mason, "that what would be a proper tax in one State would be grievous in another?"[21]

An oft-repeated Antifederalist scenario explained how the sword would be employed. The national government would quite possibly be too shrewd to send a standing army to enforce the laws and intimidate the people, a step that would raise specters of Caesar, Cromwell, and George III.* Rather, it would resort to the federalized militia: it would confuse the people by using the body of the people against the people. Mason had endeavored to address this fear at the Constitutional Convention. He wanted to preface the section on federalizing the militia by stating that to do so would have made it transparent that the purpose of the militia in national service was to protect freedom, not to threaten it. But Gouveneur Morris of Pennsylvania — supported by Charles Pinckney of South Carolina and Gunning Bedford of Delaware — called the Mason addition a slap in the face of American professional soldiers, "the military class of Citizens," and it met defeat.[22]

As Antifederalists saw it, the militia under federal control would possess all the evils associated with a standing army. Congress's power to impose harsh discipline would brutalize the militia into submission by fines, corporal punishment, and fear of death by court-martial. Having been thus transmogrified into myrmidons,† citizen-soldiers would become the mirror image of European professionals. These "meer machines as Prussian soldiers" would lose their devotion to freedom and to the dignity of the individual as they became walled off from the body politic. Of course, some yeomanry might be too sensitive and independent-minded to be deceived or to knuckle under. It would be terribly distasteful, for instance, for Pennsylvania militiamen, many of them doubtless Quakers opposed to military obligations in principle and antislavery in sentiment, to be sent to Georgia to suppress slaves revolting for "*sacred liberty.*" To avert such defection or disobedience, the national administration would concentrate its energies on militiamen from "the young and ardent parts of the community, possessed of but little or no property."[23]

Although the means might vary, the result would be the same: the militia would become, in effect, a standing army maintained by the states but controlled by the central government.[24] Militias might be dispatched from one end of America to the other to quell insurrections sparked by the most terrible oppressions, leaving their home states defenseless, particularly from Indians on the frontier. This military arm, the erstwhile palladium of liberty, would become an instrument of tyranny. As one Maryland "Farmer and Planter" put it, if you "think you are imposed upon by Congress[,] . . . your great Lords and Masters, and refuse or delay to pay your taxes, or do any

---

Caesar, Cromwell, George III: Americans of the Revolutionary generation would have viewed all three of these leaders as tyrants. The first two, the Roman leader Caesar and the seventeenth-century Puritan revolutionary Oliver Cromwell, were military leaders who had seized power after commanding powerful armies. George III was the king whom Americans rebelled against during the Revolution.

†*"Myrmidons":* A classical term used to describe any subordinate who willingly obeys without question.

thing that they shall think proper to order you to do, they can . . . send the militia of Pennsylvania, Boston, or any other state or place, to cut your throats, ravage and destroy your plantations, drive away your cattle and horses, abuse your wives, kill your infants, and ravish your daughters, and live in free quarters, until you get into a good humour, and pay all that they may think proper to ask of you, and you become good and faithful servants and slaves."[25] In sum, moaned John Smilie in the Pennsylvania convention, the militia, "the last resource of a free people[,] is taken away" and put in the hands of Congress. "It ought to be considered as the last *coup de grace* to the *State governments,*" lamented Luther Martin.[26]

Antifederalists objected in general to the Constitution's bestowal of concurrent powers on the federal government and the states, and nowhere did this shared authority appear more starkly than in the militia provisions. Antifederalists maintained that either the central government or the states would ultimately control the militia. This concern found vociferous expression in the Virginia convention. The new government would be consolidated in character, complained Henry, pointing to the militia language; Congress did not have to receive the approval of the states to call out the militia. The concept of shared jurisdiction was a myth: "To admit this mutual concurrence of powers will carry you into endless absurdity:— That Congress has nothing exclusive on the one hand, nor the States on the other!" All such absurdities would resolve to the advantage of the central power. If, for example, a state needed its militia at the same time as the federal government, "Which call is to be obeyed, The Congressional call, or the call of the State Legislature? The call of Congress must be obeyed."[27]

Antifederalists sought means for redress — for tilting the balance toward the states' retaining greater control of their armed forces — by changing either the text of the Constitution or by adding a national bill of rights. At the Pennsylvania convention, they tried — and failed — to delay approval of the Constitution until adoption of amendments that would have included stipulations for lessening federal authority over the militias. Beginning with the Massachusetts convention, Federalists faced stiffer opposition and increasingly agreed to propose recommendatory amendments in a variety of areas. Massachusetts and four other states offered such recommendations.[28] When the First Federal Congress took up the issue of constitutional change in 1789, it had approximately one hundred separate proposals on a broad range of topics available for consideration.[29]

Because Madison, who introduced amendments in the House of Representatives after pledging to do so at the Virginia convention, supported almost exclusively stipulations guaranteeing individual and collective rights, he avoided all recommendatory amendments that would have created structural changes in the Constitution, including weakening the power of

Congress over the militia.[30] Recommendations for limiting the militia's numbers in federal employment, restricting its time under national control, regulating its out-of-state service, subjecting its rank and file to martial law, and providing for its training all failed to find their way into what became the Second Amendment. One measure advocated by some Antifederalists, freeing conscientious objectors from military participation, passed in the House but lost in the Senate. Still another proposal popular with some Antifederalists — that the militia would remain under state control except when in the employment of the United States — was introduced in the House but received little support, perhaps because it failed to go beyond the language already in the Constitution. In any case, Congress, composed largely of Federalists, showed no inclination whatsoever to mollify Antifederalists on the subject of the militia.[31] The members, with few exceptions, shared Madison's belief that a bill of rights should be a statement of general principles rather than a document that included particulars and policies that, in their view, were more properly determined by statute law.

The Federalists, in refusing proposals for change, responded as they had done during ratification. They dismissed Antifederalist apprehensions as totally unrealistic. In The Federalist, Hamilton branded them as "far fetched and . . . extravagant," and Madison dismissed them as "misguided exaggerations."[32] Denying that Congress would enact legislation that would be harsh or discriminatory toward states or large numbers of people, Federalists further contended that civilian officials, including judges, would almost always have the means to uphold federal law and maintain the peace without resorting to the nationalized militia or the army. William Samuel Johnson of Connecticut argued that the Constitution goes to great lengths to avoid military responses to internal difficulties: rather than "armed force. . . . the power which is to enforce these laws is to be a legal power vested in proper magistrates."[33] Consequently, as Virginia Federalists repeatedly pointed out, militias, with very rare exceptions, would remain under direct control of the states, which would be free to increase their arms and their training as they saw fit. Edmund Randolph reminded Virginia's convention that militia officers, appointed by and subject to removal by the states, would hardly give up their state loyalties if and when they entered federal service. Randolph, reflecting other supporters' sentiments, ridiculed the opposition's lack of "common sense" in "interpreting this Constitution."[34]

The rhetoric of Antifederalists and Federalists will never enable us to understand fully what the members of the First Congress intended by the language of the Second Amendment: "A well-regulated militia, being necessary to the security of a free State, the right of the people to keep and bear arms shall not be infringed." The problem is that, with exceedingly few exceptions, we do not know how individuals in either camp understood the amendment as it moved through the Congress to the state legislatures. Neither side displayed unanimity of views about the strengths and weaknesses of the Constitution. Much has been said over the years about the difficulty of determining the original intent of the authors of the Constitution; the same holds true of those who voted — warmly or halfheartedly — for rights amendments or for the Bill of Rights itself, a subject that gained the serious attention of Congress only as a result of Madison's prodding in 1789.[35]

We can only speculate about Madison's motives in introducing the Second Amendment. He may well have done so partly for psychological or symbolic reasons and partly to satisfy — in some measure, at least — the Virginia convention, which wanted not only alterations in the body of the Constitution that would have weakened jurisdiction over the militia but also a bill of rights containing militia language fairly close to Madison's own Second Amendment wording. By conceding something heavy in emotional content but thin in substance, something that could be interpreted as each reader chose to do, Madison and his supporters in Congress probably hoped to calm Antifederalist fears. Without dealing with specifics, the amendment seems to imply that the concurrent power of the state and federal governments over the militia will not threaten the states or obstruct their use of the militia when not in federal service. That would include the states' arming and equipping their respective militias if Congress failed to do so. It can surely be seen as a confirmation of their views by that small number of Antifederalists who are known publicly to have favored citizens' right to keep arms for private purposes as well as for collectively defending society as members of the militia.[36] If most Antifederalist writers feared that the central authority would make the militias so muscular that they might serve as a standing army, others saw another disturbing possibility: that the national government would keep the militias too weak to resist the power of a future standing army.[37]

It is clear, in any case, that Congress was less than enthusiastic about a bill of rights and that some Antifederalists were disappointed with the Bill of Rights, including Virginians Richard Henry Lee and William Grayson, the former judging the amendments "much mutilated and enfeebled," the latter calling them "good for nothing."[38] Also opposed was Gerry of Massachusetts, like the two Virginians an Antifederalist member of the First Congress. Gerry singled out the militia amendment as his most serious objection to the Bill of Rights. He saw in it the continuation of a dangerous precedent that had begun with the militia provisions of the Constitution: the sacrificing of the states' total control of the militia to a central government that also had the authority to create a standing army. It reminded him of Britain's efforts during the earlier imperial crisis to keep the Massachusetts militia weak at the same time that royal troops were sent to coerce the Bay Colony.[39]

The new national charter remained in 1789 a skeleton to be fleshed out by laws and judicial interpretation. President Washington's administration encountered difficulty in getting Congress to implement the Constitution's provisions for bringing the state militias under federal jurisdiction for training. The reasons are complex and not always ideological. The large Federalist majority in the First Congress had refused to weaken Congress's control of the militia in the Second Amendment but was not of one mind about creating a centralized militia establishment.

Congressional divisions on that subject became apparent immediately after Secretary of War Knox, borrowing liberally from militia plans that he and Washington had advanced in the Confederation years, presented an implementation package to the national lawmakers in January 1790.[40] Stressing the need for quick legislative action because of Indian uprisings on the frontier, Knox once again called for a system of classing the militia by age and providing summer encampments and standardized weapons and equipment for the younger militiamen, who would constitute the elite class. Knox, like Washington and other former generals of the Continental army, knew that not all militiamen were well armed and familiar with their weapons.[41] Equally bold, and certainly unprecedented, was Knox's recommendation that young men should be denied the full benefits of citizenship until they completed their terms of service in the elite class.

Knox's proposals produced heated opposition in and out of Congress. Critics asserted that classing and summer camps for younger men would be unworkable and exceedingly expensive. The cost, estimated at over $400,000 a year for the "advanced corps," prompted Benjamin Goodhue of Massachusetts, a Federalist member of the House of Representatives, to exclaim, "I believe Knox to be" nearly "the most extravagant man . . . living." Others called for exceptions for numerous occupations and for conscientious objectors, and they denounced Knox for stipulating that citizenship rights should be linked to compulsory military service.[42] According to a satirical piece in Benjamin Bache's Philadelphia *General Advertiser,* one Charlotte informed her friends Sophia and Thalestris that, because Quakers, tradesmen, students, and farmers sought exemptions from militia duty, "I suppose that we young women must learn militia duty, and turn out with both musquet and bayonet." Two authorities state that "nothing [the First Federal Congress] considered raised as much organized public opposition as Knox's militia plan."[43]

Congress backed off, taking the customary route of legislative bodies that seek to escape the heat: a committee drafted a bill, encouraged further public commentary, and put the controversial measure aside for months while lawmakers dealt with other divisive issues such as Hamilton's financial program and the location of the national capital.[44] The Knox legislation eventually limped through a succession of ad hoc committees in 1790 and 1791, each one further weakening its original contents. The first and only full debate on the much-revised militia bill terminated with the end of the First Congress in early 1791. The national legislators, hopelessly divided on the subject, went home without voting on it.[45]

When the Second Congress finally passed the Uniform Militia Act of 1792, it eliminated almost all the parts Washington and Knox considered crucial. The act lumped together all men between the ages of eighteen and forty-five in a huge, undifferentiated militia force, with every man responsible for securing his own weapon, regardless of its condition, unless the states elected to furnish arms. The law provided only loose guidelines for training and organizing the militia under state, not federal, supervision. It provided no penalties if the states proved unwilling to enforce these guidelines.[46] The statute continued to be the basic structural legislation for the militia until the twentieth century, despite reform-minded efforts of various presidents. None made more persistent attempts than Thomas Jefferson, who addressed the matter in seven of his annual messages to Congress. Like Washington and Knox before him, Jefferson embraced the idea of Congress's classing the militia and supplying the best-trained component with standardized weapons. But when he persuaded lawmakers to consider the matter seriously in 1805–1806, he met a resounding defeat.[47]

Congress in 1792 also enacted the Calling Forth Act to define procedures for federalizing state militias. Some Federalists wanted to leave the decision to the president, but a majority of the lawmakers insisted on safeguards against hasty action by the administration. In the event of an insurrection against a state government, the act made it "lawful for the President . . . on the application of the legislature of such state, or the Executive (when the legislature cannot be convened)" to call out militia from other states. The new law also passed on some of Congress's power relative to executing national law to the chief executive, mostly pertaining to when it was not in session. To act, however, the president needed notification from a federal judge that civil authority was inadequate to bring order. Furthermore, before ordering out militia, he had to issue a cease-and-desist proclamation.[48]

The first and greatest test case, practically and constitutionally, for the employment of the federalized militia came soon after Congress enacted the 1792 militia laws. In 1794, Washington called out 13,000 militiamen from four states to suppress the Whiskey Rebellion in western Pennsylvania, where angry farmers blocked the collection of a federal tax on distillers of spirituous liquors. Though Washington received criticism from within the emerging Republican Party, the protesters could hardly argue that the president had failed to remain inside the letter of the law; their concerns focused on the need to resort to force and the number of men taken into national service. Most congressmen, however, approved Washington's performance: he had delayed forceful means until after conciliation had apparently failed; he released most of the militiamen after a short time in arms; and he pardoned the two rebels convicted of treason.[49]

Congress subsequently reinforced and strengthened the "calling forth" authority of the federal government in general and of the president in particular. Revising the Calling Forth Act in 1795, it made the law permanent and deleted the stipulations that the president, before implementing part of it, had to obtain a judicial certificate and secure Congressional approval if the lawmakers were in session.[50] In 1799, President John Adams, displaying less hesitancy than Washington in 1794, dispatched federalized militia to put down Fries Rebellion in Pennsylvania where, again, an unpopular federal tax generated agrarian resistance. Even Jefferson, who had faulted both Washington and Adams for federalizing militia for use against Pennsylvania farmers, when president followed their lead during the Burr Conspiracy* and again during the disorders stemming from his controversial Embargo† in 1807.[51] Once the leaders of both political parties had turned to federalized militia, the question of employing that military force to maintain or restore domestic tranquility could hardly arouse as much dispute as a party issue as it had in the 1790s.

Remaining constitutional issues were resolved by the Supreme Court under Chief Justice John Marshall in the 1820s. From time to time, militia had been reluctant or unwilling to serve the federal government. President Jefferson had a greater problem in this respect than his predecessors, owing to the extreme unpopularity of the Embargo in New England, and Federalists saw danger in Congress's enabling Jefferson to deploy both the army and the militia to enforce the Embargo. The Massachusetts legislature condemned Jefferson's assembling militia at the ports as "irregular, illegal, and inconsistent with the principles of the constitution . . . subversive of the militia system, and highly dangerous to the liberties of the people."[52] In *Houston* v. *Moore* (1820), the Supreme Court ruled that a militiaman who refused to respond to a federal call-up violated national law. Justice William Johnson, in a concurring opinion, found the central government empowered to

---

Burr Conspiracy: An alleged plot by former Vice President Aaron Burr to sever part of the Southwest from the United States by force.

†*Embargo of 1807:* A prohibition on the import of British goods enacted by Jefferson in response to violations of American rights on the high seas. The embargo prompted serious protests and disturbances in Northeast port cities.

stipulate "both the officer and private who shall serve, and to call him forth or punish him for not coming."[53] Even more sweeping was the court's unanimous decision in *Martin* v. *Mott* (1827) that, in the words of Justice Joseph Story, upheld the constitutionality of all portions of the Calling Forth Act of 1795. Addressing concerns about presidential tyranny, Story declared that it must be assumed that chief executives would demonstrate "public virtue and honest devotion to the public interests." He added that Congressional oversight and frequent elections would ever "guard against usurpation or wanton tyranny."[54]

The settlement of constitutional questions about militia control hardly guaranteed that Americans would live comfortably with the outcome. Rather, a combination of laws and judicial opinions and the infrequency of federal militia call-ups explain why the militia-control issue in peacetime became moot. Since the time of Jefferson's Embargo, the central government has seldom assembled state units under its direction, and in every instance they have acted in conjunction with troops of the United States army.[55] For ninety years following the Civil War — from 1867 to 1957 — although often activated by a state to maintain order, the militia saw no federal service in internal disturbances. Beginning in the latter year and continuing into the next decade, the militia, by then known as the National Guard, performed short-term duty in enforcing racial integration in the South and restoring order in several northern cities racked by racial violence. Since the 1960s, the Guard's responsibilities have been carried out under state jurisdiction, with only a single two-day exception in Arkansas in 1980.[56]

The Antifederalists lost the battle but, in a sense, won the war. They largely prevailed in that the federal government showed small interest in federalizing the militia for domestic reasons or in subjecting it to intensive training overseen by the national military establishment. Presidential administrations have not dispatched militiamen from one end of America to the other or, typically, kept them on duty for more than a few days to a few months. With the major exception of the Civil War, federal law could normally be upheld and enforced by civil authorities and by the judiciary. Strong sentiments of localism and states' rights also are factors that worked against federalizing the militia and subjecting it to demanding training. So too is the fact that America hardly had an activist government in Washington, D.C., before the twentieth century.

Ironically, state control, a reality during by far the greater part of American history, failed to produce the positive results that its admirers predicted. Although Antifederalists feared that national authorities either would fail to train the militia or would remove it from the states, the truth is, as the Federalists maintained at the time, the states could train their militias above and beyond whatever regulation the central government imposed. The states have displayed scant initiative in providing substantial appropriations and rigorous training for their units — to the point that, by 1861, save for volunteer units (usually elitist in character), the state militias had virtually ceased to exist, especially in the South, and they revived but slowly after the Civil War.[57] The deterioration of the militias provides the explanation why, after the War of 1812, the federal government took into active service in time of national conflict very few militia units as such prior to the twentieth century, preferring instead to fight its wars with the regular army and federal volunteers.

Nor has state control insured that the militia would be the bulwark of liberty its proponents had claimed it to be from the time of seventeenth-century English opponents of the Stuarts through the colonial period and the Revolution to the Antifederalists and beyond. When called out by state authorities, the militia and the National Guard have often been accused of heavy-handed behavior against various minorities, including Catholics in antebellum cities, labor unionists, Native Americans, Asian Americans, African Americans, and Vietnam War protesters.[58]

The militia and National Guard never served as splendid repositories of freedom and equality. They were highly politicized instruments that reflected majoritarian views in the states, except during Reconstruction. Because governors or legislatures appointed general and staff officers, political affiliation became a critical factor in the selection process; this can be seen as early as 1802 in Tennessee when Andrew Jackson won the post of commanding general over John Sevier. The opportunity to be a member of the Guard has always been influenced by political factors. Just as some antebellum northern states limited participation to non-Irish whites, so blacks by 1900 had all but disappeared from the Guard in the southern states. Conversely, the Guard became a haven for countless young men seeking to avoid the draft during the Vietnam War, their ability to join often depending on their having political or social connections.[59]

Since the adoption of the Constitution in 1788, control of the militia has never been an either-or matter. It rarely received a call-up for peacetime domestic duty. Patrick Henry, who doubted that concurrent powers could work, was wrong, but for reasons he could not have foreseen, which have been enumerated in this essay. Rather than becoming agents of oppression in the name of the national government, as Antifederalists feared, the militia and National Guard have more often been agents of state-level discrimination against minorities, in acting against such elements, excluding them from joining the state forces, or both.[60]

James Madison, at the Constitutional Convention and in The Federalist

No. 10, declared that personal rights were more likely to be endangered by the state governments than by the national government. That is why he included in his initial draft of the Bill of Rights in the House an amendment that "No state shall violate the equal rights of conscience, or the freedom of the press, or the trial by jury in criminal cases." (Though this prohibition failed to gain the Senate's approval, Madison considered it "the most valuable amendment on the whole list.") [61] Hence, in still another way, the Antifederalists were mistaken in believing, as they did, that freedom was more secure in small, homogeneous republics. History vindicates Madison's new and daring counterargument of 1787: namely, that rights are more secure in large and diverse republics in which majorities are slow to form and thus have difficulty discriminating against minorities. The history of the militia and the National Guard, viewed from a comparison of their federal and state services, points in that direction.

Notes

1. Robert E. Shalhope, "The Ideological Origins of the Second Amendment," *Journal of American History,* 69 (1982): 599–614; Lawrence Delbert Cress, "An Armed Community: The Origins and Meaning of the Right to Bear Arms," ibid., 71 (1984): 22–42; Shalhope and Cress, "The Second Amendment and the Right to Bear Arms: An Exchange," ibid., 587–93; Joyce Lee Malcolm, *To Keep and Bear Arms: The Origins of an Anglo-American Right* (Cambridge, Mass., 1994). Cress, rejecting any Second Amendment guarantee of gun ownership as a basic right, sees the amendment solely as reflective of Americans' belief in the citizen's collective obligation to defend society as a member of the militia. Shalhope and Malcolm view the amendment as recognizing both the individual's personal right and the collective rights to possess arms. Unlike Cress and Shalhope, Malcolm, in her very recent book, pushes the argument back beyond the ratification struggle over the Constitution and the Revolution itself to the English Bill of Rights and subsequent British laws and judicial writings. She contends that the ownership of guns, apart from any responsibility for the common defense, became a well-recognized right in England long before the American Revolution. In time, according to Malcolm, this attitude about gun rights became conventional wisdom in British America, as did certain other dimensions of English common law. It evolved and became generally understood and accepted, regardless of how often or in what form it received articulation. According to Malcolm, this "English influence on the Second Amendment is the missing ingredient that has hampered efforts to interpret its intent correctly," in *To Keep and Bear Arms,* xii.

2. Scott Heller, "The Right to Bear Arms: Some Prominent Scholars Are Taking a New Look at the Second Amendment," *Chronicle of Higher Education,* 41 (July 21, 1995): A8, A12. *See also* "An Open Letter on the Second Amendment," a full-page ad from "Academics for the Second Amendment," ibid. (Aug. 11, 1995), A23. Thirty-one of the 51 signers are members of the legal academy. For a scathing attack on the individual rights view of the Second Amendment, *see* Garry Wills, "To Keep and Bear Arms," *New York Review of Books,* 42 (Sept. 21, 1995): 62–73.

3. Levy, *Original Intent and the Framers' Constitution* (New York, 1988), 341.

4. T. A. Critchley, *The Conquest of Violence: Order and Liberty in Britain* (London, 1970); Tony Hayter, *The Army and the Crowd in Mid-Georgian England* (London, 1978); Pauline Maier, *From Resistance to Revolution: Colonial Radicals and the Development of American Opposition to Britain, 1765–1776* (New York, 1972); Hiller B. Zobel, *The Boston Massacre* (New York, 1970); John Shy, *Toward Lexington: The Role of the British Army in the Coming of the American Revolution* (Princeton, 1965).

5. The substantial literature on friction concerning control of provincial forces in wartime includes Jack P. Greene, *The Quest for Power: The Lower Houses of Assembly in the Southern Royal Colonies, 1689–1776* (Chapel Hill, 1963), 297–309; Don Higginbotham, *The War of American Independence: Military Attitudes, Policies, and Practice, 1763–1789* (New York, 1971), chap. 1; Alan Rogers, *Empire and Liberty: American Resistance to British Authority, 1755–1763* (Berkeley, 1974); Fred Anderson, *A People's Army: Massachusetts Soldiers and Society in the Seven Years' War* (Chapel Hill, 1984); and Douglas Edward Leach, *Roots of Conflict: British Armed Forces and Colonial Americans, 1677–1763* (Chapel Hill, 1986).

6. "Virginia Bill of Rights," in S. E. Morison, *Sources and Documents Illustrating the American Revolution,* 2nd ed. (Oxford, 1929), 151; Ruth Bogin, *Abraham Clark and the Quest for Equality in the Revolutionary Era, 1774–1794* (Rutherford, N.J., 1982), 22, 25.

7. Lawrence Delbert Cress, *Citizens in Arms: The Army and the Militia in American Society to the War of 1812* (Chapel Hill, 1982), 73.

8. George Washington, "Sentiments on a Peace Establishment," in *The Writings of George Washington from the Original Manuscript Sources, 1745–1799,* ed. John C. Fitzpatrick, 39 vols. (Washington, D.C., 1931–1944), 26:374–98, quotations on 389, 389–90. An overall assessment of the Revolutionary militias' performance appears in Higginbotham, *War and Society in Revolutionary America: The Wider Dimensions of Conflict* (Columbia, S.C., 1988), 106–31.

9. Henry Knox, *A Plan for the General Arrangement of the Militia of the United States* (Philadelphia, 1786). The best treatment of militia reform efforts, including congressional attitudes on the subject, is Cress, *Citizens in Arms,* chap. 5.

10. Articles of Confederation, Article VI.

11. Ramsay to Knox, Mar. 12, 1786, in *David Ramsay, 1749–1815: Selections from His Writings,* ed. Robert L. Brunhouse, American Philosophical Society, *Transactions,* New Ser., 55, pt. 4 (Philadelphia, 1965): 98–99.

12. Washington, "Sentiments on a Peace Establishment," 394.

13. Robert Porterfield, quoted in Harrison E. Ethridge, "Governor Patrick Henry and the Reorganization of the Virginia Militia, 1784–1786," *Virginia Magazine of History and Biography,* 85 (1977): 436. Madison, in describing the opposition to the new law as limited to a minority of counties, may have underestimated the number of critics; Madison to Thomas Jefferson, Jan. 22, 1786, in *The Papers of James Madison,* ed. William T. Hutchinson et al., Congressional Series, 17 vols. (Chicago and Charlottesville, 1962–1991), 8:478.

14. Robert J. Taylor, *Western Massachusetts in the Revolution* (Providence, R.I., 1954), chap. 7; David P. Szatmary, *Shays' Rebellion: The Making of an Agrarian Insurrection* (Amherst, Mass., 1980), chaps. 6–7; Cress, *Citizens in Arms,* 95–97. For recent interpretations of Shays's Rebellion *see* Richard D. Brown, "Shays's Rebellion and the Ratification of the Federal Constitution in Massachusetts," in *Beyond Confederation: Origins of the Constitution and American National Identity,* ed. Richard Beeman, Stephen Botein, and Edward C. Carter II (Chapel Hill, 1987), 113–27, and Robert A.

Gross, ed., *In Debt to Shays: The Bicentennial of an Agrarian Rebellion* (Charlottesville, 1993).

15. Jeremy Belknap, *History of New Hampshire . . .* , 3 vols. (Boston, 1813), 2:360–64; Alan Taylor, "Regulators and White Indians: The Agrarian Resistance in Post-Revolutionary New England," in *In Debt to Shays,* ed. Gross, 145–50. Debtor violence on a lesser scale also took place in the backcountry from New Jersey to South Carolina. *See* Richard B. Morris, *The Forging of the Union, 1781–1789* (New York, 1987), 264–65.

16. John K. Alexander, *The Selling of the Constitutional Convention: A History of News Coverage* (Madison, Wis., 1990), 20–21, 34, 54–55, 99–101, 142–43, 169–70n. 65; Washington to Knox, Dec. 26, 1786, in W. W. Abbot et al., eds., *Papers of George Washington,* Confederation Series, 6 vols. (Charlottesville, Va., 1992–1997), 4:482.

17. Max Farrand, ed., *Records of the Federal Convention of 1787,* rev. ed., 4 vols. (New Haven, 1937), 2:182, 323, 326, 330–33, 352, 355–56, 380–81, 382, 384–88, 390.

18. Whitehill, resolution 11, in *The Documentary History of the Ratification of the Constitution,* ed. Merrill Jensen, John P. Kaminski, Gaspare J. Saladino, et al., 12 vols. to date (Madison, Wis., 1976–), 2:598, hereafter cited as *Documentary History Ratification.* For similar views expressed by Pennsylvania Antifederalist delegate John Smilie, *see* ibid., 508–09.

19. Henry's speeches, ibid., 10:1277, 1300.

20. "Federal Farmer," ibid., 14:29.

21. George Mason's speech, ibid., 9:937; "Centinel I" and "Dissent of the Minority of the Convention," ibid., 2:162, 635–39 passim; Henry's speech, ibid., 10:1300; Jackson Turner Main, *The Antifederalists: Critics of the Constitution, 1781–1788* (Chapel Hill, 1961), 143–45.

22. Mason's proposed preface to the militia language in Article I, Section 8 of the Constitution declared: "And that the liberties of the people may be better secured against the danger of standing armies in time of peace"; Farrand, ed., *Records of the Federal Convention of 1787,* 2:616–17.

23. Quotations from "Centinel III," "Philadelphiensis II," and "Federal Farmer," in *Documentary History Ratification,* Jensen et al., eds., 14:60, 253–54, 37–39; "Aristocrotis," "The Government of Nature Delineated," in *The Complete Anti-Federalist,* ed. Herbert J. Storing, 7 vols. (Chicago, 1981), 3:16.9; Jonathan Elliot, comp., *The Debates in the Several State Conventions on the Adoption of the Federal Constitution, as Recommended by the General Convention at Philadelphia in 1787,* 5 vols. 2nd ed. (Philadelphia, 1861–1863), 2:552; Mason's speech, in *Documentary History Ratification,* ed. Jensen et al., 10:1269–70, 1271–72. A broadside published in Maryland, signed J. T. Chase and J. F. Mercer, endeavored to generate public opposition to the Constitution without a bill of rights, which should include "no whipping militia, nor marching them out of the state, without consent of the general assembly"; *Documentary History of the Constitution of the United States of America,* 5 vols. (Washington, D.C., 1894–1905), 4:641–42. Daniel Carroll informed Madison that the broadside had "alarm'd" many people with its "positive assertions"; May 28, 1788, in *Madison Papers,* ed. Hutchinson et al., 11:63.

24. Connecticut Antifederalists voiced some of the earliest fears that the federalized militia would become a standing army; *Documentary History Ratification,* ed. Jensen et al., 3:378, 427, 428–29.

25. "Essay by a Farmer and Planter," in *Complete Anti-Federalist,* ed. Storing, 5:2.3. For examples of other predictions of federalized militia outrages *see Documentary*

History Ratification, ed. Jensen et al., 2:509, 13:540. I find no evidence of Antifederalists' quoting an intellectual ally, Sir William Blackstone, who wrote that English militiamen "are not compellable to march out of their counties, unless in case of invasion or actual rebellion, nor in any case compellable to march out of the kingdom," in *Commentaries on the Laws of England,* 4 vols. (Oxford, 1765–1769), 1:399.

26. Smilie's speech in the Pennsylvania convention and Martin, "Genuine Information VII," in *Documentary History Ratification,* ed. Jensen et al., 2:508–09, 15:411.

27. For examples of attacks on the concurrent powers idea *see* Henry's speeches, ibid., 9:957–58, 10:1276 (quotation), 1309–11, 1419; Mason's speech, ibid., 9:936–37; William Grayson's speech, ibid., 10:1306.

28. For a state-by-state analysis of the tactics and strategies of the Federalists and Antifederalists in the ratifying conventions *see Ratifying the Constitution,* ed. Michael Allen Gillespie and Michael Lienesch (Lawrence, Kan., 1989).

29. Helen E. Veit, Kenneth R. Bowling, and Charlene Bangs Bickford, eds., *Creating the Bill of Rights: The Documentary Record from the First Federal Congress* (Baltimore, 1991), xi, 14–28; Edward Dumbauld, *The Bill of Rights and What It Means Today* (Norman, Okla., 1957), 173–205. The number can be placed as high as 210 if one counts duplicate proposals, many of which did not relate to rights but instead focused on structural changes in the central government. In fact, structural "alterations formed a clear majority of both the 210 and the 100"; Bowling, "'A Tub to the Whale': The Founding Fathers and Adoption of the Federal Bill of Rights," *Journal of the Early Republic,* 8 (1988): 228.

30. Stuart Leibiger, "James Madison and Amendments to the Constitution, 1787–1789: 'Parchment Barriers,'" *Journal of Southern History,* 59 (1993): 441–68.

31. Veit, Bowling, and Bickford, eds., *Creating the Bill of Rights,* 12, 30, 38–39n, 182–85, 267. Charles A. Lofgren argues that the conscientious objector issue came up mainly in discussions of the militia rather than in regard to federal armies and navies because both Federalists and Antifederalists considered the Constitution as limiting the citizen's military obligation to compulsory service in the militia, in "Compulsory Military Service under the Constitution: The Original Understanding," *William and Mary Quarterly,* 3rd ser., 33 (1976): 61–88.

32. Nos. 29, 46, in *The Federalist,* ed. Jacob E. Cooke (Middletown, Conn., 1961), 185, 321.

33. Jensen et al., eds., *Documentary History Ratification,* 3:546. For the same point *see* Hamilton, No. 27, in Cooke, ed., *Federalist,* 171–75. In Federalist No. 28, ibid., 176–80, Hamilton conceded that there might be rare exceptions when force would be needed. Although he was unclear whether the federalized militia or regular troops would be employed in such circumstances, he stated that the decision would be made by the representatives of the people. He went on to say, in Federalist No. 29, ibid., 181–87, that the well-trained, properly disciplined federalized militia is preferable because standing armies are more likely threats to liberty.

34. Jensen et al., eds., *Documentary History Ratification,* 9:1014, 1074, 1102, 10:1288 (quotation), 1289, 1293–94, 1296, 1311–12, 1324–25, 1486, 1531. Hamilton and Madison also stressed officers' loyalty to the states that appointed them as a safeguard against federal misuse of the militia, in Federalist Nos. 29, 46, in *Federalist,* ed. Cooke, 185, 321–22.

35. Because the Senate did not initially hold open sessions, little is known about the details of its members' response to Madison's amendments. John Randolph, in New York City at the time the future Second Amendment reached the Senate,

informed his stepfather, St. George Tucker, that "a Majority of the Senate were for not allowing the militia arms & if two thirds had agreed it would have been an amendment to the Constitution. They [the senators] are afraid that the Citizens will stop their full Career to Tyranny & Oppression." The House held open sessions, which enabled several men from the press to record its debates, though none did so in a full and systematic way. Much of what later appeared in print on the Bill of Rights debates in the House is technical and procedural rather than substantive. *See* Veit, Bowling, and Bickford, eds., *Creating the Bill of Rights,* 55–213 passim, quotation on 293.

36. Ibid., 19, 20. Although Jefferson, from Paris, plied Madison with suggestions for changes in the Constitution, particularly for adopting a national bill of rights, he failed to express any reservations about the militia clauses of the document. *See* especially Jefferson to Madison, Dec. 20, 1787, July 31, 1788, Aug. 28, 1789, in *Madison Papers,* ed. Hutchinson et al., 10:336, 11:212–13, 12:364.

37. "Essays of John DeWitt," in *Complete Anti-Federalist,* ed. Storing, 4:3.27–28; Martin's speech, in *Documentary History Ratification,* ed. Jensen et al., 14:290–91; Henry's speech, ibid., 9:957–58; Mason's speech, ibid., 10:1270, 1271; Grayson's speech, ibid., 1306; Henry's speech, ibid., 1535. A Federalist writer correctly noted that the Antifederalists tried to have it both ways: they spoke of the dangers of the federal government's both arming and its failing to arm the state militias; "The Landowner No. X," ibid., 16:267.

38. Richard Henry Lee to [Francis Lightfoot Lee], Sept. 13, 1789, in *The Letters of Richard Henry Lee,* ed. James Curtis Ballagh, 2 vols. (New York, 1911–1914), 2:500; Grayson to Henry, Sept. 29, 1789, in *Patrick Henry: Life, Correspondence, and Speeches,* ed. William Wirt Henry, 3 vols. (New York, 1891), 3:406. There is a disappointing lack of information about the public's reaction to Congress's proposed amendments that became the Bill of Rights, probably because there seems to have been strong public support for most of them. The subject is not even mentioned in Donald H. Stewart, *The Opposition Press of the Federalist Period* (Albany, N.Y., 1969), x, based on "nearly all" of the approximately 550 newspapers published between 1789 and 1801. The existing sources are mainly skeletal outlines of legislative measures. The ratification literature is listed and evaluated by Saladino, "The Bill of Rights: A Bibliographic Essay," in *The Bill of Rights and the States: The Colonial and Revolutionary Origins of American Liberties,* ed. Patrick T. Conley and John P. Kaminski (Madison, Wis., 1992), 484–85. The continued strength of Antifederalism in post-1788 Virginia is discussed in Richard Beeman, *The Old Dominion and New Nation, 1788–1801* (Lexington, Ky., 1972), 61–66, and J. Gordon Hylton, "Virginia and the Ratification of the Bill of Rights, 1789–1791," *University of Richmond Law Review,* 25 (1991): 433–74 passim. These accounts suggest that Virginia Antifederalists were less interested in the Congressionally proposed individual rights amendments than in the absence of amendments that would have specifically restricted the powers of the federal government in its dealings with the states. Richard Henry Lee and William Grayson to the Speaker of the Virginia House of Representatives, Sept. 28, 1789, cited in Beeman, *Old Dominion,* 61. In contrast, Georgia, whose convention unanimously ratified the Constitution, appears to have taken the view, as reflected in the action of its legislature in rejecting the Bill of Rights, that amendments were premature until the people had a chance to observe the actual workings of the new government after the Constitution went into effect; Julia M. Bland, comp., *Georgia and the Federal Constitution: Proceedings of the State Constitutional Convention, and Proceedings of the State Legis-*

lature with Respect to the Amendments Proposed by the United States Congress on September 25, 1789 (Washington, D.C., 1937), 9–15.

39. George Athan Billias, *Elbridge Gerry: Founding Father and Republican Statesman* (New York, 1976), 232–35; Veit, Bowling, and Bickford, eds., *Creating the Bill of Rights*, 182–84.

40. Knox, "A Plan for the General Arrangements of the Militia of the United States," in *Documentary History of the First Federal Congress*, ed. Bickford, Bowling, Grant DePauw, and Veit, 14 vols. to date (Baltimore, 1972–), 5:1435–57, hereafter cited as *Documentary History First Congress*.

41. In 1794, Secretary of War Knox stated that of 450,000 men in the militias, probably 100,000 at most owned guns or had been supplied them by their states; *American State Papers: Documents, Legislative and Executive, of the Congress of the United States,* class V, *Military Affairs,* 7 vols. (Washington, D.C., 1832–1861), 1:70. Several scholars are currently looking into the subjects of gun ownership and regulation in early America. None has yet produced a major study, but Michael A. Bellesiles has written two preliminary offerings. *See* "Gun Laws in Early America: The Regulation of Firearms Ownership, 1607–1794," paper delivered at the Second Annual Institute of Early American History and Culture Conference, Boulder, Colorado, June 1, 1996, and "The Origins of Gun Culture in the United States, 1760–1865," *Journal of American History,* 83 (1996): 425–55.

42. As early as April 16, 1790, about seven months before Congress formally debated the measure, Senator William Maclay of Pennsylvania predicted that it had no chance of adoption; Bowling and Veit, eds., *The Diary of William Maclay and Other Notes on Senate Debates, March 4, 1789–March 3, 1791* (Baltimore, 1988), 246–47. An excellent summary of the early reaction to Knox's plan is in Richard H. Kohn, *Eagle and Sword: The Federalists and the Creation of the Military Establishment in America, 1783–1802* (New York, 1975), 128–33, Goodhue quotation on 131.

43. Bickford and Bowling, *Birth of the Nation: The First Federal Congress, 1789–1791* (Madison, Wis., 1989), 82–83. For the satire on militia legislation see "C. to Mr. Bache," Philadelphia *General Advertiser,* Jan. 20, 1791; copy provided through the courtesy of Kenneth R. Bowling.

44. *Documentary History First Congress,* 3:256–69 passim, 379, 484, 631–48 passim.

45. First Congress militia debates, ibid., 14:48–189 passim.

46. *Annals of Congress,* 2nd Congress, 1st Session, 103, 418–24, 436, 1392–95; *Statutes at Large,* 271.

47. James D. Richardson, ed., *A Compilation of the Messages and Papers of the Presidents, 1789–1902,* 10 vols. (Washington, D.C., 1896–1899), 1:329, 345, 372, 385, 410, 428–29, 455; Paul Leicester Ford, ed., *The Writings of Thomas Jefferson,* 10 vols. (New York, 1892–1899), 8:409–12; *Annals of Congress,* 9th Congress, 1st Session, 69–70, 141, 327–30.

48. *Annals of Congress,* 2nd Congress, 1st Session, 554–55, 574–80; 1 *Statutes at Large,* 264. *See also* for the 1792 militia legislation Robert W. Coakley, *The Role of Federal Military Forces in Domestic Disorders, 1789–1878* (Washington, D.C., 1988), 19–23, and John K. Mahon, *History of the Militia and the National Guard* (New York and London, 1983), 51–54.

49. There is a sizable literature on the Whiskey Rebellion. Accounts of the martial dimensions are in Kohn, *Eagle and Sword,* 157–73; Coakley, *Role of the Federal Military Forces,* chaps. 3–4; and Bennett Milton Rich, *The Presidents and Civil Disorder* (Washington, D.C., 1941), chap. 1. The subject is treated more broadly in

Leland D. Baldwin, *Whiskey Rebels: The Story of a Frontier Uprising* (Pittsburgh, 1939), and Thomas P. Slaughter, *The Whiskey Rebellion: Frontier Epilogue to the American Revolution* (New York, 1986).

50. 1 *Statutes at Large*, 422.

51. W. W. H. Davis, *The Fries Rebellion, 1798–99* (Doylestown, Pa., 1899); Coakley, *Role of Federal Military Forces*, 69–77.

52. 2 *Statutes at Large*, 506. Massachusetts General Court, quoted in Coakley, *Role of Federal Military Forces*, 89. Jefferson's military enforcement of the Embargo is criticized in Levy, *Jefferson and Civil Liberties: The Darker Side* (Cambridge, Mass., 1963), chaps. 5–6, and viewed somewhat sympathetically in Dumas Malone, *Jefferson the President: Second Term, 1805–1809* (Boston, 1974), chaps. 28, 32–35.

53. 5 Wheat. 1, 12–32, 37 (U.S., 1820).

54. 12 Wheat. 19, 29–39 (U.S., 1827).

55. Coakley, *Role of Federal Military Forces*, is a detailed account covering the years through Reconstruction, the first of a projected three-volume work on military interventions.

56. Robin Higham, ed., *Bayonets in the Streets: The Use of Troops in Civil Disturbances*, 2nd ed. (Manhattan, Kan., 1989), although comprehensive, focuses on post–Civil War activity. *See also* Jerry M. Cooper, "Federal Military Intervention in Domestic Disorders," in *The United States Military under the Constitution of the United States, 1789–1989*, ed. Kohn (New York, 1991), 120–50.

57. Mahon, *History of the Militia and the National Guard*, chaps. 6, 8; Higginbotham, "The Martial Spirit in the Antebellum South: Some Further Speculations in a National Context," *Journal of Southern History*, 58 (1992): 3–26; Kenneth Otis McCreedy, "Palladium of Liberty: The American Militia System, 1815–1861" (Ph.D. diss., University of California at Berkeley, 1991).

58. Robert Reinders, "Militia and Public Order in Nineteenth-Century America," *Journal of American Studies*, 11 (1977): 81–101; Mahon, *History of the Militia and National Guard*, chaps. 6, 8, 16; Stephen E. Ambrose, "The Armed Forces and Civil Disorder," in *The Military and American Society: Essays and Readings*, ed. Ambrose and James A. Barber, Jr. (New York, 1972), 241–48. Few state Guards displayed more partisan behavior than that of Colorado. *See* Alvin R. Sunseri, "The Ludlow Massacre: A Study in the Mis-employment of the National Guard," *American Chronicle: A Magazine of History*, 1 (1972): 21–28; Clarence C. Clendenen, "Super Police: The National Guard as a Law-Enforcement Agency in the Twentieth Century," in *Bayonets in the Streets*, ed. Higham, 90–91; George G. Suggs, Jr., *Colorado's War on Militant Unionism: James H. Peabody and the Western Federation of Miners* (Detroit, 1972); and Alan M. Osur, "The Role of the Colorado National Guard in Civil Disturbances," *Military Affairs*, 46 (1982): 19–24. At least three Vietnam-era studies address the Guard's performance on the homefront: *Report of the National Advisory Committee on Civil Disorders* (New York, 1968), 497–506; American Civil Liberties Union, *The National Guard and the Constitution* (New York, n.d.); and Renata Adler, "A Reporter at Large," *The New Yorker*, 46 (Oct. 3, 1970): 40–64, which in some respects remains the most penetrating analysis of the Guard's domestic role at the time.

59. Mahon, *History of the Militia and National Guard*, chap. 8 passim, 149, 212, 236–37, 243, 246, 264; Willard B. Gatewood, Jr., "North Carolina's Negro Regiment in the Spanish-American War," *North Carolina Historical Review*, 48 (1971): 370–87. On none of the four major occasions the Guard was called out by state governors in the 1950s to deal with racial strife are blacks known to have served; W. Ronald Wachs,

"'Off Guard': The National Guard and Race Relations in the 1950s" (Ph.D. diss., University of North Carolina at Chapel Hill, 1977), 416. The political activities of the militia and National Guard, especially at the federal level, are developed in William H. Riker, *Soldiers of the States: The Role of the National Guard in American Democracy* (Washington, D.C., 1957), and Martha Derthick, *The National Guard in Politics* (Cambridge, Mass., 1965).

60. Perhaps the harshest scholarly judgment is in Ambrose, "Armed Forces and Civil Disorder," 241–48.

61. Veit, Bowling, and Bickford, eds., *Creating the Bill of Rights*, 13, 41, 41 n 19, 188.

Edmund S. Morgan

The People in Arms: The Invincible Yeoman

From *Inventing the People: The Rise of Popular Sovereignty in England and America*

Prior to his retirement, Edmund S. Morgan was Sterling Professor of History at Yale University. This chapter, taken from his Bancroft Prize–winning book, *Inventing the People: The Rise of Popular Sovereignty in England and America,* explores the evolution of ideas about the militia in England and America. The central issue that Morgan examines is why early Americans continued to idealize the militia despite widespread recognition of its inability to function as an effective military force. To unravel the complex connections between rhetoric and reality leads the historian away from a close examination of printed texts such as constitutions and pamphlets, to a wider examination of the social and political context. Morgan's analysis of the way the militia functioned in Virginia captures an important context of the Second Amendment that has often been ignored by scholars who take the rhetoric of the Founders at face value. While praising the ideal of the militia, Virginia's political elite were able to use the structure of the militia to reinforce social hierarchy. Seemingly democratic rhetoric could be used to achieve goals that were decidedly undemocratic in reality. The myth of the militia helped the gentry, who dominated Virginian society, to secure the consent of the broad ranks of yeomen, who were the majority of the population.

Questions for a Closer Reading

1. One of the central concepts Morgan uses is the idea of "political fictions." What is a political fiction?

2. Who exactly were the yeomanry in America? What was the myth of the invincible yeoman, and what led Americans to embrace it with such intensity?

3. Explain the concept of deference. How did individuals such as George Mason believe the militia might be used to inculcate the principle of deference in the yeomanry?

4. How does Morgan's analysis help us understand the context out of which the Second Amendment emerged?

5. How should historians deal with situations in which rhetoric and reality are at odds with one another?

The People in Arms: The Invincible Yeoman

The sovereignty of the people is a much more complicated, one might say more fictional, fiction than the divine right of kings. A king, however dubious his divinity might seem, did not have to be imagined. He was a visible presence, wearing his crown and carrying his scepter. The people, on the other hand, are never visible as such. Before we ascribe sovereignty to the people we have to imagine that there is such a thing, something we personify as though it were a single body, capable of thinking, of acting, of making decisions and carrying them out, something quite apart from government, superior to government, and able to alter or remove a government at will, a collective entity more powerful and less fallible than a king or than any individual within it or than any group of individuals it singles out to govern it.

Edmund S. Morgan, "The People in Arms: The Invincible Yeoman," from *Inventing the People: The Rise of Popular Sovereignty in England and America* (New York, 1988), 153–73.

To sustain a fiction so palpably contrary to fact is not easy. And to begin with, it had to make its way in societies — England and England's colonies — where political authority was strongly linked with social class. The fact that it became the reigning fiction in such societies is not easily explained. But part of the explanation may lie in the operation of another fiction that accompanied and supported it. This was the notion that the ability of the people to exercise sovereignty and control their government rested on the righteousness, independence, and military might of the yeoman farmer, the man who owned his own land, made his living from it, and stood ready to defend it and his country by force of arms.

The notion existed at least as early as Aristotle, but it reappeared with new vigor in England and America during the seventeenth and eighteenth centuries. The germs of the idea, as it came to prevail in England, can be found even before the emergence of popular sovereignty there, at least as early as Sir John Fortescue* in the fifteenth century and Niccolò Machiavelli† in the sixteenth. Fortescue praised the laws of England because they protected the subject's property, and he contrasted the condition of ordinary Englishmen with that of the abject French peasantry, racked by arbitrary rents and taxes. The people of England, according to Fortescue, were "rich, abounding in gold and silver and all the necessaries of life." And as proof he offered a characteristically English piece of evidence: "They do not," he said, "drink water, except those who sometimes abstain from other drinks by way of devotional or penitential zeal." Englishmen ate well, drank well, lived well because their property was secure from arbitrary exactions. And property for Fortescue, despite the mention of gold and silver, surely meant land.[1]

It seems unlikely that Machiavelli had read Fortescue, but he entertained the same notion of Englishmen that Fortescue did, and he made his own invidious comparison of Englishmen to Frenchmen. "Quite lately," he wrote, sometime early in the sixteenth century, "the king of England attacked the kingdom of France, and employed for that purpose no other soldiers except his own subjects; and although his own kingdom had been for over thirty years in profound peace, so that he had at first neither soldiers nor captains who had seen any active military service, yet he did not hesitate with such troops to assail a kingdom that had many experienced commanders and good soldiers, who had been continually under arms in the Italian wars."[2]

Fortescue and Machiavelli between them contributed the basic elements for the concept of the invincible yeoman: England was a country filled with

---

Sir John Fortescue: fifteenth-century English jurist and political philosopher.

†*Niccolò Machiavelli:* sixteenth-century Italian Renaissance political theorist who helped revive and reshape republican thought.

prosperous property owners, and they made good soldiers without previous experience. In 1622 Francis Bacon* combined the two elements in his biography of Henry VII, giving Henry credit for keeping landed property widely spread through the population, by means of a statute forbidding alienation of land from farms of twenty acres or more. Henry thus perpetuated and increased the strength of the English yeomanry and prevented land-grabbing nobility and gentry from debasing them. By strengthening the yeomanry Henry made England strong, and to prove the point Bacon went on to the comparison with France, against which, he said, "England, though far less in territory and population, hath been (nevertheless) an overmatch; in regard the middle people of England make good soldiers, which the peasants of France do not." [3]

Even before Bacon's exposition of it, this view of the English yeoman had become standard fare in Parliamentary debates, and quite properly so, because the security of property that allegedly — and indeed actually — differentiated England from France was sustained by the exclusive authority of the English Parliament to levy taxes. European monarchs, including England's, had made use of parliaments in order to obtain grants of property in taxes, but except in England the grants had generally become perpetual. Englishmen had somehow managed to keep most of their grants temporary. Now, when the king, in need or revenue, threatened to levy a tax without the consent of Parliament, he would be warned against the national weakness that must ensue from reducing the security of the subject's property. The strength of the king, it was argued, came from the strength of his people, and the strength of the people came from the security of their property. [4]

That was before the 1640s, when Oliver Cromwell† came upon the scene and demonstrated that the strength of the people could be used against the king as well as for him. England became a republic, and it remained only for James Harrington‡ to give classic expression and a republican twist to the belief in the invincible yeoman. Harrington's version of the now familiar comparison of England with France differed only in emphasis from previous ones: "the true cause whence England hath been an overmatch in arms for France lay in the communication or distribution of property unto the lower sort." And for the same reason the lower sort had been an overmatch for their king. Quoting liberally from Bacon, Harrington showed how the

---

Francis Bacon: sixteenth-century English philosopher and statesman.
†*Oliver Cromwell:* seventeenth-century Puritan who led the Parliamentary forces in the English Civil War.
‡*James Harrington:* seventeenth-century English republican theorist.

steps taken by Henry VII to protect the land of the yeomanry had begun a process that little-by-little in the course of a century had reduced the property both of the crown and of the nobility while increasing that of the yeomanry and gentry. With less income from land the crown became more dependent on taxation, the province of the House of Commons. And so, concluded Harrington, "by these degrees came the house of commons to raise that head, which since hath been so high and formidable unto their princes that they have looked pale upon those assemblies." And Harrington went on to affirm not merely that English yeoman made better soldiers than French peasants but that an army built or bought by a king out of debased peasants or paupers would inevitably fall before an army of yeoman citizens, "wherefore an example of such an one [that is, an army of yeomen] overcome by the arms of a monarch, is not to be found in the world. . . ."[5]

Henceforth the tradition that began with Machiavelli and Fortescue, or perhaps earlier, flourished in England and America in Harrington's version. In that form it contained three or four distinct propositions:

1. That the freedom characteristic of popular governments depends on the independence of the voting population and their representatives, and that their independence in turn rests on the secure possession of sufficient property in land to support them and thus render them free of coercion by employers or landlords, a coercion to which landless men must yield or else lose their livelihood. The vulnerability of the landless made them unfit to be given the suffrage. The ability to vote independently made the yeomanry the political guardians of the internal freedom of a popular government.

2. That these independent yeomen, armed and embodied in a militia, are also a popular government's best protection against its enemies, whether they be aggressive foreign monarchs or scheming demagogues within the nation itself.

3. As a corollary to the second proposition, that standing armies of professional soldiers are an internal threat to freedom and that popular governments must avoid them at all costs. A militia is the only safe form of military power that a popular government can employ; and because it is composed of the armed yeomanry, it will prevail over the mercenary professionals who man the armies of neighboring monarchs. The superiority of Englishmen to Frenchmen has become in Harrington the superiority of a militia to a professional army.

4. An additional proposition stressed by Aristotle was not so conspicuous in Harrington, but appealed strongly to Americans. The

proposition was that farmers are somehow more virtuous than other people and the success of popular government must rest in part on their virtue as well as on their arms and property.

Harrington expounded, or rather buried, these ideas in his tiresome Utopian fantasy. But the fact that *Oceana* is virtually unreadable did not prevent the ideas in it from finding their way into popular tracts and gaining wide acceptance in both England and America in the seventeenth and eighteenth centuries.

Harrington's propositions could not have prevailed so widely without bearing some relation to fact. The English yeomanry did have something worth fighting for: they did, by definition, own land, and their ownership was protected by a government over which they at least had more control than the French peasantry had over theirs. The enjoyed, relatively speaking, a large degree of economic and political independence, and their counterparts in America, constituting a majority of the adult males there, had even more. On both sides of the water they prided themselves on the rights of Englishmen, of which none was more sacred than the security of their property.

Nevertheless, if Harrington's propositions rested on a substratum of reality, they were more fiction than fact. We should be warned from taking them as fact by the serious error into which Harrington himself was led by them. Writing in 1656, while England was a republic, he predicted that the widespread distribution of property among England's armed people, among its yeomanry, would make it impossible henceforth for England to be anything but a republic. Four years later the armed people submitted to their hereditary king.[6]

But this miscalculation aside, Harrington's propositions betray their fictional character when measured against the role that property-holding yeomen actually played in government and warfare in England and America. The yeoman's role in government did not rise much above the casting of votes for members of Parliament, and the way yeomen cast their votes discloses the narrow limits of their independence. Before the English revolution, during the Cromwellian republic, and after the restoration of the king, the yeomen never made a practice of electing their own kind. Through all the changes of government they used their votes, as they had traditionally always done, to man the House of Commons with untitled noblemen and higher gentry.

The enduring deference of the English yeomanry to their social superiors does not mean that they were reduced to the position that Englishmen attributed to the French. Eighteenth-century Englishmen still prided themselves on their standard of living, so much better than that of those peasants across the channel, who wore wooden shoes and fed on black bread and gruel. Liberty and property and no wooden shoes was the standard chant to put down any ministerial measures that seemed to threaten the security of property in England.[7] Yet we know that the House of Commons remained throughout the eighteenth century in the hands of an oligarchy that bullied or bought its way into office. And from whom did it buy the votes? Whom did it bully? Among others it bullied those very yeomen whose sturdy independence was supposed to be proof against bullies and bribes.

The independence in voting that the ownership of land was supposed to confer on the yeomanry rested on the assumption that a man of property would be less susceptible to bribery or coercion than one without. There may have been some validity in the assumption but not much. As we shall see, the limitation of the suffrage to property-holders did not in fact eliminate widespread coercion and corruption in eighteenth-century elections. Indeed it can be argued more convincingly that the limitation of suffrage to property-holders invited the most effective form of bribery. In English electoral contests it was less common for a candidate to buy his votes by outright purchase from individuals than by a promise to pay borough or county expenses, such as poor relief or the building of a bridge or market-house.[8] And who would benefit from such payments? Who but the property owners, the landowners, the yeomanry, who would otherwise be taxed for the purpose. The very ownership of property thus became the means by which voters could be bribed in a body. Property was the handle by which they could be twisted this way or that, perhaps as readily as any laborer could have been twisted by threats to his livelihood had he been able to vote. A bought vote was no more an independent vote than a coerced vote, and yeomen, it appears, were quite willing to be bought en masse.

But bribery was seldom necessary, because voters were seldom offered a choice of candidates. In order to avoid the expense of an election contest the big families in a county increasingly agreed in advance on a single set of candidates to stand for the local seats. And since contests were so expensive when they could not be avoided, the members of the House of Commons in 1716 minimized the number of them by extending the interval between elections from three to seven years. The desire to save their own property thus warped the gentlemen candidates as much as the yeomen voters. There were, of course, Englishmen who decried septennial elections as betrayals of popular liberty. But the yeomanry themselves seem to have accepted the state of affairs without serious resistance, unless we count as resistance the abortive attempts to return the Stuarts to the throne, and it requires a certain degree of eccentricity to interpret the Jacobite movement as a thrust for popular government.[9] The sturdy yeomanry of the eighteenth century even allowed themselves to be disarmed by the laws which their representatives passed in order to preserve game for the hunting pleasure of nobility and gentry.[10]

The case was a little different in the American colonies, where the ownership of land and of arms was much more widespread than in England and where uncontested elections seem to have been less common. The power and independence of the yeomanry were accordingly more in evidence, especially in New England, where yeoman farmers did elect men of their own kind to represent them. In the political contests of the middle and southern colonies, however, we can see the same use as in England of property ownership as the handle by which to move voters in one direction or another. Candidates would obtain election by agreeing to oppose taxes and also by agreeing to serve without pay,[11] a form of bribery not possible in England, where representatives were unpaid anyhow and sought election for the prestige and profits that attached to their office. Candidates also resorted to more direct forms of bribery, common in England too, by treating the voters to dinners and drink in staggering quantities. And in the southern colonies, the site of the most ardent advocates of the independent yeoman farmer, candidates were not above outright intimidation of voters who preferred a different candidate.[12] . . . Suffice to say that even in the colonies the supposed independence and virtue of the yeoman farmer as a voter scarcely squares with the facts.

Equally at odds with fact is that cherished tenet of the yeomanry in arms, embodied in the militia, as the best and only safe form of military protection for a republic. What was the actual wartime record of those wonderful English yeomen who could allegedly dispose so easily of the debased peasantry or mercenaries in the armies of France? It is true that England was able to mount effective forces against France in the age of the longbow, before Machiavelli offered his flattering analysis of English strength. But for a century and a half after Machiavelli wrote, until the 1690s, when England created a permanent professional army, England mounted no formidable land force against France or another country.[13] It was not because England remained at peace with the world during those years. She went to war repeatedly with Spain, with France, and with the Netherlands. And she did build a powerful navy. But her soldiers, her land forces, proved an overmatch for nobody. English seamen might singe the king of Spain's beard, but the only land forces sent to the continent were feeble and ineffectual, composed mainly of the country's paupers and ne'er-do-wells, rather than the valued yeomanry. We will never know whether the yeoman would have done any better, because they stayed comfortably by their firesides. England did defeat France in the long series of wars that ended with the Peace of Paris in

1763, but that was after England had established a professional army. The eighteenth-century wars were fought on both sides by professional armies, and in their ranks yeomen were conspicuous by their absence. England's yeomen remained invincible, to foreign foes at least, by virtue of not having to fight.

In England's American colonies yeoman militia did prove sufficient in the sporadic, guerilla-type warfare that the first settlers carried on with the Indians. But the colonists' success owed much to the mere fact of their possessing firearms. And though the Indians quickly acquired firearms too, they did not have the skills or the equipment to keep them in repair or to make ammunition for them. Moreover, their social organization and culture were even less well adapted to sustained military operations than was the militia system that the colonists relied on. It was a different story when the Indians were organized and supplied by the French. In the final contest for the continent, the so-called French and Indian War that lasted from 1754 to 1763, the victory was not one of colonial militia over Indians but of British professionals, assisted by colonists, over French professionals, assisted by the Indians.[14]

The colonists chafed over the subordinate position assigned them in that war and may have nourished illusions about their own military skills. In 1775, when they challenged the professionals who had so recently defeated the French, their initial successes at Concord and Bunker Hill gave new support to the notion of the invincibility of amateurs and impeded the creation of a professional American army. The Continental Congress was all too ready to believe that stout-hearted American farmers, enlisted for a short stretch, would win the war quickly against the hired mercenaries of George III.[15] But George Washington did not make that mistake. Even before the professionals trounced him in the Battle of Long Island, he knew that he needed professionals to beat them. In the end he got his professionals: in the end he was allowed to enlist a small number of men for long enough periods to make professionals of them. But these were mostly men who did not have property that they wanted to stay home to look after. In the words of Commissary General Jeremiah Wadsworth, the Continental army was ultimately constituted of "very idle and very worthless fellows, which did not hinder them from doing their duty."[16] They did their duty because they could be made to do it, because there was no fireside waiting to shelter them from the stern discipline an army required. And in the eyes of their contemporaries they earned no credit for their submission to that discipline.

Popular hostility to a standing army grew not only out of the danger it posed to republican government but also out of contempt for the persons who would subject themselves to the tyranny of military discipline. "Can a friend to liberty," asked one pamphleteer, "entertain a tender regard for men, who without any motive but a dislike to labour, have relinquished voluntarily the blessings of freedom, for a state in which they are arbitrarily beaten like slaves?" Regular soldiers were "a species of animals, wholly at the disposal of government." They were "the dregs of the people"; and what made them "fit instruments of tyranny and oppression" was "the severity of discipline" by which they were themselves reduced "to a degree of slavery."[17]

It may be argued whether the men of the Continental army were moved by a dislike of labor or by patriotism, but statistical studies do confirm the fact that they were generally drawn from the lowest ranks of society, from the poor and landless.[18] The trouble was that there were never enough of these "idle fellows" in America, the land of the yeoman farmer. The French king's despised peasants, drilled into a regular army at their monarch's command, contributed as much to the final American victory at Yorktown as the freeborn Americans did at the behest of their popular governments. Cornwallis surrendered to Washington, but Washington's forces at Yorktown, if we include the indispensable naval forces, numbered more French than Americans.

It would be difficult to demonstrate that militia either in England or America have prevailed in any sustained contest with professionals. What made them ineffective was the very quality that Bacon and Harrington and others saw as the source of the militia's alleged superiority, namely the independent spirit that went with their possession of property. After England came to rely on a professional army, a knowledgeable member of Parliament explained why it was not and should not be composed of men with property. "Battles," he said, "are not won by fury, but by discipline." Independent yeomen might show a certain fury against the enemy for a short time — their independent spirit — but it was too hard to discipline an army made up of such men. And he explained with unusual candor: "The last man I desire to have the command of, is the substantial tenant or freeholder . . . it were an ungracious business to bring a constituent to the halberds, or too bitterly to animadvert on *him* for getting drunk, whom courteously I entreated, and invited by example, to do the same but yesterday."[19]

In America, George Washington expressed a similar opinion. As a general it was the bane of his existence that he had so often to rely on militia to supply deficiencies in his Continental army. "Men just dragged from the tender Scenes of domestick life; unaccustomed to the din of Arms" he found worse than useless on the battlefield. Their impatience to be back home again made them desert in droves, and it was all but impossible to bring them to discipline. "Men," he observed, "accustomed to unbounded freedom, and no control, cannot brook the Restraint which is indispensably necessary to the good order and Government of an Army; without which, licentiousness, and every kind of disorder triumphantly reign." Reliance on militia, in Washington's view, was the way to lose a war. Militia simply could not stand up against regular troops.[20]

If we turn to the question of domestic safety, of militia not endangering popular liberties in the way that a professional army does or can, the fiction is again betrayed by the facts. At first glance it would appear that the militia, by virtue of their very ineffectiveness, could not have been a serious threat to anything. Moreover, militia did sometimes seem to support liberty by joining a popular protest they had been called out to suppress. The people, as so often stated, would not be likely to oppress themselves. The very independence that made militia unreliable in battle would lead them to refuse the orders of a government that wished to use them against their fellow citizens.[21]

But the actual record, while it does contain instances of this kind, is just as replete with cases where the government did use militia successfully to suppress popular dissent. In England during the sixteenth and seventeenth centuries the government underwent a number of abrupt and radical shifts that provoked resistance and rebellion from subjects adversely affected. To suppress resistance, the government, whatever its current complexion, relied heavily on militia. When the government went Catholic under Mary Tudor, the militia suppressed Protestants. When it went Protestant under Elizabeth, militia disarmed Catholics. Although the militia failed Charles I, it was under circumstances that ultimately required the formation of a professional army. And when Charles II reclaimed the throne, it was again the militia that put down those who opposed the Restoration or were suspected of opposing it. Militia disarmed the die-hard Puritans, hanged them, deported them, levelled the fortifications of their towns, and broke up the conventicles in which they carried on their Sunday worship.[22]

In the colonies, as in sixteenth- and seventeenth-century England, the militia was the principal, indeed the only, method of forcibly suppressing discontent, not only the discontent of slaves, but the discontent of the free as well. Granted, in the largest colonial rebellion before the American Revolution, that of Nathaniel Bacon in 1676, the militia were at first completely without effect (most of them were with Bacon) and England dispatched an expeditionary force to uphold Virginia's government. Before it arrived, however, the rebellion had subsided, and Governor Berkeley with a handful of loyal militia had regained control. Against most other American rebels militia proved adequate: against the North Carolina Regulators at Allamance in 1771, against Shays's Rebellion in Massachusetts in 1787, against the Whiskey Rebellion in Pennsylvania in 1794. In every instance militia enabled the established government to ignore grievances that had moved people to take up arms. And the people so readily suppressed by the yeoman militia were not urban mobs, not proletariat, but other yeoman farmers.

In sum, it appears that in both England and America actual experience was at odds with the beliefs that elevated the yeoman to so high a place in the folklore of popular government. We are left with the question why. If yeoman farmers were vulnerable to bribery and intimidation in politics, why did people insist that they were independent and virtuous upholders of civil liberty? If as militia they were neither effective in warfare nor a bulwark against tyranny and oppression, why did people keep insisting that they were? Did the political and military exaltation of the yeoman contribute to popular government in ways that do not appear in the repeated but undeserved eulogies of the armed people? If we say yes, if we go on the assumption, as I think we must, that the persistence of a set of beliefs in apparent defiance of facts must have served some not so apparent social and political purpose, a couple of possibilities suggest themselves.

The first relates only to the notion that the militia make a mightier force than a professional army. Obviously this notion was viable only where a country's security was not seriously threatened by aggressive neighbors. It could thrive in England and America because the English Channel in the one case and the colonists' superior technology in the other made it possible to do without a professional army for more than a century. During that time the prevalence of the idea of a mighty militia made it possible for government to eliminate what is always the largest element in any country's budget. The mighty militia offered a cheap rhetorical substitute for an expense that might otherwise have placed a heavy and unnecessary drain on the economy. It helped to prevent the government from burdening the people with taxes to pay for an army at times when an army was not needed.

That in itself was enough to make the fiction attractive, but relief from taxes may also point to the intricate way in which this particular fiction shaped reality and helped to mold a society in which the larger fiction of popular sovereignty could flourish. By relieving the yeoman of the taxes that arbitrary governments levied in support of their expensive armies, the fiction of the mighty militia enabled him to keep his land, to enlarge his acreage, free of mortgages and free of rents, free of seizure for taxes. And it gave to larger and larger numbers the disposable income to acquire land and become yeomen. Thus the fiction of the mighty militia, by nourishing the economic independence of the yeoman farmer, helped to create a factual base on which the fiction could rest. It is not, perhaps, a coincidence that the rise of popular sovereignty in England and America was accompanied for so long by reliance on militia and by acceptance of the notion, however dubious, that English yeomen could fight better than French peasants and that militia could overpower professional armies.

But the magnification of the militia was only one of the ways in which the fictional glorification of the yeoman may have contributed to the success of popular sovereignty. The notion of the independent yeoman as the bulwark of civil liberty, we have seen, was equally persistent in defiance of fact. In this case we may find a clue to the persistence of the notion and to the purpose it served if we ask what the seventeenth- and eighteenth-century champions of the yeoman wanted him to be independent of and what sort of liberty they conceived him to be guardian of. It was independence, not of his lordly neighbors, but of the king and his court and of anyone else who might threaten the security of landed property. Spokesmen for the Country party in England, while extolling the yeomanry, urged the gentry to wield over them and over all their inferiors "that Influence which their Family and Fortune procure them."[23] They had, they were told, "a Right to interfere in those elections that are carrying on round about you."[24] The liberty that the yeoman must guard was the liberty to follow his local superiors in defying the influence of the court and its minions.

In the seventeenth century Harrington, though down on hereditary kings, had been no enemy of aristocracy. And the neo-Harringtonians of the eighteenth century emphasized the necessity of the landholding aristocracy as well as the landholding yeomanry for the maintenance of popular liberty.[25] The danger, as they saw it, was that an ambitious king would seek arbitrary power through a standing army and a venal commercial aristocracy. The way to head off royal thrusts of this kind was through the yeomanry, embodied in a militia, on the one hand, and through the landed aristocracy, embodied in Parliament, on the other. The two were closely linked: the landed aristocracy were the natural leaders of the landed yeomanry. Accordingly the neo-Harringtonians, the Englishmen who were most vociferous in idolizing the independent yeomen, showed no concern to keep the yeomen independent of the big country gentlemen and county families that had traditionally commanded their votes and led their militia. And the yeomen, secure in their idealized independence, showed no concern to strike out on an independent unfamiliar political course of their own.

In other words, the glorification of the yeoman farmer in England and America during the eighteenth century functioned as an expression of solidarity among landowners, large and small, against the changing but continuous threats to the security of their property. Or perhaps it would be fairer to say that it was an exhortation by large landowners to stand behind them against the protean political dangers that threatened them both.

In England the greatest threat still came from the court, but backed now by the rise of a money power, a commercial and financial class against which large and small landowners must stand together. The villains in England were the corrupt ministry surrounding the king and the stockjobbers and financiers, who were hand-in-glove with the ministry in schemes for getting rich out of the pockets of both yeomen and gentlemen by means of financial manipulations. We may recall that Trenchard and Gordon's famous *Cato's Letters* began in 1720 in the *London Journal* as an attack on the South Sea bubble as well as on the ministry that permitted stockjobbers to fleece the public.[26]

The colonists in America, avid readers of Trenchard and Gordon, feared the spread of ministerial schemes across the water and after establishing independence in the Revolution remained alert for any similar danger in their new nation. They found it in the programs of Alexander Hamilton. In the 1790s when Madison and Jefferson sought to organize the yeoman farmers of America in what became the Republican party, they worked against the money power, against the unnatural aristocracy created and nurtured by Hamilton — not against America's natural aristocracy, not against men like themselves who had traditionally, since the beginning of settlement, furnished the country with leaders. Those leaders, whatever their personal faults, had demonstrated in the Revolution their vigilance against threats to the colonists' property rights. With independence won, their vigilance was needed more than ever to fend off new and more insidious threats. For the voters to be bullied or bought by their natural leaders, the proven protectors of their property, was no cause for alarm. What the voters, indeed the whole country, needed protection from was the sinister and hidden influence of the "paper aristocracy" that Hamilton seemed to be fabricating.

A distinct but related threat to property, greater in England than in America, came from the poor. The glorification of the yeoman had begun with a denigration of the peasant and carried on with a denigration of paupers and landless laborers, who spent their earnings on drink and went on relief when the jobs gave out, people whom landowners had to support with taxes that ate away at their property.[27] Nor did glorification of the yeoman involve much sympathy with the slaves who manned the American plantations of the South. When Thomas Jefferson talked about those who labored in the earth being the chosen people of God, he did not mean slaves. Englishmen and Americans in the eighteenth century regarded slaves, paupers, and destitute laborers as an ever-present danger to liberty as well as property. From the poor an ambitious monarch or executive might forge an army and impose a tyranny. And they were also the material out of which the new capitalists would recruit workers for their factories. If they were allowed to vote, their employers might march them to the polls to vote down the independent yeomen. The best way for the yeoman to deal with the danger was to line up behind his big neighbor, who had the experience, the resources, and the political clout to defend the land and the liberty of both of them.

In other words, the glorification of the yeoman in the seventeenth and eighteenth centuries, which seemed to elevate the ordinary man, served paradoxically as the central ideological tenet of deferential politics (especially for the so-called country parties whether in England or America). The paradox appears only from our modern perspective. We assume too easily that popular sovereignty was the product of popular demand, a rising of the many against the few. It was not. It was a question of some of the few enlisting the many against the rest of the few. Yeomen did not declare their own independence. Their lordly neighbors declared it, in an appeal for support against those other few whom they feared and distrusted as enemies to liberty and to the security of property — against irresponsible kings, against courtiers and bankers, stockjobbers and speculators — and against that unsafe portion of the many whom they also feared and distrusted for the same reason: paupers and laborers who held no land.

In the last resort the yeomen might have to be bullied or bought, along with other voters; but just as the fictional exaltation of the king could be a means of controlling him, so the fictional exaltation of the yeomen could be a means of controlling them. Landed gentlemen, those who touted themselves as "the country" against "the court," proclaimed the yeoman's independence — and claimed his vote as the proper exercise of that independence. They were the "natural" superiors the yeoman would defer to, if his independence were not subverted by the wiles of courtiers and court politicians (even if those courtiers were themselves landed gentlemen). In their common ownership of land, yeomen and gentlemen could make common cause and join hands, in election time at least, in a curious combination of camaraderie and condescension on the part of the big men and of deference and self-respect on the part of the small.[28]

Another look at the militia will reveal that the military glorification of the yeoman could serve similarly as a prop for deferential politics. The militia, besides suppressing revolts, were also a means of forestalling them and of fostering consent to government, not by force but by instruction. Service in the militia was a school of subordination, where the structure of society was most visibly displayed, especially on the annual or semiannual or even monthly training days. Officers of the militia in sixteenth- and seventeenth-century England and in seventeenth- and eighteenth-century America were selected, not for their military skill but for their social position. There are recorded instances not only in Elizabethan England but in revolutionary America of militia refusing or objecting to serve under officers with insufficient social standing.[29] High social position helped officers to secure obedience to their commands, and conversely, subordination to an officer in uniform helped to secure subordination to him out of uniform. In some colonies militia officers were popularly elected and their men therefore the more devoted to them. The officers they elected were generally men whom they recognized as their social superiors.[30]

In the absence of titles of honor, which no colonial government had authority to confer and which of course were formally forbidden by both the Articles of Confederation and the Constitution, military titles were the most important designation of social status in America, and they were seldom attained except by large landholders, who also held the lion's share of political offices. Contests for captaincies or colonelcies in the militia were often more bitter than those for political office.[31] And the winners were correspondingly more proud of their military titles than of those that might attach to political office. John Leverett, who was governor of Massachusetts from 1673 to 1679, continued for the rest of his life to be addressed, not as Governor Leverett but as Captain Leverett, the rank he had held in the militia.[32] And George Washington himself continued to be referred to most commonly as General Washington, even after he became president.

Training days for the militia were much alike throughout the colonies. The officers put the men through their paces, and then they all got drunk together, at the officers' expense.[33] There was that same strange combination of camaraderie and condescension, of deference and conviviality that bound high and low together politically. It was a time for showing both the structure and the tone of society. And those who thought that the structure needed tightening and the tone needed elevating would accordingly call for a tightening of discipline in the militia. Timothy Pickering, for example, an ardent conservative, argued in 1769 that a better disciplined militia would "in a great measure prevent *domestic* jars, by promoting good *Order*, and *a just Sense of the Subordination, necessary not only to the Well-Being but to the very Existence, of Society;* as one Act of Obedience and Respect leads to another; and Acts repeated grow into Habit."[34] And in 1788 another New England conservative, Jonathan Jackson, arguing for a stronger militia, insisted that "the most important thing to be learned [from militia service] and for which alone the institution would be wise, is — that discipline of the mind — subordination."[35]

But most Americans were content with the festivity and the easier, looser variety of subordination that went with training days, when the soldiers delighted in surrounding a pretty girl and firing their muskets in the air, while officers dashed about in glittering uniforms that bespoke social rank more than military prowess.[36] The subordination taught in the militia was not the kind that deprived a man of his independence and made a professional army effective, not a forced subordination or a blind subordination but a willing social subordination, the kind of subordination that made orderly government possible. It was subordination to one's large landholding neighbors, men whom one knew and might with confidence elect to government office. It was not the kind of subordination that George Washington wanted in the Continental army or Alexander Hamilton in the Army of the United States, but a considered deference of free men to their acknowledged superiors, a kind of subordination that did not violate the yeoman's independent spirit.

Patrick Henry, as governor of Virginia, was brought up short along with his legislature, when he and they momentarily ignored the social function of the militia. George Washington, fresh from his disappointments with militia performance in the revolutionary war, recommended to Henry in 1784 that the state militia be strengthened by the replacement of existing officers with former Continental army officers, adding only the caution "so far as can be done without creating uneasiness and jealousy." The Virginia legislature obliged the general with an act authorizing the change but left it up to the governor to do the job. Henry tried to move cautiously by consulting "respectable characters" in different counties for nominations, but many of them refused to have anything to do with so wild a scheme and refused to make recommendations. When Henry went ahead and made appointments, he met with a political storm. Prominent citizens were furious at being displaced from positions on which their prestige and local influence had in part rested; and the rank and file were furious at the prospect of being treated like regular soldiers. The next year the legislature repealed the act and restored the old officers to their commands and the militia to its military incompetence and its social and political effectiveness.[37]

In teaching the yeoman his place in the social order the militia performed an undesignated but crucial political function as well as a social function and performed both more successfully than its military function. In the American Revolution, as John Shy has shown us, the militia, however lacking in armed prowess, was a formidable means of lining up indifferent citizens on the side of the gentlemen who led the popular opposition to England and created popular governments in America.[38] But the militia's most valuable service during the seventeenth and eighteenth centuries was in reconciling the incongruity of popular sovereignty with a hierarchical society. The willing deference of men to their officers, in or out of uniform, was of particular importance in America, because militia office generally went hand-in-hand with political office and because the American militia included all able-bodied free men, most of whom were voters, conditioned by their militia service to support their officers.

Throughout the colonial period in America the formal presence of militia was not uncommon at political ceremonies and elections. And after the Revolution, when politics took on a new character with the development of political parties, the militia for a time was the obvious organizing unit at the local level. Militia officers made campaign speeches at musters and sometimes marched their companies to the polls. In Maryland in the 1790s, the state militia organization formed an interlocking directorate with the Republican party.[39] And in South Carolina a grand jury complained in 1800 that "There is nothing more common, than for a militia officer to have a place appointed for his men to meet him, or some other influential character that he may appoint, in order to prepare their votes for such person or persons as he may think proper; indeed, some of them have the assurance to march them in a body to the very election, and others to march at their head even into the house to give their votes."[40] In the early years of the republic the militia thus continued to function as a prop for deferential politics, and the politicians in Congress and the state governments thwarted every effort to turn it into an effective military organization.

To sum up, then, the fiction of popular sovereignty, conceived by gentlemen contending with an irresponsible king, had to be buttressed by other fictions that would leave the hegemony of gentlemen intact. The imaginary invincible yeoman served that purpose admirably. He was not really needed either for valor in battle or independence at the hustings, he was needed as an ideological shield against arbitrary monarchs and conniving courtiers on the one hand and against scheming demagogues and pliant paupers on the other. And his ingrained deference to his big neighbors was needed to reconcile popular sovereignty with a social hierarchy that was too deeply entrenched to be overthrown, even had there been a widespread desire to overthrow it. The fiction of the invincible yeoman thus embodied the same ambiguities as the larger fiction it supported: it sustained the government of the many by the few, even while it elevated and glorified the many.

Notes

1. Sir John Fortescue, *De Laudibus Legum Angliae,* ed. and trans. S. B. Chrimes (Cambridge, England, 1949), 80–91. Quotation at p. 87.
2. Niccolò Machiavelli, *The Prince and the Discourses* (New York, 1950), 175. (Discourse No. 21.)
3. Francis Bacon, *Works,* ed. James Spedding, R. L. Ellis, and D. D. Heath (London, 1857–74), VI:94–95, 405–06, 446–47. Quotation at p. 447.
4. *See,* for example, the eloquent speech by Thomas Hedley in the Parliament of 1610 (Elizabeth Foster, ed., *Proceedings in Parliament, 1610* [New Haven, Conn. 1966], II:194–95): "So if the liberty of the subject be in this point impeached, that their lands and goods be any way in the king's absolute power to be taken from them, then

they are (as hath been said) little better than the king's bondmen, which will so discourage them and so abase and deject their minds, that they will use little care or industry to get that which they cannot keep and so will grow both poor and base-minded like to the peasants in other countries, which be no soldiers nor will be ever made any, whereas every Englishman is as fit for a soldier as the gentleman elsewhere." Cf. Walter Raleigh, *Remains of Sir Walter Raleigh* (London, 1702), 226.

5. James Harrington, *The Political Works of James Harrington*, ed. J. G. A. Pocock (Cambridge, England, 1977), 198, 443, 688.

6. Cf. David Hume, *Essays Moral and Political*, 3rd ed. (London, 1748), 70–77.

7. The association of wooden shoes with the supposed degradation of the French peasantry began early. *See* Henry Parker, *Some Few Observations* (London, 1642), 15; *Vox Pacifica* (London, 1644), 11.

8. Edward and Annie G. Porritt, *The Unreformed House of Commons: Parliamentary Representation before 1832* (Cambridge, England, 1903), I:151–203.

9. But it is possible to make a powerful argument that the Tories were the political radicals of the eighteenth century before Wilkes. *See* Linda Colley, "Eighteenth-Century English Radicalism before Wilkes," Royal Historical Society, *Transactions* 31 (1981): 1–19. *See also* Colley, *In Defiance of Oligarchy: The Tory Party 1714–60* (Cambridge, England, 1982).

10. C. H. Kirby, "The English Game Law System," *American Historical Review* 38 (1932–1933): 240–62.

11. Alexander Spotswood, *The Official Letters of Alexander Spotswood*, ed. R. A. Brock (Richmond, 1882–1885, Virginia Historical Society, *Collections*, n.s. I–II), I:140, II:1–2; H. R. McIlwaine, ed., *Journals of the House of Burgesses of Virginia 1752–1755, 1756–1758* (Richmond, 1909), 360–61.

12. *See* Morgan, *Inventing the People*, 184–189.

13. For a differing view of the English military, *see* Stephen Saunders Webb, *The Governors-General: The English Army and the Definition of the Empire, 1569–1681* (Chapel Hill, N.C., 1969); and *1676: The End of American Independence* (New York, 1984). Cf. Richard R. Johnson, "The Imperial Webb: The Thesis of Garrison Government in Early America Considered," *William and Mary Quarterly*, 3rd ser., 43 (1986): 408–30; and Webb, "The Data and Theory of Restoration Empire," ibid., 431–59.

14. Douglas E. Leach, *Roots of Conflict: British Armed Forces and Colonial Americans 1677–1763* (Chapel Hill, N.C., 1986), 176–233; Fred Anderson, *A People's Army: Massachusetts Soldiers and Society in the Seven Years' War* (Chapel Hill, N.C., 1984).

15. Charles Royster, *A Revolutionary People at War: The Continental Army and American Character 1775–1783* (Chapel Hill, N.C., 1979); E. Wayne Carp, *To Starve the Army at Pleasure: Continental Army Administration and American Political Culture* (Chapel Hill, N.C., 1984).

16. *The Debates and Proceedings of the Congress of the United States*. Third Congress, first session (Washington, D.C., 1855) (*Annals of Congress*, III), 162, Jan. 6, 1794. Cf. ibid., II, 796.

17. Alexander Smyth, *The Third and Last Letter from Alexander Smyth to Francis Preston* (n.p., 1796), 15. Herbert J. Storing, ed., *The Complete Anti-Federalist* (Chicago, 1981), III:202; V:181. John Steele, representative from North Carolina in congressional debate in January 1793, giving yeoman militia credit for winning the revolutionary war, argued that "Such men will not enlist in regular armies, nor will any one who has the disposition or the constitution of a freeman." (*Annals of Congress*, II, 796.)

18. The question of motivation is discussed in Robert Middlekauff, "Why Men Fought in the American Revolution," in *Saints and Revolutionaries,* ed. D. D. Hall, J. M. Murrin, and T. W. Tate (New York, 1984), 318–31, and in Royster, *A Revolutionary People at War,* 373–78, where the relevant statistical studies are cited.

19. Sir George Savile, *An Argument Concerning the Militia* (London, 1762), 15–16.

20. George Washington, *Writings,* ed. John C. Fitzpatrick (Washington, D.C., 1931–1944), VI:110–11. Cf. ibid., IV:124; VI:5.

21. John Trenchard and Walter Moyle, *An Argument Showing, That a Standing Army Is Inconsistent with a Free Government* (London, 1697), 20; E. S. and H. M. Morgan, *The Stamp Act Crisis* (Chapel Hill, N.C., 1953), 124, 131, 197–98.

22. J. R. Western, *The English Militia in the Eighteenth Century: The Story of a Political Issue 1660–1802* (London, 1965), Chapters 1 and 2, *passim;* John Miller, "The Militia and the Army in the Reign of James II," *The Historical Journal* 16 (1973): 659–79.

23. *Common Sense,* July 19, 1740; *Gentleman's Magazine* 10 (1740): 346.

24. *A Serious Exhortation to the Electors of Great Britain* (London, 1741), 51–53. Cf. the statement by Thomas Carew, *Parliamentary History* 13:1061, that "If elections were allowed to go in their natural course [i.e., without court influence] such men only [i.e., gentlemen of substance] would be chosen." This was a point regularly made in debate on place-bills and on bills to repeal the Septennial Act. *See,* for example, ibid., 9:430–31, 448.

25. J. G. A. Pocock, "Machiavelli, Harrington and English Political Ideologies in the Eighteenth Century," *William and Mary Quarterly,* 3rd ser., 22 (1965): 549–83.

26. John Trenchard and Thomas Gordon, *Cato's Letters; or Essays on Liberty, Civil and Religious, and Other Important Subjects* (London, 1723). Isaac Kramnick, *Bolingbroke and his Circle: The Politics of Nostalgia in the Age of Walpole* (Cambridge, Mass., 1968).

27. I have discussed the association of these ideas in *American Slavery American Freedom: the Ordeal of Colonial Virginia* (New York, 1975), 316–87.

28. *See* Morgan, *Inventing the People,* pp. 197–200.

29. Lindsay Boynton, *The Elizabethan Militia 1558–1638* (London, 1967), 101–09; *Archives of Maryland,* XI:350–51.

30. Timothy H. Breen, *Puritans and Adventurers: Change and Persistence in Early America* (New York, 1980), 25–45; Robert Gross, *The Minutemen and Their World* (New York, 1976), 70–74, 156–59; Ronald L. Boucher, "The Colonial Militia as a Social Institution: Salem, Massachusetts 1764–1775," *Military Affairs* 37 (1973): 125–28; John K. Rowland, "Origins of the Second Amendment: The Creation of the Constitutional Rights of Militia and of Keeping and Bearing Arms," (Ph.D. diss., The Ohio State University, 1978), 335.

31. *See,* for example, the account of the riots in Mifflin County, Pa., in 1791, raised by disgruntled candidates for commissions. *The Universal Asylum and Columbian Magazine for September, 1791* (Philadelphia, 1791), 214–15.

32. Norman Dawes, "Titles as Symbols of Prestige in Seventeenth-Century New England," *William and Mary Quarterly,* 3rd ser., 6 (1949): 69–83, at p. 79.

33. *Essex Gazette,* Jan. 29–31, 1769.

34. Ibid., Feb. 14–21, 1769.

35. Jonathan Jackson, *Thoughts Upon the Political Situation* (Worcester, Mass., 1788).

36. *Essex Gazette,* Jan. 29–31, 1769; *Connecticut Gazette,* May 8, 1762; John Sullivan, *General Sullivan's Address to the Freemen of New Hampshire* (Portsmouth, N.H., 1785), 7.

37. Harrison M. Ethridge, "Governor Patrick Henry and the Reorganization of the Virginia Militia 1784–1786," *Virginia Magazine of History and Biography* 85 (1977): 427–39.

38. *A People Numerous and Armed* (New York, 1976), 195–224.

39. Frank A. Cassell, *Merchant Congressman in the Young Republic: Samuel Smith of Maryland* (Madison, Wis., 1971), 71, 87–89, 92.

40. *City Gazette and Daily Advertiser* (Charleston, S.C.), Dec. 23, 1800. I owe this reference to Professor Rachel Klein.

Michael A. Bellesîles

The Origins of Gun Culture in the United States, 1760–1865

Michael A. Bellesîles is associate professor of history at
Emory University. He has written about the early American frontier, the history of American violence, and gun regulation. In this provocative article, which won the Binkley-
Stephenson Award in 1997 for the best essay published in
the *Journal of American History* in 1996, Bellesîles takes on
the myth of America's gun culture. Many commentators
on the problem of gun violence in modern America have
traced its origins to the role that the frontier played in shaping American values. They contend that America was always
a gun culture because the frontier forced Americans to depend on guns for survival. Surveying a wide range of sources
from probate records to militia muster rolls, Bellesîles concludes that guns were far less pervasive in American culture
than the frontier myth would suggest. Although this essay
does not deal extensively with the meaning of the Second
Amendment, it does suggest another context for understanding the right to bear arms and the militia. In Bellesîles's view, the threat to the viability of the militia came not
from a powerful federal government, but ironically from the
states who refused to provide sufficient funds to adequately
arm their militias.

Questions for a Closer Reading

1. How does the frontier myth inform the way Americans interpret the meaning of the Second Amendment?

2. What sorts of evidence does Bellesîles use to prove that guns were not as common as the frontier myth would suggest? Does the evidence support his claims?

3. How are Bellesîles's sources different from those used by Shalhope and Cress?

4. Does Bellesîles's argument support or contradict Edmund Morgan's discussion of the role of the militia in early American culture?

5. What forces helped transform America into a gun culture?

6. If Bellesîles is correct, how should his argument alter the way we interpret the meaning of the phrase "the right to bear arms"?

The Origins of Gun Culture in the United States, 1760–1865

An astoundingly high level of personal violence separates the United States from every other industrial nation. In 1993, when the number of murders in Canada reached a high of 630, the United States (with nearly ten times the population) experienced 24,526 murders, out of a total of nearly two million violent crimes. The weapon of choice in 69.6 percent of those murders was a gun, and thousands more are killed by firearms every year in accidents and suicides.[1] More people are killed with guns in the United States in a typical week than in all of western Europe in a year. It is now thought normal and appropriate for American urban elementary schools to use metal detectors to check students for firearms.

Michael A. Bellesîles, "The Origins of Gun Culture in the United States, 1760–1865," *Journal of American History*, Vol. 83, no. 2 (1996): 425–55.

We are familiar with the manifestations of American gun culture; the sincere love and affection with which our society views its weapons pours forth daily from the television and movie screens. Every form of the media reinforces the notion that the solution to your problems can be held in your hand and provide immediate gratification. Since the United States does not register guns, we have no idea how many there are or who actually buys them. The FBI (Federal Bureau of Investigation) estimates that there are 250 million firearms in private hands; an additional 5 million are purchased every year. The National Sporting Goods Association estimates that 92 percent of all rifles are bought by men (94 percent of the shotguns). Most of those men fall into the 25- to 34-year-old age group, make between $35,000 and $50,000 annually, and do not need to kill animals for their survival.[2]

The consequence of this culture is also very familiar. To select just a few more statistics as indicators: The chief of police and mayor of New York City were nearly euphoric that the number of murders in the city dropped below two thousand (to 1,995) in 1993; it reached a contemporary low of 1,581 in 1994. Yet the total number of murders in New York City in those two years exceeds by over 500 the 3,000 killed in Northern Ireland since the beginning of the "Troubles" in 1969.[3]

It is assumed that the nation's love affair with the gun is impervious to change, since its roots are so deep in our national history and psyche. The origin of this culture of violence is routinely understood to lie in our frontier heritage. With guns in their hands and bullets on their belts, the American frontiersmen conquered the wilderness and created modern America. In the imagined past, "the requirements for self-defense and food-gathering," as Daniel Boorstin has said, "had put firearms in the hands of nearly everyone."[4] The almost universal ownership of guns in the eighteenth century was enshrined in the Second Amendment to the Constitution, and its continuation is defended with ferocity by the National Rifle Association today. That frontiers elsewhere did not replicate our violent culture is thought irrelevant. The frontier experience simply required that every westward migrant carry a gun. The result was a deep inward faith that, as Richard Slotkin so eloquently put it, regeneration came through violence. In short, we have always been killers.[5]

Such statements are often presented as logically obvious. An examination of the social practices and cultural customs prevalent in the United States in the late eighteenth and early nineteenth centuries, however, will show that we have it all backwards. Before we accept an individual right to gun ownership in the Second Amendment, we must establish who were "the people" who were allowed to "keep and bear arms." Did they in fact own guns? What was the popular attitude toward firearms? Did such perceptions change over time? We will find that gun ownership was exceptional in the eighteenth and early nineteenth centuries, even on the frontier, and that guns became a common commodity only with industrialization, with ownership concentrated in urban areas. The gun culture grew with the gun industry. The firearms industry, like so many others, relied on the government not just for capital development but for the support and enhancement of its markets. From its inception, the United States government worked to arm its citizens; it scrambled to find sources of weapons to fulfill the mandate of the Second Amendment. From 1775 until the 1840s the government largely failed in this task, but the industrialization of the arms industry from 1820 to 1850 allowed the government to move toward its goal with ever-increasing speed, though against residual public indifference and resistance.

Probate Records

The evidence for this contrary thesis began with the dog that did not bark. In Sir Arthur Conan Doyle's "Silver Blaze," the Scotland Yard inspector asked Sherlock Holmes, was there "any other point to which you would wish to draw my attention?" Holmes responded, "To the curious incident of the dog in the night-time." "The dog did nothing in the night-time." "That was the curious incident."[6]

While studying county probate records (inventories of property after a death) for a project on the legal and economic evolution of the early American frontier, I was puzzled by the absence of what I assumed would be found in every record: guns. An examination of more than a thousand probate records, which listed everything from acreage to broken cups, from the frontiers of northern New England and western Pennsylvania for the years 1765–1790 revealed that only 14 percent of the inventories included firearms; over half of those guns (53 percent) were listed as broken or otherwise dysfunctional. A musket or rifle in good condition often drew special notice in the probate inventories and earned a very high valuation. Obviously guns could have been passed on to heirs before the death of the original owner. Yet wills generally mention previous bequests, even of minor items, and they list only a handful of firearms.

Integrating Alice Hanson Jones's valuable probate compilation into this general study and examining counties in sample periods during the eighty-five years from 1765 to 1850 reveals a startling distribution of guns in early America. Probate records are not a perfect source for information, and there has been a long, instructive debate on their reliability as historical sources.[7] Nonetheless, they do provide much information on common household objects and can be used as a starting point for determining the level of gun ownership. Stated briefly, the probate inventories reveal that gun ownership was more common in the South and in urban centers than in the countryside or on the frontier, and that it rose slowly up to the 1830s;

Table 1. Percentage of Probate Inventories Listing Firearms

	1765–1790	1808–1811	1819–1821	1830–1832	1849–1850
Frontier[a]	14.2	15.8	16.9	20.4	32.9
Northern coast, urban	16.1	16.6	17.3	20.8	27.3
Northern coast, rural	14.9	13.1	13.8	14.3	18.7
Southern	18.3	17.6	20.2	21.6	39.3
National average	14.7	16.1	17.0	20.7	30.8

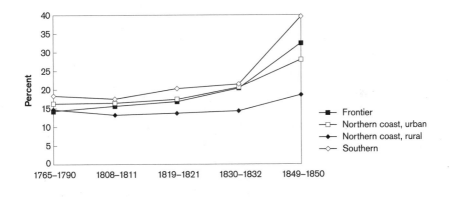

[a]Frontier counties moved into other categories with each new time period.
Source: Probate records for the following 38 counties (modern names): Bennington, Rutland, Windham, and Windsor, Vermont; Luzerne, Northampton, Philadelphia, Washington, and West-moreland, Pennsylvania; Litchfield and New Haven, Connecticut; Essex, Hampshire, Plymouth, Suffolk, and Worcester, Massachusetts; Burlington, New Jersey; Kent, Delaware; Anne Arundel and Queen Anne, Maryland; Fairfax, Spotsylvania, Chesterfield, Charlotte, Halifax, Mecklenburg, Brunswick, and Southampton, Virginia; Orange and Halifax, North Carolina; Charleston, South Carolina; Baldwin, Chatham, and Glynn, Georgia; Jefferson and Knox, Indiana; Adams and Washington, Ohio.

it increased to half again as much over the next twenty years. By 1849–1850, guns appeared in nearly one-third of all probate inventories.[8]

Almost all of the probate inventories studied are for white males. Most states had laws forbidding blacks to own guns, and no woman's inventory lists a gun. The inventories, therefore, are from the people most likely to own guns. The figures indicate that few people actually had guns in their possession, at least at the time of death. White males older than fifteen made up just under a quarter (23.8 percent) of the population in 1820; if we dare to include women and blacks in our definition of Americans, it would appear that at no time prior to 1850 did more than a tenth of the people own guns.

Militia Records

Looking at militia records can also provide some sense of gun ownership in early America. Militia units were based in their home communities or counties, but they existed under state authority. "All adults" (white, Protestant, non-immigrant, property-owning males) were expected to serve, with exceptions for those with specific jobs; in time, the list of those expected to serve expanded, as did the list of exceptions. Age and other requirements varied widely with time and place.

In the colonial period, the militias drew their authority from colonial legislatures operating in the name of the king. After the ratification of the Constitution, the authority was in the state governments as authorized and regulated by Congress (Article I, Section 8). On several occasions states and communities ordered censuses of the firearms in the possession of their citizens. Militia records also sometimes include accurate counts of total number of guns in the possession of those eligible for militia service. Such records are scattered, but they do provide a sampling of the number of firearms and a reflection of the public attitude toward them.

The old myth of the military effectiveness of the militia has taken a battering over the last twenty years as historians have studied its performance more carefully. Military historians have debated the utility and commitment of the militia, and they generally doubt both. Those scholars have noted the absence of a well-armed and efficient militia in the period from the French and Indian War through the War of 1812.[9] Those findings are strongly supported by extant military records, though the period of militia ineffectiveness should be extended into the 1850s. Right up to the beginning of the Civil War, nearly every militia officer's report, even from the frontier, complained of the shortage and poor quality of the weapons available and the routine failure of their rank and file to care for the weapons they did possess. Regular army officers noted this same paucity and inferiority of firearms and commented often on the recruits' unfamiliarity with guns. Such comments ran right up the chain of command. For instance, Capt. Charles Johnston reported to the New Hampshire Provincial Congress in June 1775 that his company was "in difficult circumstances; we are in want of both arms and ammunition. There is but very little, or none worth mentioning — perhaps one pound of powder to twenty men, and not one-half our men have arms." On the top of the military hierarchy, Gen. George Washington complained incessantly about his lack of arms. Every volume of *The Papers of George Washington: Revolutionary War Series* has dozens of letters with such complaints as "Being in the greatest distress here for Arms with-

Table 2. Census of American Militia Members and Firearms, 1803–1830

	1803[a]	1810[b]	1820[c]	1830
Militia members	524,086	677,681	837,498	1,128,594
Muskets	183,070	203,517	315,459	251,019
Rifles	39,648	55,632	84,816	108,036
Other[d]	13,113	49,105	0	0
Total arms	235,831	308,254	400,275	359,055

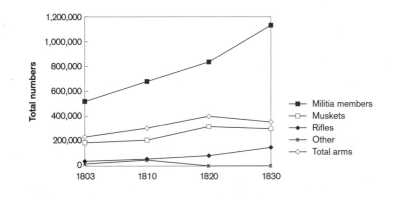

[a]In 1803 Tennessee, Delaware, and Maryland did not respond to Secretary of War Henry Dearborn's request for information. Population is based on the 1800 census, producing an overstatement in percentages since the population had grown in the intervening three years. On the other hand, Dearborn's study would not have indicated those instances in which an individual owned several firearms, nor the arms of those avoiding the militia officers who conducted this survey (though there is no evidence of anyone doing so).
[b]The 1810 returns from Michigan, Orleans, and Illinois territories were incomplete and are therefore not included.
[c]By 1820 statistics were becoming significantly less reliable. The adjutant general noted that Delaware last made a return in 1814, Maryland in 1811, South Carolina in 1815, Mississippi in 1812, Arkansas never, Alabama's return left out sixteen regiments, and the District of Columbia's returns vanished. Most surveys were actually conducted in 1821. The 1820 census was used for population figures, leading to a slight overstatement in percentages.
[d]*Other* includes pistols, fowling pieces, blunderbusses, and other curiosities. From 1820 on, such pieces are included with *muskets.*
Source: Frederick Bernays Wiener, "The Militia Clause of the Constitution," *Harvard Law Review,* 54 (Dec. 1960): 181–219.

out the most distant prospect of obtaining a Supply." The shortage of guns and ammunition even led Washington to dismiss troops he could not arm. He concluded that he and his officers were but "amusing ourselves with the appearance of strength, when at the same time we want the reality."[10]

A quarter century later, the situation remained unaltered. In 1801, Gov. William Claiborne of Mississippi Territory informed James Madison that

Total Firearms as a Percentage of Selected Populations, 1803–1830

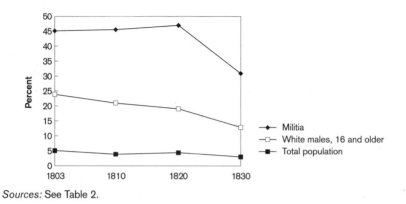

Sources: See Table 2.

the settlers did not have guns, nor could they acquire any. Six years later, as governor of Orleans Territory, Claiborne reported that he had 126 muskets for 4,971 members of the militia. That same year, three of Delaware's five regiments had no serviceable firearms at all; Gov. Nathaniel Mitchell told the legislature that the militia was effectively unarmed and that it was ridiculous to expect the people to arm themselves.[11] During the interminable Seminole wars of the 1830s, Gen. Winfield Scott discovered that the Florida militia was essentially unarmed, and he frantically sought firearms from Washington for those frontier militia companies.[12]

Quantitative evidence supports the views of those officials. In the first official inventory of American arms in 1793, Secretary of War Henry Knox found that 37 percent of the 44,442 muskets owned by the government were unusable, and an additional 25 percent were either archaic or in serious need of repair and cleaning. The following year Knox estimated that there were 450,000 militia members in the United States, of whom no more than 100,000 either owned or had been supplied with guns.[13] A decade later Secretary of War Henry Dearborn conducted a more precise census of the militia and its arms. Counting weapons both privately and publicly owned, Dearborn discovered that 45 percent of the militia bore arms. His census of weapons, which was certainly incomplete, indicated that just 4.9 percent of the nation's population was armed, or 23.7 percent of its white adult males. In 1810 Secretary of War William Eustis, in what was probably the most thorough and exact of all the studies, found that almost nothing had changed: 45.4 percent of the militia bore arms; the total number of guns recorded was sufficient for 4.3 percent of the American population, or 20.9 percent of the white adult males. Ten years later, John C. Calhoun found some slight improvement, with 47.8 percent of the militia bearing arms, and enough guns for 4.7 percent of the American population, or 19.9 percent of the white adult males (down a point). But Calhoun found it rather disturbing that several states had simply ceased bothering to issue militia returns; their governments just no longer cared if their militia carried guns or not. In 1830, Secretary of War J. H. Eaton found that just 31 percent of America's militia bore arms. With only enough arms for 3 percent of the population (12.5 percent of the adult white males), the militia was obviously no longer able to defend the United States — if it ever was.

By comparison, the current figures, based on FBI estimates, indicate enough firearms for 102.5 percent of the total population, 334.9 percent of the adult white male population, and 49,765.8 percent of the militia (the current National Guard, which has 512,400 members, or 0.2 percent of the population). Under Article 1, Section 8 of the Constitution, only congressionally regulated militia can be the legal militia of the United States. Since the Dick Act of 1903, the National Guard, and only the National Guard, has held that status.[14]

The early national audits depended on the willingness and ability of the states to count accurately the number of firearms within their borders. With several states ignoring the whole procedure, the results cannot be considered entirely reliable. The complete absence of any debate within the state legislatures over the right of the national government to conduct these censuses is surprising; nor were there external protests. Apparently the public did not question government action on this issue.

Massachusetts made concerted efforts to determine the level of its gun ownership. On several occasions the state government counted all privately owned guns. As their findings indicate, at no point prior to 1840 did more than 11 percent of that state's citizens own firearms (30 percent of the adult white males); and Massachusetts, together with Connecticut, was the center of arms production in the United States.[15]

In 1812, a similar census in Pennsylvania found that there were 30,366 guns, both publicly and privately owned, for the 99,414 men in the militia (30.5 percent, or 3.7 percent of the population). An 1837 census in New York revealed that of 84,122 state troops, 30,388 (36.1 percent) had neither private nor public arms in their possession, and 15,500 (18.4 percent) of those who had guns had no flints. Even in the heavily armed and deeply paranoid state of South Carolina, militia officers continually expressed shock over the shortage of firearms. In 1825 Gen. Robert Y. Hayne reviewed Charleston's 2,060 troops, finding that 509 had no arms at all. Of those who had guns of some kind, the majority bore muskets "in bad order." The following year, one militia company rejected a shipment of arms from the government as inadequate; its commander wrote to the governor, "I have taken the sense of my company and they refuse to make use of such arms."[16]

Improperly armed, the militia could not do its duty. During Nat Turner's rebellion in Southampton County, Virginia, in 1831, newspapers reported

Table 3. Private Gun Ownership in Massachusetts

	Number of Privately Owned Muskets or Rifles	Population	% of Population with Guns	
			Total Population	White Males 16 or Older
1789	27,619	475,327	5.81%	23.00%
1795	34,000	524,946	6.48%	25.60%
1808	50,000	675,509	7.40%	28.70%
1812	49,000	482,289	10.16%	27.80%
1815	50,000	497,664	10.05%	29.80%
1824	32,128	557,978	5.76%	19.40%
1839	21,760	724,931	3.00%	9.50%

Note: Population estimates are based on per year increase during the decade. The adjutant general tended to round up the number of muskets in the state.
Sources: Adjutant General, annual Return of the Militia for Massachusetts, Commonwealth of Massachusetts Military Division, Military Records (National Guard Armory, Natick, Mass.); Quartermaster General's Letter Book 6, p. 9, ibid.

that the local militia were "very deficient in proper arms, accoutrements and ammunition." Gov. John Floyd spent weeks trying to acquire arms and ammunition to supply these units, and he continued to do so even after the rebellion had been repressed. Similarly, militia units on both sides of the Dorr Rebellion in Rhode Island in 1842 lacked sufficient arms to exercise effectively their political will.[17] Given that the supposed purpose of the militia was to protect American liberty and order, it is ironic that neither the state nor the rebels were well armed. As New York's General J. Watts de-Peyster said of his own troops in 1855, "We always associate the term militia with the rag-tag and bob-tail assemblages armed with broomsticks, cornstalks, and umbrellas."[18]

Statistics alone give no indication of the condition of these firearms nor of the ability of the citizenry to employ them. Practically every adjutant general and militia commander in the United States in the antebellum period complained of the indifference with which Americans treated their weapons, and many state governments discovered that their armories were full of useless firearms.[19] Unlike today's glistening beauties, firearms in the eighteenth and nineteenth centuries were made mostly of iron and, as a consequence, required constant attention to keep them from rusting. Most people who owned guns brought them forth but once a year, on muster day; it is little wonder that those who did not have servants tended to let their weapons rot. In 1817 Virginia's adjutant general, G. W. Gooch, warned that the state's militia companies did not keep their arms "in good order —

indeed, I might say, [not even] to preserve them from ruin." Gooch tried issuing orders demanding greater attention to the care and maintenance of the militia's weapons, but he found such efforts worthless; he finally ordered that all public arms be collected and stored in a single location. An awareness of this lack of enthusiasm for firearms by the public led a House special committee on the militia, chaired by William Henry Harrison, to propose in 1818 that the government keep its arms in armories under federal control and maintenance rather than giving them directly to the people. The committee felt that the nation's guns, so grossly abused by the public, should be left in the care of experts who could keep them operational. Their recommendation was ignored, only to be repeated time and again over the next twenty years. In 1838, Secretary of War Joel R. Poinsett complained to Congress that military expenses were nearly four times what they should be, largely because the militia did not seem capable of caring for their arms. The following year he reported that "when mustered, a majority of [the militia] are armed with walking canes, fowling pieces, or unserviceable muskets."[20] Nothing had changed.

Even those with arms lacked experience in their use. Musters were, after all, usually held but once a year; parading, drinking, and partying clearly took priority over target practice; and uniforms evoked far more passion and interest than musket fire.[21] For example, the militia records of Oxford, Massachusetts, which begin in 1755, devote more space to uniforms than to any other subject. The company argued over the color of their pantaloons (white or blue) from just after the Revolution until 1823, and of their plumes (white or black) until 1824. They spent a year debating whether to require each member to powder his beard when appearing at muster, voting in May 1821 to so require, repealing that act in October. There were instances of companies disbanding because of a change in uniform. In 1819 Charles K. Gardner wrote an instruction manual for use by militia companies after discovering during the War of 1812 that "so many militiamen . . . are not skilled in the use of the Rifle or Musket." Drills in muster books involved marching, not shooting. The Oxford, Massachusetts, militia voted for the first time in May 1819 to meet once a year "for the purpose of firing at a mark." In 1823 they voted 35–5 to stop this annual target practice in order to avoid public humiliation.[22]

Target-shooting contests, which began in the 1820s, were often major embarrassments. When the Second Company of New York's Seventh Regiment held their first target-shooting contest in 1825, it was a miserable show. As the company's official historian admitted, it was "not a very brilliant exhibition of sharp shooting"; but then very few members had ever fired a musket before. When the prestigious New Haven Grays held its first target-shooting contest in 1822, forty-three men fired 172 shots at a target six feet high by twenty inches wide at one hundred yards. Only twenty shots (11 percent) hit any part of the target. The winner, Frederick T. Stanley, admitted that he had "but little experience in the use of firearms, and have neither before or since owned a pistol, rifle, musket, or fowling piece." His gun was on loan from the state arsenal. In 1826 the Grays shortened the distance to one hundred feet, which improved their ratio to 65 hits out of 198 shots fired (33 percent). Shortening the distance again over the next several years raised their percentage of successful shots as high as 48 percent in 1827. As a Pennsylvania newspaper unkindly said of one company's effort at target shooting: "The size of the target is known accurately having been carefully measured. It was precisely the size and shape of a barn door." The prize went to the man "who came nearest to hitting the target."[23]

Several historians have suggested that proficiency with a gun carried a necessary definitive power for manliness.[24] If so, we must wonder what it means that American men were generally such terrible shots. There are instances of militia units shooting their officers, bystanders, and one another during target practice. Even that man's man, Robert E. Lee, could bag but four birds in a pigeon shoot (a captured pigeon is placed in a black box, shaken, and released, whereupon the shooter raises his gun and hopes to blow the bird away) that lasted all afternoon and was outshot by his British opponent.[25]

It is not surprising that the militia entered a period of rapid decline after the War of 1812. Many people opposed the very institution of the militia, some because they were idealistic pacifists, others because they found no utility in the institution now that the United States was not threatened by an external foe. To the contrary, many Americans feared that the presence of the militia could encourage a democratic government to declare an unnecessary war — a fear seemingly confirmed by the Mexican War in 1846.[26] *Brother Jonathan,* a popular magazine, described a militia muster as "useless and unseemly," its members "obstructions of humanity" and "extraordinary looking individuals, with . . . rusty muskets dangling at the end of their arms . . . waiting with an indifference certainly highly praiseworthy in professional soldiers." This journal, at least, felt that "this shamefully ridiculous practice has continued too long already, and should be abolished forthwith. What is the object — what the utility of it?" T. L. Hagood, a company commander, described the militia to New York Governor William Bouck as "mere *mobs* of half-drunken men." Even children's books derided the militia. In one from the mid-1820s, a boy described seeing a militia muster: "I saw many drunken men. One was crawling on his hands and feet like a dog, being too much intoxicated to walk upright. Two of them were fighting; the blood ran down their faces, and they looked like furies." Not much of a role model for young men and patriots.[27]

Militia companies reflected this public sentiment; many made a deliberate mockery of the whole enterprise. Officers were often elected specifically on their promise that they would not call musters. Jean Baptiste Beaubien was elected colonel of Chicago's militia every year from 1834 to 1847, calling only one muster during that entire period. The ever-pained William H. Sumner, adjutant general of Massachusetts, complained in 1834 that "The records of my office are disgraced with returns of persons of infamous character to honorable places,—of town paupers, idlers, vagrants, foreigners, itinerants, drunkards and the outcasts of society" elected militia officers. Most militia companies died from inattention or hostility by the early 1830s.[28]

When the members of a militia did not mock themselves, the crowds would. Locals, including many who should have been taking part in the exercises, often gathered to make fun of the militia. The crowd's favorite target was the poor marksmanship of the militia. Some state legislatures attempted to outlaw heckling the militia; for instance, in 1835 South Carolina passed a law fining any person who heckled or disrupted a militia muster $50. In 1841 the legislature added to the fine a five-day jail sentence. Both efforts apparently proved ineffective.[29]

In the years after the War of 1812, avoidance of militia duty reached crisis levels. Much of it was perfectly legal, as state laws exempted ever more citizens from the need to serve. The South Carolina act of 1833 excluded from militia duty most government officials, clergymen, teachers, students, doctors, pilots, ferrymen, sheriffs, and jailers; toll bridge, grist mill, and forge operators; canal, railroad, bank, and lunatic asylum employees; arsenal and lock keepers; toll collectors and all federal officials; and, most significant, all members of volunteer fire companies. In South Carolina, as in nearly every other state, fire departments proved the premier method of avoidance — indicating that antebellum American males would rather run around with hoses than guns.[30]

Generally individuals were saved the trouble of fabricating excuses to avoid militia duty as state governments themselves undermined the entire militia structure. Several states followed the lead of Delaware, which passed "An Act to Repeal Military fines for non-attendance on days of parades" in 1816. With the state then lacking any coercive power to enforce attendance, scores of militia companies vanished within a few years, leaving the militia effectively dormant in Delaware. In 1827, the legislature attempted to reverse direction by enacting a new militia law that carried heavy fines for nonattendance. The response of the public was immediate: they turned out most of the old legislature and voted in a new governor, Charles Polk, who led the drive to repeal the offending act. In 1829 the legislature repealed all fines and penalties, and the state issued no new commissions for the next seventeen years. Delaware's militia ceased to exist, leaving only a few scattered private volunteer companies. In 1846, Delaware was unable to respond to President James K. Polk's call for militia to fight Mexico. Fifteen years later Governor William Burton responded to yet another presidential call for a regiment of militia by stating that Delaware did not have one.[31]

Hunting

This widespread rejection of the militia was paralleled in public attitudes toward hunting. From the time of the earliest colonial settlements, frontier families had relied on Indians or professional hunters for wild game, and the colonial assemblies regulated all forms of hunting, as did Britain's Parliament.[32] Also as in England, most hunters were actually trappers, finding the use of traps more efficient and less expensive than the time-consuming process of tracking animals with guns. Most Americans in the seventeenth and eighteenth centuries got nearly all their meat from domesticated animals, and it was rather unusual to use a musket to slaughter a cow or pig. From the start, hunting was an inessential luxury. In the first decades of the nineteenth century, hunting was held up to ever-increasing ridicule as a waste of time, money, and resources and mocked as the play of insufficiently grown-up boys. In the popular press, hunting had become both exotic and foolish. Hunters themselves were often portrayed as little more than tedious bores looking for any opportunity to tell the same tired story of the glorious hunt.[33] An 1825 article in the *Atheneum* described the incredible number of animals killed by various aristocratic hunters, the thousands of deer, ducks, and rabbits, and expressed amazement at the pride that those aristocrats took in totting up such statistics: "A magnificent list of animal slaughter carefully and systematically recorded as achievements." Another article warned that citizens of Philadelphia interested in a walk in the country should "go a considerable distance from the city, to avoid the showers of shot" sent skyward by a few overenthusiastic bird hunters.[34]

Judging from the popular literature of the day, the public seemed completely uninterested in firearms. In 1843, the first book to lavish attention on the details of gun production, part of the Marco Paul's Adventures series for children, closes with a long condemnation of the gun. Carrying weapons makes men "fierce in spirit, boastful, and revengeful." Men with guns are like little boys with sticks, bound to hit each other with them.[35]

Even western magazines showed a decided coolness toward hunting and militarism, with occasional opposition to both. For instance, the *Western Monthly Magazine* of Cincinnati stated, "We aspire to be useful"; yet it found no need to publish anything on guns, hunting, or the military or militia, being much more concerned with education. In its first three years, 1833–

1835, it published thirty-six issues and 356 articles; there was one article on hunting, one on a shooting match, and four on Indian wars — and not a single other article on any gun-related themes. Likewise, the *Western Miscellany* published 300 articles in its first year, 1849, but only two were hunting articles. An article "On Western Character" in *Western Miscellany* describes westerners as marked primarily by autodidacticism and ingenuity, insisting that respect for the law and the avoidance of violence were far more notable in the West than in the East. While these magazines were, in part, promoting the West, their observations that eastern and European cities were more violent are valid. In those few instances when guns appeared in articles, it is surprising how often firearms prove useless in combat. Again and again in these and other magazines, hunters and soldiers fire and miss. After the first errant shots, battle descends to tomahawks and knives, the real weapons of frontier combat. Sometimes the descriptions border on the comic, as in one historical account of the siege of Ft. McIntosh, Ohio, in 1782. Volley after volley is exchanged without anyone getting injured. Finally a relief column appears, the Indians run away, and the "battle" is over.[36]

The most famous frontier novel is James Fenimore Cooper's *The Pioneers*, first published in 1823. This book begins with an unusual meeting between Cooper's representative of frontier mores, Leather-Stocking, and that of the cultivated elite, Judge Temple. The judge, shooting his fowling piece from the seat of his carriage, believes he has hit a deer, which Natty Bumppo has claimed for himself and his protégé, Oliver Effingham. Bumppo contemptuously rejects the judge's "pop-gun" as a toy rather than a tool. The reader soon learns that Judge Temple actually shot Effingham, while it was the frontiersman, with his plain but utilitarian long rifle, who has hit the deer. Of the two archetypes of frontier gun owners, the gentleman and the hunter, only one knows what he is doing; only one really deserves to carry a gun.[37]

Murder Methods

As a final measurement of the marginal role of guns in American life prior to the Civil War, it should be noted that the gun was not then the preferred weapon for murder, as it is now. It is difficult to build up a compelling statistical base on this issue since murder was so rare in the antebellum period. For instance, during Vermont's frontier period, from 1760 to 1790, there were five reported murders (excluding those deaths in the American Revolution), and three of those were politically motivated.[38] A study of 685 nineteenth-century murders indicates that prior to 1846 the gun was the weapon of choice in just 17.2 percent of the murders committed; for the years from 1846 to 1860, that figure nearly doubled, to 32.6 percent; for the

Table 4. Nineteenth-Century Murder Methods

	1800–1845	*1846–1860*	*1861–1899*	*Total*
Beating, drowning, and strangling	92	36	59	187
Stabbing	53	31	48	132
Using an ax	33	11	21	65
Using a gun	41	46	145	232
Using poison	15	14	22	51
Other[a]	5	3	10	18
Total	239	141	305	685

Nineteenth-Century Murder Methods by Percent

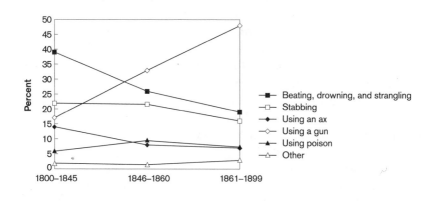

Notes: The execution of rebellious slaves has not been included in these statistics, though they certainly were unjustifiable homicide. The beating deaths of slaves have been included, though the law did not consider them murder. Also excluded from this data are all Civil War–related murders and deaths in the New York City draft riot of July 1863.

The year 1846 has been chosen as a demarcator because of Colt's introduction of the revolver into the mainstream of American life.

[a]*Other* includes abortion, cannon, bomb, and chloroform.

Sources: 501 cases are drawn from Thomas M. McDade, *The Annals of Murder: A Bibliography of Books and Pamphlets on American Murders from Colonial Times to 1900* (Norman, 1961); an additional 184 cases were drawn from the following newspapers and magazines: *Baltimore Weekly Magazine; Niles' Weekly Register,* Baltimore; *Boston Gazette; Southern Patriot,* Charleston, S.C.; *Western Monthly Magazine,* Cincinnati; *Western Miscellany,* Dayton; *Connecticut Courant,* Hartford; *Southern Recorder,* Milledgeville, Ga.; *New York World; New York Tribune; Graham's American Monthly Magazine,* Philadelphia; *Pennsylvania Packet,* Philadelphia; *Southern Literary Messenger,* Richmond; *Vermont Journal,* Windsor.

remaining forty years of the century, it climbed to 47.5 percent. Prior to the Mexican War, the knife was the weapon of choice. By the end of the century, guns were being used three times as often as knives. Samuel Colt's own brother, John C. Colt, preferred an ax to one of his brother's revolvers when he murdered a rival in 1841. Samuel Colt did take advantage of the publicity surrounding the trial to give a shooting display in the courtroom, convincingly demonstrating the superiority of his revolver to his brother's ax as a murder weapon.[39]

Gun Production

Until the 1830s, guns were tools, luxury items, or broken relics. Guns were either mass-produced for the military or handmade for specific customers rather than for general sale. A truism, repeated "by the best gunmakers," ran that no two guns were alike, not even the double barrels of a shotgun.[40] The few gunsmiths in colonial America seem to have enjoyed a brisk business, but their production remained minuscule. The first known gunsmith in colonial America, Eltweed Pomeroy of Windsor, Connecticut, established a family business in 1630 that lasted until 1849, yet this family enterprise rarely produced more than two dozen guns per year. There were a few successful efforts to found larger operations, most notably those of Hugh Orr in Bridgewater, Massachusetts, and William Henry in Lancaster, Pennsylvania, in the mid-eighteenth century. But even at these forges, each gun was an individual product, handmade by a highly skilled artisan. Hand cranks, foot treadles, treadmills, and water wheels supplied the power for such crude machinery as the pole lathe and rifling bench, and all metal parts had to be imported from Europe. At both those establishments, axes and scythes made up the greater part of their business, and the demand for guns dropped to almost nothing at the end of the Revolution.[41]

Most communities lacked gunsmiths and had to rely on blacksmiths to make the necessary repairs to guns — and they did not always know what they were doing. Even qualified gunsmiths often found far more work available in more general smithing. For instance, David Reese, the first gunsmith in Buffalo, had a sign in the shape of a large ax and took pride in his ax-making skills. Reese did repair several firearms, but he made no guns from 1800 to 1825. Oddly, there did not seem to be much of a market for guns in this frontier town. In 1817 M. D. Mann arrived in Buffalo, announcing that he would commence making and repairing guns. In 1819 he declared bankruptcy and closed his shop. The same fate awaited Peter Allison, who opened his gun shop in May 1825 and was gone by the end of the year.[42]

Guns of any quality tended to be either rugged and serviceable, made to order for those who made their living from hunting, or beautifully crafted, to grace the study and, on special occasions, the hands of a member of the elite. The overwhelming majority of guns in circulation were poorly cared for; they were passed on from generation to generation as family heirlooms and not kept in operational order. The consequence was that most states made frantic efforts at the beginning of military campaigns to get their militias' guns into working order.[43]

The federal government had been trying to overcome these resistances since 1775 in an effort to arm its citizens, but the nation just simply did not have the productive capacity. Throughout the colonial period, Americans had relied almost entirely on Great Britain for firearms, yet they never really had enough even for their most immediate defensive needs; even those who wanted them could not get them. Frontier settlers commonly petitioned their assembles for firearms during time of war, as they neither owned nor could they purchase guns, but they were not alone in having a shortage. Assemblies were hesitant to expend the necessary funds, but they often gave way to pressure and sent agents to England to try to purchase guns for private and public use.[44] Throughout the seventeenth and eighteenth centuries, Americans had been almost entirely dependent on Europe for arms and ammunition. Locks (firing mechanisms), the most important parts of firearms, were not made in America; gunpowder too was imported from Europe. During the American Revolution, the United States acquired 80 percent of its firearms and 90 percent of its gunpowder from France and the Netherlands. Most of the remaining 20 percent of the firearms had been supplied by Britain during the French and Indian War. Not surprisingly, the British Parliament imposed a complete embargo of firearms and gun parts on its rebellious colonies in October 1774.[45]

After the Revolution, Congress attempted to bolster the supply of American arms by outlawing the export of firearms and removing all import duties on foreign-made guns. In 1792, Congress, fearing war with France, ordered the purchase of 7,000 muskets. By 1793 the United States government, paying above market prices, had only been able to acquire 400 guns from American manufacturers. As a consequence, Congress voted to purchase arms from Europe. In 1800, 6,000 used muskets arrived, eight years late and still 500 muskets short. Every effort to promote domestic arms production seemed to end in failure. In 1819, G. Gregory's *A New and Complete Dictionary of Arts and Sciences* argued that the "manufacture of fire-arms is now carried to such a degree of perfection by different European nations, that it may perhaps be justly doubted whether any farther improvement . . . can be made." There was therefore almost no reason to try to make firearms in the United States.[46]

Congress's most notable effort came in 1808, when it voted to devote a large proportion of the federal budget every year "for Arming and Equiping the whole body of the Militia of the United States." Like the colonial and

Table 5. Average Yearly Arms Production at the Harpers Ferry and Springfield Armories, 1795–1870

	Harpers Ferry	Springfield
1795–1800		2,102
1801–1810	3,107	5,099
1811–1820	7,318	10,473
1821–1830	11,855	14,770
1831–1840	10,264	13,047
1841–1850	8,551	12,603
1851–1860	8,081	12,586
1861–1870[a]		90,992

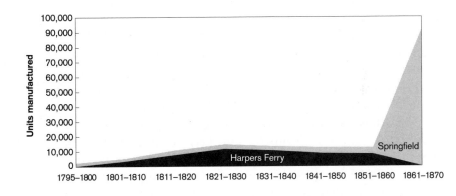

Note: The statistics include all firearms made at these armories (muskets, rifles, pistols, carbines, and pattern arms).
[a]Confederate troops destroyed most of the armory at Harpers Ferry in June 1861.
Sources: Merritt Roe Smith, *Harpers Ferry Armory and the New Technology: The Challenge of Change* (Ithaca, 1977), 342–47; Felicia J. Deyrup, *Arms Makers of the Connecticut Valley* (Northampton, 1948), 233.

revolutionary legislatures, Congress understood that most militia members could not afford to provide for themselves what they saw as an expensive luxury. The members of Congress intended to accomplish what colonial and state legislatures could not: arm their constituents. With an initial appropriation of $200,000 per year, Congress hoped to see every adult white male in the nation in possession of a firearm; arms were allotted to each state based on population, with the firearms remaining the property of the state. Drawing upon the two major arsenals in Springfield, Massachusetts, and Harpers Ferry, Virginia, as well as private companies throughout the United States, the government absorbed the vast majority of guns produced prior to 1840, and still it was not enough. The government made every conceivable effort to promote production, not just at its own arsenals but in privately owned gun shops as well. No shop was too small to escape the government's efforts at financial encouragement. Yet even with these efforts, Congress failed to fulfill its constitutional mandate of arming the militia in any year prior to the Civil War.[47]

Production levels in the United States just could not keep up with congressional demands. The 1808 congressional call for 170,000 firearms was only half fulfilled by the beginning of the War of 1812, and most of them were channeled to the federal army instead of to the states. By 1813 Massachusetts had received none of the promised 5,688 muskets. The state government responded by withholding taxes from the federal government in order to try and purchase arms elsewhere. This extortion actually worked; Massachusetts received 2,300 muskets in five shipments, but it did not receive its full 1808 allotment until 1817. Allotments were never large enough to meet state needs. For instance, in 1818, New Hampshire reported 23,399 men in the state militia, a quarter of whom needed guns; the federal government supplied 750 stands of muskets. New York reported 40 percent of its adult white males, or 109,990 men, in need of arms and received 3,522 stands.[48]

The individual states also attempted to fill their armaments needs by entering into contracts large and small. At the beginning of the War of 1812, the Massachusetts quartermaster general reported the state's total ordnance as "177 spears . . . 35 muskets 'out of repair', and 124 firearms, good." During the crisis of the War of 1812, Massachusetts gun makers (excepting the Springfield Armory) could produce just over a thousand muskets a year. With state and federal governments competing for guns, few American-made arms were left for the public market.[49]

The first hindrance to arming the nation was swept away in the 1840s as American arms manufacturers reached new heights of productivity. Industry created the supply and encouraged the demand for firearms. Production took off in the late 1840s and 1850s with the organization of a series of large gun manufacturers: Colt, Sharps, Remington, Robbins and Lawrence, Smith and Wesson, and Winchester. But the government's participation was vital in this as in many other early industries; the federal government provided capital, patent protection, technological expertise, and the largest market for guns.[50]

Gun Promotion

The increased production fed a gradual expansion of interest in and appreciation for guns. Hunting became increasingly popular with an urban middle class seemingly desperate for the instant status granted by possession of a gun. Largely through the efforts of John Stuart Skinner's *American Turf Register and Sporting Magazine,* which began publication in 1829, and William T. Porter's *Spirit of the Times,* first published in 1831, hunting became an appropriate enterprise for would-be gentlemen.[51] It is extremely difficult to find an article published in either of those journals or a gun advertisement in any newspaper that did not use the word "gentleman" in describing a hunter. Amateur hunters looked for legitimacy to the British aristocracy, modeling their notions of sportsmanship, hunting styles, clothing, appropriate game, and even patterns of speech after the British elite. The very portraits of hunters the magazines published mimic the style of those available in British sporting journals. Porter and his colleagues sought to rescue hunting from public disdain and to translate it into "the very corinthian columns of the community," the mark of the true gentleman and of a real man. The magazines pushed for the acceptance of the idea that "our rifles and our liberties are synonymous." Owning and using a firearm is therefore "a moral decision."[52]

There is much in mid-nineteenth-century hunting literature that we would recognize. The male bonding and the deep romantic affection for a favorite gun stand out. In the 1830s the first loving descriptions of every detail of firearms appear in print. No longer is it sufficient simply to say "He held a musket in his arms." From this date the dedicated author of hunting articles must have the precise name and maker of the piece noted, with sensual descriptions of the well-oiled stock and the long, gleaming barrel, as well as the delicate intricacies of the lock. The gun is no longer held; it is now "cradled," "caressed," "hugged," and ultimately "grasped with firmness" in order to fulfill its "deadly purpose." Real men hunt, while "the effeminate young man may die at home, or languish in a dead calm for the want of some external impulse to give circulation to the blood."[53]

On the other hand, the magazines sought to separate the participants in their luxurious sport from hoi polloi. Thus there are constant references to servants almost as necessities for the hunt. Close attention is paid to the quality of the dogs, horses, food, and spirits appropriate for a fruitful hunt. The decadence of this elite romanticism is savored by connoisseurs, those with the education and intelligence to appreciate the deeper meanings of this close contact with nature.[54] The mixture of nature, sociability, and killing comes together perfectly in one of the many hunting songs popular at the time:

> The cordial takes its merry round,
> The laugh and joke prevail,
> The huntsman blows a jovial sound,
> The dogs snuff up the gale;

> The upland hills they sweep along,
>   O'er fields, through breaks they fly,
> The game is roused; too true the song,
>   This day a stag must die.[55]

Samuel Colt initially appealed to these gentleman hunters with his elegant revolvers; but his ambitions demanded a broader market. Colt had hit on the perfect weapon for a gun culture: his revolvers were relatively inexpensive; fired several rounds quickly, negating the need for skill; were perfect for urban life, being easy to conceal; had no function other than "self-defense," being useful in neither hunting nor militia service; and, in short, were clearly intended for personal use in violent situations. Unable to discover a large demand for such weaponry, Colt tried to create one through the cleverest advertising yet seen in America. He engraved his guns with heroic scenes, such as a man protecting his wife and child against a pack of savage Indians, armed only with a Colt revolver. He filled eastern newspapers with advertisements identifying his revolver with the romance of the West, commissioning Currier & Ives to craft beautiful portraits of Colt hunting buffalo with a revolver. His most ingenious move was to include instructions, carefully printed on the cleaning rag that came with every Colt firearm; he realized that most Americans did not actually know how to use a gun.[56]

Despite the subtle cultural shifts exemplified by Skinner and Porter, and despite the efforts of Colt and his fellow gun makers, the vast majority of Americans remained apathetic toward guns and what they represented. The complete lack of interest on the part of most states in taking advantage of the federal government's arms giveaway program is stunning. In order to receive firearms from the federal government, a militia company simply needed to file a return listing its current membership. Yet in 1839, 230 of the 490 militia companies in Massachusetts did not bother to make returns. In 1851 the United States Army Ordnance Office informed Congress that only *seven* states had made militia returns in 1850. In fact, seven states and the District of Columbia itself had made no returns for the previous decade. Ironically, the one state that took advantage of the disinterest of the others to maximize its armaments was the Quaker State. Pennsylvania paid a penny for each name enrolled on the militia lists and was thus able to return the largest number of militia. As the New York Senate complained, even though Pennsylvania's "population is less by at least one million than our own," that state continually reported more militia to the federal government and received more arms.[57]

Incredibly, even when they took federal arms, states rarely expended any money for the maintenance of these weapons, and Congress made no provisions for the verification of numbers or for the storage of weapons. States were thus entirely free to do what they would with the weapons, perhaps most commonly just letting them rot in inadequate storage facilities. State militias almost never repaired broken weapons, rarely discarded obsolete ones, and simply stored the vast majority of weapons without regular servicing in the most inappropriate locations. Certainly this official lack of interest reflected the general population's inattention to military and firearms concerns.[58]

What the government needed was a constituency for its arms program. It found that support in middle-class militarists. The same people who revived hunting in the 1830s breathed new life into the militia in the 1840s. But just as they sought to separate hunting from its plebeian American roots, so urban militia companies rejected the traditional republican ideal of universal citizen service and embraced the notion of elite volunteer companies, creating for the first time a gun subculture.[59]

The volunteer movement got off the ground in Massachusetts. The state legislature finally got tired of trying to make its tradition-bound but nearly invisible militia system work, so in 1840 it created a volunteer militia. A new "active militia" of no more than ten thousand soldiers would form the core of this reorganized structure; all other adult males were theoretically in the inactive "enrolled militia."[60] The state also acknowledged its other key problem of arming its soldiers by no longer requiring each soldier to supply his own musket; the new volunteer militia companies were to apply to the Adjutant General's Office for arms, which they were required to maintain. The volunteers were thus not only better armed than the old militia but they kept their arms in good repair — a drastic innovation. Volunteer companies attracted those who valued guns and enjoyed the military style, and the state rewarded them with all the arms they needed. Within four years the state had issued more than 10,000 of its 17,000 muskets to the active militia.[61]

There were dangers in these better-armed volunteer militia units. The companies included a small minority of their communities, were usually organized along ethnic and class lines, and demonstrated a disturbing willingness to use their guns. The Philadelphia riots of 1844 devolved into a battle between nativist, Irish, and state militias that ended with twelve deaths. In 1849, the Astor Place riot in New York City culminated with the Seventh Regiment firing on a crowd and killing twenty people. For the first time, American militia opened fire on unarmed fellow citizens.[62]

And volunteer companies effectively began the greatest carnage in American history: the Civil War. As Southern states were seceding through the winter of 1860–1861, volunteer militia companies around the South seized federal property; from Harpers Ferry in Virginia to Fort Moultrie in South Carolina to the United States Arsenal at Apalachicola in Florida, they grabbed all the federal armaments they could. It was a wise move; the South lacked a single gun manufacturer other than Harpers Ferry, which they destroyed. In Texas, volunteer companies forced the regular United States Army forces under Gen. D. E. Twiggs to abandon the state and all United States military property. When war came in April 1861, South Carolina turned first to the volunteers, not calling out the regular militia until May 27.[63]

North and South, volunteers rushed to do battle. North and South, state governments discovered that most of these new soldiers — except those in volunteer companies — owned no arms and that the state arsenals were empty. In Ohio, 30,000 volunteers sprang forth to fill the state's quota of 13,000 troops. But George McClellan reported that the state arsenal contained only a few boxes of rusty muskets, leaving the state no choice but to send its first two regiments to Washington without guns. An Indiana inventory in 1861 found 3,436 firearms "of sixteen different kinds, but of uniform inferiority." In 1860 Maryland's adjutant general reported that the state's three arsenals held 780 muskets and 19 rifles that were "tolerable good," plus an additional 700 that desperately needed repair, 44 condemned rifles, and 687 condemned and entirely worthless muskets. Mississippi found that the state arsenal contained 110 rifles and 234 muskets in fair order. Like other Southern states, Mississippi responded by calling for contributions of arms, and many wealthy planters exchanged personal arms caches for field commands. Northern states turned to the federal government for their weapons.[64]

The Civil War

The Civil War dramatically accelerated the slow cultural shift that had been instigated by the increase in arms production in the 1840s. By 1865 it would seem that most Americans believed that the ability to use a gun made one a better man as well as a patriot more able to defend the nation's liberties — they certainly showed a willingness to act on that assumption. Technological innovation coupled with government support had powerfully altered the national character and sensibilities within a single generation. The Civil War established these attitudes permanently by demonstrating the need for one American to be able to kill another. In 1865 the army allowed Union soldiers to take their firearms home with them. The government had finally succeeded in arming America.[65]

The initial consequence of all those guns is easy to guess: a rising murder rate. It was not simply that the number of murders increased; the very nature of the crime shifted dramatically. The rare prewar murders had been seen in the public imagination as outbursts of madness or acts of demons.

After the war, murder took on an air of calculation or anonymity. The gun itself changed the workings of murder. The face-to-face fury of strangling or the ax attack gave way to the bullet in the back of the head.[66] Prior to the war, the emerging middle class viewed with disdain the ugliness of personal confrontation and violence, though workers tended to find some defining manliness in the ability to fight well. Yet resorting to violence in antebellum America rarely involved the use of firearms. That attitude changed considerably after the war, most especially in the cities, with revolvers now small enough to fit in a coat pocket. Inexpensive and readily available guns changed many social equations, as the Ku Klux Klan demonstrated in their terror campaigns in the South, most notoriously in Louisiana's Colfax Massacre of 1873.[67]

Despite the war's end, firearms production levels remained high, while prices fell. Coupled with the expansion of advertising that built on Samuel Colt's antebellum equation of firearms possession and manly security, high levels of production led to the wide distribution of guns, both geographically and socially. It was now possible for anyone to own a gun. But the production of firearms is not in itself sufficient to create a gun culture; otherwise Britain would have developed such a culture sooner than did the United States. There needed to be a conviction, supported by the government, that the individual ownership of guns served some larger social purpose; for instance, that they preserved the nation's freedom or the security of the family. The advertising campaigns of all the gun manufacturers played up those two angles, with the added incentive of low prices. Having finally succeeded in arming its citizens, the government generally maintained a benign neutrality in the further promotion of the gun culture, with one exception: subsidies to the National Rifle Association (NRA).

The very existence of the National Rifle Association is a testament to the absence of a widespread gun culture in the antebellum period. Many former Union officers recalled their soldiers' lack of familiarity with firearms and hoped to avoid that situation in the future. The NRA's founders, the veterans William Conant Church and George Wood Wingate, sought to maintain widespread familiarity with firearms in times of peace. Doing so required teaching a new generation of American men to shoot. Church and Wingate understood that accuracy was irrelevant with the traditional muzzle-loading musket, while the new mass-produced breech-loading rifle offered the opportunity to develop sharpshooting skills. But American men had to own guns and use them regularly to develop these skills. With support from the state of New York — monetary backing that would later be taken over by the federal government — the NRA opened its first target-shooting range at Creedmore in 1872. The NRA's influence, along with its emphasis on individual gun ownership, spread west from Long Island.[68]

These developments may appear, and have generally been treated as, arcane historical details. But recently, the arguments of scholars have spilled over into more public forums. In looking back over the nation's obsession with firearms, historians, political scientists, and politicians usually come to rest at the Second Amendment. Those who adhere to the self-described "standard model" of the Second Amendment insist on their understanding of the original intent of the Framers. Looking to the second half of the amendment — "the right of the people to keep and bear Arms, shall not be infringed"— adherents of the standard model argue for an individualist reading of the amendment. The Framers intended free access to firearms for every American. The historical roots of this right lie deep in the British heritage and drew intellectual validation from Niccolò Machiavelli and the British commonwealth writers. Good republican citizens did not bear arms simply for the protection of the state; there was also the presumption of a right to self-protection and even armed insurrection — despite the Constitution's treason clause in Article III, Section 3.[69] But as Garry Wills and others have pointed out, the second is the only amendment with a preamble establishing its purpose, clearly stated to be "a well regulated Militia" preserving national security and civic order. The context for the amendment was the antifederalist fear that the Constitution diminished state power, particularly in granting Congress authority to "provide for organizing, arming, and disciplining the Militia" (Article I, Section 8). The debates addressing the Second Amendment demonstrate that no one cared about an individual right to bear arms; they were concerned with the fate of the militia. James Madison formulated this amendment as a political response to the antifederalists, guaranteeing state control of the militia yet promising federal support.[70]

The point this article seeks to make is that Madison attempted to deliver on that promise. Since the passage of the Second Amendment, the federal government has worked to arm and regulate the militia. The first and most persistent problem was that there just were not enough guns available for the militia to arm itself, or even for the government to provide free to the militia. The government also ran into resistance — not from adherents of states' rights, for the southern states actually took greater advantage of federal largess than did the northern and western states — but from the people at large. It took seventy years of government and industrial efforts to produce sufficient firearms for the American market and twenty years of promotion to convince even a proportion of the public that private gun ownership was a necessity. The Civil War finally presented the federal government with the opportunity to fashion a well-regulated militia. The war brought home the idea that firearms were necessary for social control and order: guns preserved the Union and, in the Reconstruction years, helped to reestablish white supremacy in the South. And, perhaps most important, the war's end brought guns into the home, making them part of the domestic environment and an unquestioned member of the American family.

Notes

1. In 1990 there were 36,866 deaths involving firearms in the United States. The high point for American murders so far was 24,703 in 1991. In 1993 there were 22,526 murders and 1,932,270 violent crimes reported; in 1994, 1,924,188 violent crimes. U.S. Department of Justice, *Uniform Crime Reports for the United States, 1993* (Washington, 1994), 10, 13; *The World Almanac, 1994* (Mahwah, 1994), 963–64, 967; *Statistics Canada, 1995* (Ottawa, 1995).

2. *Atlanta Constitution,* June 18, 1992.

3. *New York Times,* Jan. 3, 1994, Jan. 2, 1995.

4. Daniel J. Boorstin, *The Americans: The Colonial Experience* (New York, 1958), 353; see also, for instance, Richard Maxwell Brown, *Strain of Violence: Historical Studies of American Violence and Vigilantism* (New York, 1975); Robert Elman, *Fired in Anger* (Garden City, 1968); and John Hope Franklin, *The Militant South, 1800–1861* (Cambridge, Mass., 1956), 20–25.

5. Richard Slotkin, *Regeneration through Violence: The Mythology of the American Frontier, 1600–1860* (Middletown, 1973).

6. Arthur Conan Doyle, *Memoirs of Sherlock Holmes* (1893; Garden City, 1990), 23.

7. Alice Hanson Jones, *American Colonial Wealth: Documents and Methods* (3 vols., New York, 1977), I:13–24, III:1847–59. On the value of probate records, see Gloria L. Main, "Probate Records as a Source for Early American History," *William and Mary Quarterly,* 32 (Jan. 1975): 89–99; Daniel S. Smith, "Underregistration and Bias in Probate Records: An Analysis of Data from Eighteenth-Century Hingham, Massachusetts," ibid., 100–10; Lois Green Carr and Lorena S. Walsh, "Inventories and the Analysis of Wealth and Consumption Patterns in St. Mary's County, Maryland, 1658–1777," *Historical Methods,* 13 (Spring 1980): 81–104; Peter Benes, ed., *Early American Probate Inventories* (Boston, 1989); and Carole Shammas, *The Pre-Industrial Consumer in England and America* (Oxford, 1990), 18–46, 95–112.

8. No differentiation is made between functioning and dysfunctional firearms.

9. Don Higginbotham, *War and Society in Revolutionary America: The Wider Dimensions of Conflict* (Columbia, S.C., 1988), 106–31; George D. Moller, *Massachusetts Military Shoulder Arms, 1784–1877* (Lincoln, 1988), xi; Donald R. Hickey, *The War of 1812: A Forgotten Conflict* (Chicago, 1989), 33–34, 221–23; Kenneth O. McCreedy, "Palladium of Liberty: The American Militia System, 1815–1861" (Ph.D. diss., University of California, Berkeley, 1991). The entire militia system has been blamed for the debacle of the War of 1812: Emory Upton, *The Military Policy of the United States* (Washington, 1907), 91–106; and Harry L. Coles, *The War of 1812* (Chicago, 1965), 265.

10. Frederic P. Wells, *History of Newbury, Vermont* (St. Johnsbury, 1902), 72–73; George Washington to Artemus Ward, June 26, 1776, in *The Papers of George Washington: Revolutionary War Series,* ed. Philander D. Chase (5 vols., Charlottesville,

1993–), V:111; Washington to James Clinton, July 7, 1776, ibid., V:232. For a later period, see, for instance, Worcester County Regiment of Cavalry, Records, 1786–1804, Local Records (American Antiquarian Society, Worcester, Mass.); Oxford, Mass., Militia Muster Records, ibid.; and Records and Orderly Book of the Boston Rifle Corps, ibid. All three companies found that the majority of their members did not own guns.

11. Mark Pitcavage, "Ropes of Sand: Territorial Militias, 1801–1812," *Journal of the Early Republic,* 13 (Winter 1993): 485, 494; *Delaware Archives, Military Records* (5 vols., Wilmington, 1911–1919), IV:155–56, 271–76, 307–9.

12. Winfield Scott's inspection of the militia was validated by numerous observers, including Gov. John Eaton. U.S. Congress, *House Document 78,* 25 Cong., 2 sess., 1839, 52, 145, 334, 420; U.S. Congress, *Senate Document 278,* 26 Cong., 1 sess., 1840, 126, 179; *Niles' Weekly Register,* July 2, 1836, pp. 309–10; *Florida Herald* (St. Augustine), March 14, 1839; Clarence E. Carter, ed., *The Territorial Papers of the United States* (28 vols., Washington, 1934–), XXV:299. The citizens of Key West bought guns for their militia from the Spanish in Havana: *Key West Inquirer,* Feb. 3, 1836. For nearly identical concerns about the Michigan militia during the Black Hawk war, see Gen. John R. Williams to Lewis Cass, May 27, 1832, in "The Black Hawk War, Papers of Gen. John R. Williams," ed. Burton, in *Collections and Researches Made by the Michigan Pioneer and Historical Society,* XXXI, 388–89; and Williams to Stevens T. Mason, May 31, 1832, ibid., 397–98.

13. Henry Knox, "Return of Ordnance, Arms, and Military Stores," Dec. 16, 1793, in *American State Papers: Documents, Legislative and Executive, of the Congress of the United States,* class V: *Military Affairs* (7 vols., Washington, 1832–1861), I:44–60, 70. Censuses of firearms for the militia generally ignored fowling pieces, which were not considered to have any military value.

14. Frederick Bernays Wiener, "The Militia Clause of the Constitution," *Harvard Law Review,* 54 (Dec. 1960): 181–219.

15. Felicia J. Deyrup, *Arms Makers of the Connecticut Valley* (Northampton, 1948), 115–23.

16. "Pennsylvania Militia," *Niles' Weekly Register,* Dec. 12, 1812, p. 240; *Army and Navy Chronicle,* 6 (1838): 168; Census of Troops in Charleston, 1825, in Williams-Chestnut-Manning Families Papers, Caroliniana Collection (University of South Carolina, Columbia). Capt. John Mathis to Governor Manning, Nov. 27, 1826, ibid.

17. Henry I. Tragle, ed., *The Southampton Slave Revolt of 1831: A Compilation of Source Material* (Amherst, 1971), 43, 255; Marvin E. Gettleman, *The Dorr Rebellion: A Study in American Radicalism: 1833–1849* (New York, 1973), 107–38.

18. *Eclaireur,* 2 (March–April 1855): 116. See also Henry Bushnell, *The History of Granville, Licking County, Ohio* (Columbus, 1889), 162; John Borden Armstrong, "General Simon Goodell Griffin's Account of Nelson and the New Hampshire Militia," *Historical New Hampshire,* 21 (Summer 1966): 43; Charles Edward Banks, *History of York, Maine* (2 vols., Boston, 1935), II:218; Everett Newton Dick, *The Dixie Frontier* (New York, 1948), 268–69; Maud Carter Clement, *The History of Spotsylvania County, Virginia* (Lynchburg, 1929), 215; David Turpie, "The Pioneer Militia," *Indiana History Bulletin,* 38 (Jan. 1961): 48; Raymond W. Albright, *Two Centuries of Reading, Pennsylvania, 1748–1948* (Reading, 1948), 153; David Duncan Wallace, *The History of South Carolina* (3 vols., New York, 1934), III:148; and Ernest C. Hynds, *Antebellum Athens and Clarke County* (Athens, 1974), 39.

19. For instance, in 1843 Massachusetts determined that 6,649 (47.5%) of the

13,994 muskets in the Cambridge Armory were useless and sold them over the next several years for less than $3 each: Annual Report of the Massachusetts Adjutant General, 1840, p. 30, Commonwealth of Massachusetts Military Division, Military Records; Annual Report of the Massachusetts Adjutant General, 1849, p. 32, ibid.; Quartermaster General's Letter Book 3, p. 76, ibid. See also Adjutant General to Gov. Pierce M. Butler, Nov. 27, 1837, Military Affairs Committee Files, Legislative Group (South Carolina Department of Archives and History, Columbia); Frederick Townsend, "Annual Report of the Adjutant General of the State of New York, Transmitted to the Legislature March 20, 1857," *Assembly Document #15* (Albany, 1857), 9; Doc. 36, *Documents Accompanying the Journal of the Senate of the State of Michigan, at the Annual Session of 1841* (2 vols., Detroit, 1841), II:83–86; *Annual Report of the Adjutant General of the State of Michigan for the Year of 1856* (Lansing, 1857), 3–5, 21; *Annual Report of the Adjutant and Quarter Master General of the State of Michigan for the Year 1858* (Lansing, 1859), 15–16.

20. G. W. Gooch to Commanding Officer, 3d Regt., Orange, Sept. 20, 1817, Barbour Family Papers, p. 919 (Virginia Historical Society, Richmond); Gooch to Regimental Commanders, March 7, 1818, sect. 58, ibid., p. 923; *American State Papers,* class V: *Military Affairs,* I:675; *Army and Navy Chronicle,* 6 (1838): 263–64; U.S. Congress, Senate, "Report of the Secretary of War," Nov. 30, 1839, *Senate Journal,* Serial Set 354, 26 Cong., 1 sess., 1839, 44. See also *American State Papers,* class V: *Military Affairs,* I:318; Thomas H. McKee, comp., *Reports of the Committee on the Militia, House of Representatives* (Washington, 1887), Report 584, 26 Cong., 1 sess. Calls for reform came from the states as well: see, for instance, H. A. S. Dearborn, Annual Report of the Adjutant General for 1839, Commonwealth of Massachusetts Military Division, Military Records.

21. *Militia Laws of the United States and Massachusetts* (Boston, 1836), viii–ix, 33–37; Jerome B. Lucke, *History of the New Haven Grays* (New Haven, 1876), 29–30; D. A. Winslow, "The Old Vermont June Training," *Vermonter,* 6 (1901): 250; J. Trasker Plumer, "The Old Times Muster," *Manchester Historical Association Collections,* 3 (1902–1903): 176; John L. Sibley, *History of the Town of Union* (Boston, 1851), 350–86; E. G. Austin, "Memorandum of the Boston Light Infantry from Its Foundation in 1798 to 1838," Military Records (Massachusetts Historical Society, Boston).

22. Members of the New Haven Grays each fired four shots at the annual muster: Lucke, *History of the New Haven Grays,* 15–17, 26, 29–31, 44, 47, 107. Charles K. Gardner, *Compend of the United States System of Infantry Exercise and Maneuvers* (New York, 1819), 247; Oxford, Massachusetts, Militia Muster Records, Local Records (American Antiquarian Society); Regimental Orders, 75th Regt., New York State Infantry, 1815–1820, June 22, 1816, Military Records (New-York Historical Society, New York); Minutes of the Charleston Washington Light Infantry, April 21, 1841, Caroliniana Collection; *American State Papers,* class V: *Military Affairs,* I:20–21, 26, II:314–19, 329–37, 389–95, 527–29; Gayle Thornbrough, *Outpost on the Wabash* (Indianapolis, 1957), 125, 155; Arthur St. Clair, *A Narrative of the Manner in Which the Campaign against the Indians, in the Year 1791, Was Conducted* (Philadelphia, 1812), 199; William Guthman, *March to Massacre: A History of the First Seven Years of the United States Army, 1784–1791* (New York, 1975), 93, 105–06; Ebenezer Denny, *Military Journal of Major Ebenezer Denny* (Philadelphia, 1860), 344.

23. William H. Zierdt, *Narrative History of the 109th Field Artillery: Pennsylvania National Guard, 1775–1930* (Wilkes-Barre, 1932), 67; Emmons Clark, *History of the Second Company, Seventh Regiment, New York State Militia* (New York, 1864), 62; Lucke,

History of the New Haven Grays, 30–31, 50–51. By 1833, with the target back at 100 feet, one-third of the company was hitting the target: ibid., 79–80.

24. Edmund S. Morgan, *American Freedom, American Slavery: The Ordeal of Colonial Virginia* (New York, 1975), 239–40, 377–79; Bertram Wyatt-Brown, *Southern Honor: Ethics and Behavior in the Old South* (New York, 1982), 357–60; Franklin, *Militant South*, 14–62.

25. Fred Anderson, *A People's Army: Massachusetts Soldiers and Society in the Seven Years' War* (Chapel Hill, 1984), 75–76; Anthony Marro, "Vermont's Local Militia Units, 1815–1860," *Vermont History,* 40 (Winter 1972): 28, 31; *American Turf Register and Sporting Magazine,* 1 (1829–1830): 338–39, 359. Outside the pages of fiction, hunters miss more often than they find their targets. See also *Western Monthly Magazine,* 3 (1835): 65–66; *Brother Jonathan,* 6 (1843): 43.

26. Edward B. Bourne, *The History of Wells and Kennebunk* (Portland, 1875), 698; Maud Burr Morris, "William A. Bradley, Eleventh Mayor of the Corporation of Washington," *Records of the Columbia Historical Society,* 25 (1923): 130–33; Wells, *History of Newbury, Vermont,* 289–90; Marro, "Vermont's Local Militia Units," 32; *Principles of the Non-Resistance Society* (Boston, 1839); New England Non-Resistance Society, *National Organizations* (Boston, 1839); William Little, *The History of Weare, New Hampshire, 1735–1888* (Lowell, 1888), 383; William H. Kilby, ed., *Eastport and Passamaquoddy: A Collection of Historical and Biographical Sketches* (Eastport, 1888), 472.

27. *Brother Jonathan,* 6 (1843): 186; T. L. Hagood to William C. Bouck, Dec. 15, 1843, box 3, William C. Bouck Papers (New York Historical Resource Center, Olin Library, Cornell University, Ithaca, New York); *Ten Dialogues on the Effects of Ardent Spirits* (n.p., c. 1826), 6–7. A favorite phrase for the militia seems to have been "a promiscuous assemblage"; *see,* for example, Adjutant General A. C. Nevin, *Report of the Adjutant General for 1843,* New York Senate Doc. #5, Jan. 4, 1844 (American Antiquarian Society). See also Johnson Jones Hooper, *Adventures of Captain Simon Suggs, Late of the Tallapoose Volunteers* (n.p., 1845), 65–103; Augustus Baldwin Longstreet, *Georgia Scenes, Characters, Incidents, &c., in the First Half Century of the Republic by a Native Georgian* (New York, 1840), 145–51.

28. A. T. Andreas, *History of Cook County, Illinois* (Chicago, 1884), 206–07; *Report of the Adjutant General and Acting Quartermaster General Accompanying the Annual Returns of the Militia of Massachusetts,* Senate Document #27 (1834), p. 91, Commonwealth of Massachusetts Military Division, Military Records. *See also* Joseph J. Holmes, "The Decline of the Pennsylvania Militia, 1815–1870," *Western Pennsylvania Historical Magazine,* 57 (April 1974): 208; Charles W. Burpee and Charles F. Chapin, "Military Life Since the Revolution," in *The Town and City of Waterbury, Connecticut,* ed. Joseph Anderson (3 vols., New Haven, 1896), III:1186; Randall Parrish, *Historic Illinois: The Romance of the Earlier Days* (Chicago, 1905), 368; Oxford, Massachusetts, Militia Muster Records, Local Records (American Antiquarian Society); *American State Papers,* class V: *Military Affairs,* II: 320.

29. Turpie, "Pioneer Militia," 48; Richard W. Musgrove, *History of the Town of Bristol, Grafton County, New Hampshire* (2 vols., Bristol, 1904), I:187; David J. McCord, ed., *The Statutes at Large of South Carolina* (10 vols., Columbia, 1836–1841), VIII:2650, XI:2856.

30. McCord, ed., *Statues at Large of South Carolina,* VIII, 2650; William H. Sumner, "Massachusetts Adjutant General's Report of 1834," 39 (American Antiquarian Society).

31. McCreedy, "Palladium of Liberty," 185–87; J. Thomas Scharf, *History of Delaware, 1609–1888* (2 vols., Philadelphia, 1888), I:816–17; Upton, *Military Policy of the*

United States, 228. For similar patterns in other states, *see* McCreedy, "Palladium of Liberty," 187; Everett Stockpole, *History of New Hampshire* (New York, 1916), 93, 159; Marro, "Vermont's Local Militia Units," 29–30; "Military Reports and Recommendations, 1830–1831" (microfilm: reel 64), Commonwealth of Massachusetts Military Division, Military Records: "Militia Reports and Recommendations, 1834," ibid.; "An Act supplemental to an act to organize the Militia," Jan. 15, 1831, in *Laws of a Public and General Nature of the State of Missouri, 1824–1836* (2 vols., Jefferson City, 1842), II:237–39; and "An Act supplemental to the several acts to organize the Militia," Jan. 14, 1833, ibid., 320–22.

32. To take just one example, see Bernard Bush, ed., *Laws of the Royal Colony of New Jersey* (5 vols., Trenton, 1980), II:294–95, III:181, 186–90, 253, 489–90, 580, IV:52–53, 237, 326–27, 582–85, V:52–53, 69–72, 162–63. In general, see Paul C. Phillips, *The Fur Trade* (2 vols., Norman, 1961), I:377–430; Thomas E. Norton, *The Fur Trade in Colonial New York, 1686–1776* (Madison, 1974), 60–82.

33. See, for instance, *Atheneum,* 2nd ser., 7 (Boston, 1827), 29–34, 53–59, 167–68, 276–77, 408, 426–27; ibid., 3rd ser., 1 (1828): 207–8; *Godey's Lady's Book,* 2 (1831): 150; *Army and Navy Chronicle,* 5 (1837): 59–60; *Anglo-American,* 5 (1845): 200–201, 390–91; *Brother Jonathan,* 6 (1843): 43; *Eclectic Magazine,* 33 (1854): 563; Norton, *Fur Trade in Colonial New York,* 83–99; Patrick Malone, *The Skulking Way of War: Technology and Tactics among the New England Indians* (Lanham, 1991), 60–66; Sarah F. McMahon, "A Comfortable Subsistence: The Changing Composition of Diet in Rural New England, 1620–1840," *William and Mary Quarterly,* 42 (Jan. 1985): 26–65; Henry M. Miller, "An Archaeological Perspective on the Evolution of Diet in the Colonial Chesapeake, 1620–1745," in *Colonial Chesapeake Society,* ed. Lois Green Carr, Philip D. Morgan, and Jean B. Russo (Chapel Hill, 1988), 176–99.

34. "Sporting," *Atheneum,* 2nd ser., 2 (1825): 444; *Ariel,* 3 (1829): 94.

35. Jacob Abbott, *Marco Paul's Adventures in Pursuit of Knowledge* (Boston, 1843), 111–12. Some children's books and magazines questioned the necessity for violence at all, even in the American Revolution: Increase N. Tarbox, *Winnie and Walter's Evening Talks with Their Father About Old Times* (Boston, 1861); Joseph Alden, *The Old Revolutionary Soldier* (New York, 1849); *Evils of the Revolutionary War* (Boston, 1846); *Parley's Magazine,* 3 (1835): 17, 81; Henry C. Wright, *A Kiss for a Blow: or, A Collection of Stories for Children* (Boston, 1842).

36. *Western Monthly Magazine,* 1 (1833): 2–3, 49–55, 238–39, 318; ibid., 2 (1834), 268; *Western Miscellany,* 1 (1849); Robert S. Dykstra, *The Cattle Towns* (New York, 1965), 112–48; Luc Sante, *Low Life: Lures and Snares of Old New York* (New York, 1991), 197–235; Elliot J. Gorn, "'Good-Bye Boys, I Die a True American': Homicide, Nativism, and Working-Class Culture in Antebellum New York City," *Journal of American History,* 74 (Sept. 1987): 388–410; Paul A. Gilje, *The Road to Mobocracy: Popular Disorder in New York City, 1763–1834* (Chapel Hill, 1987), 235–64; Carl E. Prince, "The Great 'Riot Year': Jacksonian Democracy and Patterns of Violence in 1834," *Journal of the Early Republic,* 5 (Spring 1985): 1–19; David Grimsted, "Rioting in Its Jacksonian Setting," *American Historical Review,* 77 (April 1972): 361–97.

37. James Fenimore Cooper, *The Pioneers: or, The Sources of the Susquehanna* (1823; Albany, 1980), 20–25.

38. Vermont Superior Court records (County Courthouse, Rutland, Vt.). In a study of 559 criminal actions in North Carolina from 1663 to 1740, murder accounted for 43 cases (7.7%): Donna J. Spindel and Stuart W. Thomas Jr., "Crime and Society in North Carolina, 1663–1740," in *Crime and Justice in American History: The Colonies and Early Republic,* ed. Eric H. Monkkonen (2 vols., Westport, 1991),

II:699–720. A study of Ohio County, Virginia, 1801–1810, found a total of 240 criminal indictments, 3 (1.2%) of which were for murder: Edward M. Steel, "Criminality in Jeffersonian America—A Sample," ibid., 721–26.

39. *An Authentic Life of John C. Colt, now imprisoned for killing Samuel Adams* (Boston, 1842); William B. Edwards, *The Story of Colt's Revolver* (Harrisburg, 1953), 139–75, 191–275.

40. N. Bosworth, *A Treatise on the Rifle, Musket, Pistol, and Fowling Piece* (New York, 1846), 106; G. Gregory, *A New and Complete Dictionary of Arts and Sciences, Including the Latest Improvement and Discovery* (3 vols., New York, 1819) defines a musket as a tool of war, "a fire-arm borne on the shoulder, and used in war"; s.v. "musket."

41. M. L. Brown, *Firearms in Colonial America: The Impact on History and Technology, 1492–1792* (Washington, 1980), 224–89, 371–81; James B. Whisker, *Arms Makers in Colonial America* (Selinsgrove, 1992), 9–22; S. N. D. North and R. H. North, *Simeon North, First Official Pistol Maker of the United States* (Concord, N.H., 1913), 10–36; Merrill Lindsay, *The New England Gun: The First Two Hundred Years* (New Haven, 1975).

42. *Niagara Journal,* July 1, 1817, p. 4; ibid., March 6, 1819, p. 3; *Buffalo Emporium,* May 14, 1825, p. 3; Robert W. Bingham, *Early Buffalo Gunsmiths* (Buffalo, 1934), 13–18. See, for instance, the account books of Emerson Bixby, Barre, Mass., blacksmith 1824–1855, Account Books (American Antiquarian Society); Jonathan Haight, rural New York, blacksmith, 1771–1789, ibid.; Elihu Burritt, Worcester, Mass., blacksmith, 1839, ibid.; Janes & Shumway, West Sutton, Mass., blacksmiths, 1833–1835, ibid.

43. See, for instance, Whisker, *Arms Makers in Colonial America,* 17–19; Moller, *Massachusetts Military Shoulder Arms,* 35–56; Solomon Van Rensselaer, *A Narrative of the Affair at Queenstown: In the War of 1812* (New York, 1836), appendix, 36–53; and George C. Bittle, "In the Defense of Florida: The Organized Florida Militia from 1821 to 1920" (Ph.D. diss., Florida State University, 1965), 213–14.

44. The records of every colony contain complaints of the shortage of firearms and frantic searches to complement scarce resources in arms and ammunition. See, for instance, Bush, ed., *Laws of the Royal Colony of New Jersey,* II:15–16, III:8–9, 503–4, 525–28, IV:495; *The Public Records of the Colony of Connecticut* (15 vols., Hartford, 1859), III:252–54, 429–33; J. H. Easterby, ed., *The Colonial Records of South Carolina: The Journal of the Commons House of Assembly,* vol. V: *February 20, 1744–May 25, 1745* (Columbia, S.C., 1955), 355–56, 370–71, 429–31, 434, 445–46, 460, 535, 560; R. Nicholas Olsberg, ed., *The Colonial Records of South Carolina: The Journal of the Commons House of Assembly,* vol. X: *23 April 1750–31 August 1751* (Columbia, S.C., 1974), 441; Terry W. Lipscomb, ed., *The Colonial Records of South Carolina: The Journal of the Commons House of Assembly,* vol. XIV: *November 20, 1755–July 6, 1757* (Columbia, S.C., 1989), 388–89, 445, 463–66.

45. Arcadi Gluckman, *United States Muskets, Rifles, and Carbines* (Buffalo, 1948), 44–48; *American State Papers,* class V: *Military Affairs,* V:519; Jenny West, *Gunpowder, Government, and War in the Mid-Eighteenth Century* (Woodbridge, 1991); Harold Leslie Peterson, *Arms and Armor in Colonial America, 1526–1783* (Harrisburg, 1956), 7–52, 159–225; Brown, *Firearms in Colonial America,* 1–111; Carl Parcher Russell, *Guns on the Early Frontiers: A History of Firearms from Colonial Times through the Years of the Western Fur Trade* (Berkeley, 1957), 1–141.

46. Gregory, *A New and Complete Dictionary of Arts and Sciences,* s.v. "gun-smithery"; North and North, *Simeon North,* 19; James E. Hicks, *Notes on United States Ordnance* (2 vols., Mount Vernon, 1940), I, 14.

47. Moller, *Massachusetts Military Shoulder Arms,* 19; Hicks, *Notes on United States*

Ordnance, I:11–14, 42–43. The armories at Springfield, Mass., and Harpers Ferry, Va., were the most productive gun manufacturers in the United States. As can be seen, Springfield was rather consistent in its production, not deviating far from its average 13,252 guns produced per year between 1821 and 1860.

48. Moller, *Massachusetts Military Shoulder Arms,* 49–51; "Militia Returns for the Year 1818," p. 17, entry 117, Records of the U.S. Army Ordnance Department, RG 156 (National Archives, Washington, D.C.).

49. Amasa Davis to Gov. Caleb Strong, Oct. 6, 1812, quoted in Moller, *Massachusetts Military Shoulder Arms,* 39; see also ibid., 47, 49; Account of Powder, Arms, Accoutrements, Standards & Music Delivered, Commonwealth of Massachusetts Military Division, Military Records.

50. On this new productivity, see Deyrup, *Arms Makers of the Connecticut Valley,* 115–215; Michael S. Raber, "Conservative Innovators, Military Small Arms, and Industrial History at Springfield Armory, 1794–1918," *Journal of the Society for Industrial Archaeology,* 14 (no. 1, 1988): 1–21; David A. Hounshell, *From the American System to Mass Production, 1800–1932* (Baltimore, 1984), 46–50; Robert A. Howard, "Interchangeable Parts Reexamined: The Private Sector of the American Arms Industry on the Eve of the Civil War," *Technology and Culture,* 19 (Oct. 1978): 633–49.

51. The first issue of the nation's first hunting magazine states that hunting as a sport is just beginning to attract the attention of American men: *American Turf Register and Sporting Magazine,* 1 (1829): 1.

52. *Spirit of the Times,* 7 (1837): 4; Bosworth, *Treatise on the Rifle, Musket, Pistol, and Fowling Piece,* 64, 97; see also *Spirit of the Times,* 5 (1835): 1; ibid., 9 (1839): 1; *American Turf Register and Sporting Magazine,* 1 (1829–1830): 240, 441; ibid., 5 (1834): 371–73, 474–75, 615.

53. *Army and Navy Chronicle,* 6 (1838): 209–11; *American Turf Register and Sporting Magazine,* 1 (1829–1830): 79, 338–39.

54. See, for instance, *American Turf Register and Sporting Magazine,* 1 (1829–1830): 88, 238, 400, 443–45; ibid., 5 (1834): 298–99; *American Penny Magazine,* 1 (1845): 387; *Ariel,* 3 (1829): 117; *Army and Navy Chronicle,* 6 (1838): 209–11.

55. *American Turf Register and Sporting Magazine,* 1 (1829–1830): 352. See also ibid., 447–50, 595–96; *Ariel,* 5 (1832): 308–09; *American Penny Magazine,* 1 (1845): 388.

56. James E. Serven, *Colt Firearms, 1836–1958* (Santa Ana, 1954), 99–159.

57. New Jersey, Delaware, Maryland, Georgia, Mississippi, Tennessee, and Indiana made no returns. "Report of the Colonel of Ordnance," Oct. 28, 1851, *U.S. Army Ordnance Office* Serial Set, 611, Department of War (Washington, 1851), 452; Charles W. Hall, *Regiments and Armories of Massachusetts* (2 vols., Boston, 1899), I:120. "Report of Commissioners and the Adjutant General to codify and amend [the Militia Laws], April 1, 1853," Senate Document #66, Collections of the New-York Historical Society (New-York Historical Society).

58. See, for example, *Annual Report of the Adjutant and Quarter Master General of the State of Michigan for the Year 1858,* 15–16; G. W. Gooch to Commanding Officer, 3d Regt., Orange, Sept. 20, 1817, Barbour Family Papers, Sect. 58: 919; Gooch to Regimental Commanders, March 7, 1818, ibid., Sect. 58: 923; Martin K. Gordon, "The Militia of the District of Columbia, 1790–1815" (Ph.D. diss., George Washington University, 1975), 301–03; Ebenezer Stone, *Annual Report of the Adjutant General of the Commonwealth of Massachusetts for the Year Ending Dec. 31, 1852,* Senate Document #8 (Boston, 1853), 31; *Florida Senate Journal* (Tallahassee, 1859), appendix, 7–8;

Frederick Townsend, *Annual Report of the Adjutant General of the State of New York,* Assembly Doc. no. 15 (Albany, 1857), 9; "Report of Committee on Volunteer Companies," Sept. 18, 1856, Military Affairs Committee Files, Legislative Group (South Carolina Department of Archives and History, Columbia); "Petition of Volunteer Companies of St. Philip's and St. Michael's" [1849], ibid.; George Bomford to Lewis Cass, Jan. 19, 1832, in *American State Papers,* class V: *Military Affairs,* IV, 829.

59. One sign of that new subculture was the creation of urban pistol galleries: Bosworth, *Treatise on the Rifle, Musket, Pistol, and Fowling Piece,* 82, 101.

60. This proposal replicated the suggestions of Henry Knox and George Washington back in the 1790s. There had been a few such "select militia" units in the colonial period, but they had died out in the years after the War of 1812. *American State Papers,* class V: *Military Affairs,* I: 7–8; McCreedy, "Palladium of Liberty," 16–46; Lyle D. Brundage, "The Organization, Administration, and Training of the United States Ordinary and Volunteer Militia, 1792–1861" (Ph.D. diss., University of Michigan, 1958), 52–55, 142–47.

61. See, for example, "Report of Committee on Volunteer Companies," Sept. 18, 1856, Military Affairs (South Carolina Department of Archives and History, Columbia); "Petition of Volunteer Companies of St. Philip's and St. Michael's" [1849], ibid. Committee Files, Legislative Group; Annual Report of the Massachusetts Adjutant General, 1840–1844, Commonwealth of Massachusetts Military Division, Military Records.

62. McCreedy, "Palladium of Liberty," 267–324; Michael Feldberg, *The Philadelphia Riots of 1844: A Study of Ethnic Conflict* (Westport, 1975); Richard Moody, *The Astor Place Riot* (Bloomington, 1958).

63. McCreedy, "Palladium of Liberty," 371–72, 375; T. R. Fehrenbach, *Lone Star* (New York, 1968), 352.

64. Stephen W. Sears, *George B. McClellan: The Young Napoleon* (New York, 1988), 70; McCreedy, "Palladium of Liberty," 394; Joseph A. Parsons Jr., "Indiana and the Call for Volunteers, April, 1861," *Indiana Magazine of History,* 54 (March 1958): 2; N. Brewer, *Report of the Adjutant General of Maryland to the General Assembly* (Annapolis, 1860), 7–8; Jack Gunn, "Mississippi in 1860 as Reflected in the Activities of the Governor's Office," *Journal of Mississippi History,* 23 (Oct. 1960): 185–86; Terry L. Jones, *Lee's Tigers: The Louisiana Infantry in the Army of Northern Virginia* (Baton Rouge, 1987), 3–4.

65. Officially, Union soldiers had to purchase their firearms before taking them home. But the army did not make a concerted effort to collect this money. Even most Confederate soldiers took guns home with them when the war ended. See Noah Andre Trudeau, *Out of the Storm: The End of the Civil War, April–June, 1865* (New York, 1994), 379; Edith Abbott, "The Civil War and the Crime Wave of 1865–70," *Social Service Review,* 1 (1929): 212–34.

66. Abbott, "Civil War and the Crime Wave of 1865–70"; Sante, *Low Life;* Waldo L. Cook, "Murders in Massachusetts," *Journal of the American Statistical Association,* 3 (Sept. 1893): 357–78; Harry G. Nutt, "Homicide in New Hampshire," ibid., 9 (1905): 220–30.

67. Michael Kaplan, "New York City Tavern Violence and the Creation of a Working-Class Male Identity," *Journal of the Early Republic,* 15 (Fall 1995): 591–617; Eliot J. Gorn, *The Manly Art: Bare-knuckle Prize Fighting in America* (Ithaca, 1986), 129–47; Elizabeth Pleck, *Domestic Tyranny: The Making of American Social Policy against Family Violence from Colonial Times to the Present* (New York, 1987), 49–66; Jerome

Nadelhaft, "Wife Torture: A Known Phenomenon in Nineteenth-Century America," *Journal of American Culture,* 10 (Fall 1987): 39–59; Ted Tunnell, *Crucible of Reconstruction: War, Radicalism, and Race in Louisiana, 1862–1877* (Baton Rouge, 1984), 185–202; *United States v. Cruikshank,* 92 U.S. 542 (1876); Ralph L. Peek, "Lawlessness in Florida, 1868–1871," *Florida Historical Quarterly,* 40 (Oct. 1961): 164–85.

68. There is surprisingly little historical study of the National Rifle Association (NRA): one dissertation, Russell S. Gilmore, "Crackshots and Patriots: The National Rifle Association and America's Military-Sporting Tradition" (Ph.D. diss., University of Wisconsin, 1974); an official history, James Trefethen and James Serven, *Americans and Their Guns: The National Rifle Association's Story through Nearly a Century of Service to the Nation* (Harrisburg, 1967); and a biography, Donald N. Bigelow, *William Conant Church and* The Army and Navy Journal (New York, 1952). On the modern NRA, see Osha Gray Davidson, *Under Fire: The NRA and the Battle for Gun Control* (New York, 1993).

69. Glenn Harlan Reynolds, "A Critical Guide to the Second Amendment," *Tennessee Law Review,* 62 (Spring 1995): 461–512. This entire issue of the *Tennessee Law Review* is an uncritical celebration of the "standard model." See also Robert J. Cottrol, ed., *Gun Control and the Constitution: Sources and Explorations on the Second Amendment* (New York, 1994), ix–xlviii; Joyce Lee Malcolm, *To Keep and Bear Arms: The Origins of an Anglo-American Right* (Cambridge, Mass., 1994); Don B. Kates, "Handgun Prohibition and the Original Meaning of the Second Amendment," *Michigan Law Review,* 82 (Nov. 1983): 204–73; Stephen Halbrook, *That Every Man Be Armed* (San Francisco, 1984); Robert E. Shalhope, "The Ideological Origins of the Second Amendment," *Journal of American History,* 69 (Dec. 1982): 599–614.

70. The finest critique of the "standard model" is Garry Wills, "To Keep and Bear Arms," *New York Review of Books,* Sept. 21, 1995, pp. 62–72. See also Lawrence D. Cress, "An Armed Community: The Origins and Meaning of the Right to Bear Arms," *Journal of American History,* 71 (June 1984): 22–42; Roy G. Weathrup, "Standing Armies and Armed Citizens: An Historical Analysis of the Second Amendment," *Hastings Constitutional Law Quarterly,* 2 (Fall 1975): 961–1001; and Dennis A. Henigan, "Arms, Anarchy, and the Second Amendment," *Valparaiso University Law Review,* 26 (Fall 1991): 107–29.

Making Connections

The questions that precede each selection are intended to help students deal with a particular piece of writing. But all the selections here are in dialogue with one another around one larger problem: how we can best understand the historical meaning of the Second Amendment. Although the historians in this volume do not all agree on what the Second Amendment meant to eighteenth-century Americans, they share a set of concerns that are common to all historical inquiries. How do we relate historical texts to their larger contexts? What is the relationship between rhetoric and reality? From the staggering range of voices from the past, which ones should historians privilege in their accounts? The questions that follow are intended to provide a starting point for students. Reading the essays in this volume will doubtless raise many other interesting and exciting questions. By asking new questions of this material, you will be entering the open-ended conversation among historians that allows each generation to bring fresh insights to the most well-studied topics.

1. Shalhope and Cress each focus on the ideological origins of the Second Amendment. In everyday conversation, the term *ideology* is usually something that is ascribed to those with a rigid set of beliefs. In this sense, ideology is closely linked to dogmatism. For historians, ideology is often used to describe a complex set of ideas and values shared by people within a society. For historians, ideology generally refers to a world view or a set of cultural beliefs. What ideology or ideologies shaped the way Americans interpreted the Second Amendment?

2. Shalhope and Cress use many of the same types of sources to construct their arguments. What kinds of sources are available to scholars interested in discovering how early Americans understood the Second Amendment? How should scholars weight these different sources?

3. Ultimately, Shalhope and Cress disagree about the nature of American political thought in the Revolutionary era. After reading both of these authors, how would you characterize American thinking in this era? Was America more republican or more liberal in character?

4. Edmund Morgan explores the complex relationship between rhetoric and reality in history. How does one differentiate between rhetoric and reality? How should historians deal with situations in which there is a discrepancy between rhetoric and reality?

5. If constitutional arguments depended on "political fictions," how should historians and legal scholars weight these fictions when seeking to understand the meaning of the Second Amendment?

6. Garry Wills berates lawyers for their approach to writing history. Wills is not alone in attacking "law office history." Most historians believe the goal of history is to reconstruct and explain the past, recovering as much of its complexity as is possible given the limits of the surviving sources and the power of our explanatory models. For most lawyers the goal of history is to provide the basis for constructing a legal argument that will persuade judges and juries. Can historians escape the charge that they too are advocates taking a stand?

7. Although they approach the past differently, historians and lawyers are both interested in discovering what the intentions of historical actors were with regard to the Second Amendment. In reconstructing the original debate over the Second Amendment, historians and legal scholars have explored the intents of a variety of different groups in post-Revolutionary America. What groups should historians focus on, and what types of sources provide the best guide to their different intentions?

8. For much of American history the problem of federalism has been central to constitutional struggle. How does the debate over the Second Amendment provide additional insight into the struggle to define the nature of federalism?

9. Although they focus on a different range of materials, Wills and Higginbotham both see the Second Amendment as a response to Antifederalist concerns about the structure of the federal system. Do Wills's and Higginbotham's accounts support each other or contradict one another?

10. If the Second Amendment was largely an expression of the debate over federalism, does this support the stance of Shalhope or of Cress?

11. Although many legal scholars have argued that the Second Amendment sanctioned a right of revolution, most historians reject this claim. Based on the evidence presented in these essays, what do you think about the right of revolution and the Second Amendment?

12. What does the history of gun ownership during the period in which the Second Amendment was adopted tell us about its meaning?

13. How do you account for the continuing power of the myth of the militia and the ideal of the armed citizen?

14. Does the world of the Founding Fathers seem similar to ours or does it appear to be distant and foreign — a world we have lost? If so, what, if any, wisdom can we gain from the original debate over the Second Amendment?

15. After reading all these essays, what do you think the Second Amendment means?

Suggestions for Further Reading

This volume is not intended to provide a massive bibliography, but any interested student will want to delve into the subject more deeply. For a selection drawn from a book, the best way to start is to go to that book and place the selection within the author's larger argument. Each selection is reproduced with full annotation, as originally published, to allow interested students to go to the author's original sources, study them, and compare their own readings with what the author has made of the same material.

A useful collection of historical essays on the meaning of the Constitution may be found in Edward Countryman, *What Did the Constitution Mean to Early Americans?* (Boston: Bedford/St. Martin's, 1999). Jack P. Greene and J. R. Pole, eds., *The Blackwell Encyclopedia of the American Revolution* (London: Blackwell, 1991), provides concise discussions of many topics relevant to the Second Amendment including essays dealing with the militia, the state constitutions, and the federal Constitution. Leonard W. Levy and Dennis J. Mahoney, eds., *The Framing and Ratification of the Constitution* (New York: Macmillan, 1987), contains several essays on various aspects of the Constitution and the Bill of Rights.

A concise and thoughtful introduction to the intellectual assumptions of the Founders may be found in Forrest McDonald, *Novus Ordo Seclorum: The Intellectual Origins of the Constitution* (Lawrence: University Press of Kansas, 1985). Jack N. Rakove, *Original Meanings: Politics and Ideas in the Making of the Constitution* (New York: Knopf, 1996), deals with the multiplicity of different points of view during the debate over the Constitution. Gordon S. Wood, *The Creation of the American Republic, 1776–1787* (Chapel Hill: University of North Carolina Press, 1969), is the standard work on American constitutionalism in the period between the Revolution and the ratification of the Constitution. The most comprehensive treatment of Antifederalist ideas is Saul Cornell, *The Other Founders: Anti-Federalism and the Dissenting Tradition in America, 1788–1829* (Chapel Hill: University of North Carolina Press, 1999). Studies of Federalist thought have generally focused primarily on *The Federalist,* the most intellectually rich statement of the ideas of the supporters of the Constitution. The most important of these are David Epstein, *The Political Theory of the Federalist* (Chicago: University of Chicago Press, 1984), and Charles R. Kesler, ed., *Saving the Revolution: The Federalist Papers and the American Founding* (New York: Free Press, 1987). An interesting effort to study the literary strategies of *The Federalist* may be found in Albert Furtwangler, *The Authority of Publius: A Reading of the Federalist Papers* (Ithaca, N.Y.: Cornell University Press, 1984).

A useful discussion of the individual provisions of the Bill of Rights is provided in Jon Kukla, ed., *The Bill of Rights: A Lively Heritage* (Richmond, Va.: Virginia State Library, 1987), which includes the Cress essay in this book. The origin of the Federal Bill of Rights and the struggle to define the place of rights and liberties within the individual states are addressed in the essays collected in Patrick T. Conley and John P. Kaminski, eds., *The Bill of Rights and the States: The Colonial and Revolutionary Origins of American Liberties* (Madison, Wisc.: Madison House, 1992). Several essays in this collection touch on the right to bear arms. Some sense of the range of contemporary historical writing about the Bill of Rights can be obtained from the essays in Ronald Hoffman and Peter J. Albert, eds., *The Bill of Rights: Government Proscribed* (Charlottesville: University Press of Virginia, 1997).

The modern debate over the Second Amendment among historians was inaugurated by Robert Shalhope in an influential essay, "The Ideological Origins of the Second Amendment," *Journal of American History* 64 (1982): 599–614. This interpretation was challenged by Lawrence Delbert Cress, "An Armed Community: The Origins and Meaning of the Right to Bear Arms," *Journal of American History* 71 (1984): 22–42. For an interesting exchange between Shalhope and Cress, see "The Second Amendment and the Right to Bear Arms: An Exchange," *Journal of American History* 71 (1984): 587–93. Further support for the individual rights thesis was provided by Joyce Lee Malcolm, *To Keep and Bear Arms: The Origins of an Anglo-American Right* (Cambridge, Mass.: Harvard University Press, 1994), who stresses the English origins of the Second Amendment. For a lively exchange on Malcolm's thesis, see Joyce Lee Malcolm and Michael A. Bellesîles, "Exchange: On the History of the Right to Bear Arms," *Law and History Review* 15 (Fall 1997): 339–45. Rather than stress the English origins of the Second Amendment, Michael A. Bellesîles argues that American legal culture evolved along a new path shaped by the different social and political realities that defined the lives of colonial Americans. For an elaboration of this approach, see Bellesîles, "Gun Laws in Early America: The Regulation of Firearms Ownership, 1607–1794," *Law and History Review* 16 (Fall 1998): 567–89.

Modern legal scholarship on the Second Amendment builds on the provocative essay by Sanford Levinson, "Embarrassing Second Amendment," *Yale Law Journal* 99 (December 1989): 637–59. Levinson's article is reprinted in Robert J. Cottrol, *Gun Control and the Constitution: Sources and Explorations on the Second Amendment* (New York: Garland Publishing, 1994). The individual rights thesis has won more converts among lawyers than historians. Among the most important law review essays advancing the case of the individual rights thesis are William Van Alstyne, "The Second Amendment and the Personal Right to Arms," *Duke Law Journal* 43 (April 1994): 1236–55, and Glenn Harlan Reynolds, "A Critical Guide to the Second Amendment," *Tennessee Law Review* 62 (Spring 1995): 461–512. Among the most important critiques of the individual rights thesis are Dennis A. Henigan, "Arms, Anarchy, and the Second Amendment," *Valparaiso University Law Review* 26 (1991): 107–29, and Carl T. Bogus, "The Hidden History of the Second Amendment," *University of California Davis Law Review* 31 (Winter 1998): 309–408.

Although no consensus has emerged among historians on how to interpret the Second Amendment, there appears to be an emerging consensus on the inadequacy of much recent legal scholarship on this topic. A useful sampling of historical reaction to recent legal scholarship may be found in the following essays: Saul Cornell, "Commonplace or Anachronism: The Standard Model, the Second Amendment, and the Problem of History in Contemporary Constitutional Theory," *Constitutional Commentary* 16 (Summer 1999), 221–46; Michael A. Bellesîles, "Suicide Pact: New Readings of the Second Amendment," ibid., 247–61; Don Higginbotham, "The Second Amendment in Historical Context," ibid., 263–68; and Robert E. Shalhope, "To Keep and Bear Arms in the Early Republic," ibid., 269–81.

Two useful collections of primary sources reprint much of the essential materials related to the origins of the Bill of Rights: Jack N. Rakove, ed., *Declaring Rights: A Brief History with Documents* (Boston: Bedford/St. Martin's, 1998); and Neil H. Cogan, ed., *The Complete Bill of Rights: The Drafts, Debates, Sources, and Origins* (New York: Oxford University Press, 1997).

Acknowledgments, continued from p. iv

DON HIGGINBOTHAM, "The Federalized Militia Debate: A Neglected Aspect of Second Amendment Scholarship," from *William and Mary Quarterly,* 3rd Series, Vol. 55, no. 1 (January 1998). Copyright © 1998 by Omohundro Institute of Early American History and Culture. Reprinted by permission of the Omohundro Institute of Early American History and Culture.

EDMUND S. MORGAN, "The People in Arms: The Invincible Yeoman," from *Inventing the People: The Rise of Popular Sovereignty in England and America* by Edmund S. Morgan. Copyright © 1988 by Edmund S. Morgan. Reprinted by permission of W. W. Norton & Company, Inc.

ROBERT E. SHALHOPE, "The Armed Citizen in the Early Republic" from *Law and Contemporary Problems,* Vol. 49, no. 1, pp. 125–41. Copyright © 1986 by Duke University School of Law. Used with permission.

GARRY WILLS, "To Keep and Bear Arms," from *The New York Review of Books,* Vol. 42, no. 14, pp. 62–73 (September 21, 1995) and letters by Sanford Levinson, David C. Williams, and Glenn Harlan Reynolds, *The New York Review of Books,* Vol. 42, no. 18, pp. 61–62 (November 16, 1995). Reprinted with permission from *The New York Review of Books.* Copyright © 1995 NYREV, Inc.